Enlightening Professional Supervision in Social Work

Manohar Pawar · A. W. (Bill) Anscombe

Enlightening Professional Supervision in Social Work

Voices and Virtues of Supervisors

 Springer

Manohar Pawar
School of Social Work and Arts;
Gulbali Institute for Agriculture,
Water and Environment
Charles Sturt University
Wagga Wagga, NSW, Australia

A. W. (Bill) Anscombe
Australian Centre for Christianity
and Culture;
Gulbali Institute for Agriculture,
Water and Environment
Charles Sturt University
Wagga Wagga, NSW, Australia

ISBN 978-3-031-18540-3   ISBN 978-3-031-18541-0   (eBook)
https://doi.org/10.1007/978-3-031-18541-0

This Springer imprint is published by the registered company Springer Nature Switzerland AG
The registered company address is: Gewerbestrasse 11, 6330 Cham, Switzerland

Acknowledgments

This book is about the voices and virtues of social work practitioners and supervisors. First, our appreciation and thanks go to all the social worker participants in our study, who voluntarily and generously shared their rich experiences, insights, and wisdom and enlightened us about their practice and commitment to changing the lives of people and communities. Their narratives inspired us to write this book, and we sincerely thank each one.

We would also like to acknowledge a larger research project entitled *Virtuous Practitioners: Empowering Social Workers*, which was funded by the Australian Research Council's Discovery Project scheme (DP140103730) and its other co-chief investigators, Richard Hugman and Andrew Alexandra, for their contributions. We are also thankful to Simone Engdahl, Kris Gibbs, Debra Noy, Zhaoen Pan, Nikki Scott, Jessica Russ-Smith, and Amelia Wheeler for offering research assistance for the project. The project's earlier outcomes include two books: *Empowering Social Workers: Virtuous Practitioners* (Springer, 2017) and *Virtue Ethics in Social Work Practice* (Routledge, 2021). This is the third book from the project focusing on professional supervision in professional social work.

Writing this book would not have been possible without Special Studies Program (SSP) leave provided by Charles Sturt University (CSU). We are grateful to Executive Dean John McDonald, Faculty of Arts and Education, CSU; Acting Head of School Wendy Bowles, School of Social Work and Arts, CSU; and the SSP committee for supporting the SSP application. We also thank our colleagues in the School of Social Work and Arts for supporting our work. We are grateful to Mark Filmer, Research Editor, CSU, for his editorial contribution to the book. We thank CSU's Human Research Ethics Committee for approving the research proposal (protocol no: 2014/057).

Janet Kim and her team at Springer have done a great job in carefully coordinating and producing this book, and we thank them for their cooperation throughout the publication process. We also thank the blinded peer reviewers of the book proposal for their valuable suggestions, which have further enriched the book.

Finally, and most importantly, we appreciate the love and support of our families.

Although help has come from many quarters to write and publish the book, we are solely responsible for any errors or shortcomings.

Manohar Pawar
A. W. (Bill) Anscombe

Contents

About the Authors

Manohar Pawar, PhD, is Professor of Social Work, School of Social Work and Arts and the Gulbali Institute for Agriculture, Water and Environment, Charles Sturt University, Australia; the President of the International Consortium for Social Development and the founding Editor-in-Chief of a peer-reviewed journal, *The International Journal of Community and Social Development*, published by SAGE. He has nearly 40 years of experience in social work education, research, and practice in Australia and India. He has received several honors and awards. His interests and recent publications include *COVID-19 Pandemic: Impact on and Implications for Community and Social Development* (ed., SAGE, 2021); *Virtue Ethics in Social Work Practice* (coauthored, Routledge, 2021); *Empowering Social Workers: Virtuous Practitioners* (coauthored Springer, 2017); *Future Directions in Social Development* (coedited, Palgrave Macmillan, 2017); *Reflective Social Work Practice: Thinking, Doing and Being* (coauthored, Cambridge University Press, 2015); *Water and Social Policy* (Palgrave Macmillan, 2014); *Social and Community Development Practice* (SAGE, 2014); *International Social Work: Issues, strategies and programs* (coauthored, 2nd edition, SAGE, 2013); and *SAGE Handbook of International Social Work* (coedited, SAGE, 2012).

A. W. (Bill) Anscombe, PhD, is Adjunct Associate Professor with the Australian Centre for Christianity and Culture at Charles Sturt University (CSU), Australia, and the Gulbali Institute for Agriculture, Water and the Environment at CSU. Prior to "retiring," he had 21 years at CSU, including as Course Director for CSU Social Work and Social Welfare programs. Prior to academia, he had 20 years in corrections, where he held positions from trainee to senior management roles, including Regional Operations Manager and A/Regional Director for Southern NSW, Australia. In 2000, he was seconded from the university to be the Director for Child Protection (Western) as part of the (then) New South Wales Department of Community Services, with responsibility for a geographical area of about 600,000 km^2, 25 service outlets, 1000+ children in Out of Home Care, 168 professional staff, and more than 14,000 Child at Serious Risk of Harm reports. He also operated in a joint appointment between CSU and the Department of Community

Services for four years. He is currently a voluntary director of five not-for-profit small/medium human service companies or associations. He has an active, committed Christian faith. His research interests and projects have been broad, including in the areas of First Nations housing and governance, health in multicultural Australia, rural social services, child welfare, corrections, faith in rural Australia, and numerous service evaluations. His doctoral studies were on "Consilience in social work: Reflections on thinking, doing and being." His most recent book publications are *Virtue Ethics in Social Work Practice* (coauthored, Routledge, 2021); *Empowering Social Workers: Virtuous Practitioners* (coauthored, Springer, 2017); and *Reflective Social Work Practice: Thinking, Doing and Being* (coauthored, Cambridge University Press, 2015).

Chapter 1
Professional Supervision: An Introduction

Introduction

Professional supervision in professional social work is emerging as an important area of practice in its own right. The main purpose of this chapter is to introduce the book. By discussing the concept of professional supervision in professional social work and by sharing the authors' motivations for writing this book, the chapter states the rationale for and significance of professional supervision in social work. As there is so much confusion about different types of supervision, at the outset, this book delineates nine different types of supervision with their respective purposes, features, and limitations. These include professional supervision for student social workers, post-qualification practice, and academics in the tertiary sector. Further, supervision by line managers/administration and independent supervisors is clarified. Other types include group supervision, peer supervision, mentoring, and coaching. The next section discusses the role of professional bodies in professional supervision. The objective of the book is to facilitate professional supervision in social work with a focus on building character and qualities. It outlines a mixed-methods approach followed for this research. The final section shows how the book is organized by introducing each chapter. This chapter concludes with a summary.

Professional Supervision in Professional Social Work

This book is about professional supervision in professional social work (hereafter referred to as social work) and supervisors' views about supervision, supervisees, and virtues or qualities. Professional supervision in social work (defined in Chap. 2) is not new. In fact, the origin of professional supervision is attributed to social work practice (Tsui, 1997; Davys & Beddoe, 2021). The phrase "professional supervision" is a loaded concept with several variants. To some, the term "supervision" conveys support, guidance, help, confirming performance, and the opportunity to discuss, reflect, learn, and grow. Others may think and perceive that supervision significantly compromises the whole purpose of professional supervision, as it often connotes surveillance, hierarchy, power, command and control, and some element of management. However, the practice of professional supervision does not have these elements. In some respects, the inappropriate use of these power- and control-related elements may lead to a need for professional supervision. We also wonder whether the term supervision should be taken out and replaced with development, reflection, or enhancement as professional development, professional reflection, or professional enhancement in order to remove all negative and discomforting elements associated with supervision. In some contexts, sectors, and organizations, supervision may make sense, but that kind of supervision is not intended in the professional supervision under discussion.

The meaning inherent in the term profession or professional stems from the question of what makes social work a profession. That question is provocative as some wonder whether social work is a profession. However, delving into that question is a distraction here, and we revisit it later in Chap. 2. For quick clarity, we draw on Henrickson's (2022, p. 187) delineation of seven attributes that make a profession.

1. a clearly defined and altruistic purpose;
2. transmissible theoretical knowledge (which may be trans- or interdisciplinary);
3. specialised skills or techniques;
4. a commonly held values base and enforceable ethical code;
5. a high degree of individual responsibility and autonomy in decision-making;
6. self-governing association, with a credentialling process, and accountability to others within the association; and,
7. public and political recognition as a distinct professional group (this includes prestige).

As social work has most of these attributes, at least in some nation-state contexts, we may agree that social work is a profession. Thus, professional supervision in social work should help to enhance these attributes in practitioners on an ongoing basis. Often problems and complexities in practice arise due to issues with these attributes. It may be a lack of clarity and purpose, knowledge and skills, autonomy and decision-making, and recognition and may be the presence of value conflicts. Thus, depending upon the need and context, experienced and qualified social workers help practitioners reflect on and develop clarity and purpose, transfer knowledge, strengthen skills, make decisions according to ethical standards, and connect with associations and institutions. Professional supervision in social work is about developing or improving or thinking about and reflecting on social work professional practice and professional practitioners (these two are intertwined) in order to work optimally, to the best of their ability, with individuals, families, groups, and communities within organizational and institutional contexts.

As indicated above, in addition to professional attributes in professional supervision in social work, there are three more important parts to it, as shown in Fig. 1.1. These are agency, people and communities, and their organizations and institutions. The main agency in professional supervision in social work is the social work practitioner and the social work supervisor. It is important to understand themselves and the orientation as they are the main players in the supervision. What are their

Fig. 1.1 Professional
supervision in social work.
(Source: Authors)

expectations from the supervision? Do they focus on the qualities of practitioners in the supervision? The ultimate output and outcome from professional supervision is a better service to people and communities they work with, whether it is an individual client, family, child, group, or community. Thus, practice issues and complexities to work with are critical aspects of professional supervision. Finally, as most of the time this practice occurs in the organizational and institutional context, practitioners address learnings and challenges relating to working in those contexts. This delineation suggests that professional supervision in social work revolves and reveals, and at times rebels, around professional attributes, agency of the practitioner and supervisor, people and communities, and organizational and institutional contexts. Practice experiences, challenges, and opportunities in each one of these and together make fertile ground for practitioners to discuss, reflect, and grow.

Motivation for Writing This Book

Our encounters and interviews with social work practitioners and supervisors across Australia inspired us to write and share this work with you. As part of our Australian Research Council (ARC) Discovery project, we asked a few questions relating to professional supervision in our interviews with social work practitioners and supervisors. Based on those interviews, we formed an impression that there was a great need for professional supervision in social work, but all practitioners do not have access to it, and of those who did, some desired more. Some practitioners had no provision for professional supervision in their organizations. In a few cases, social workers had organized and paid themselves for professional supervision outside of their workplace. It appears that the whole idea of supervision is shrouded in confusion. At the practice level, there seem to be terms used and approaches taken that are pragmatic and idiosyncratic responses to that confusion. This research experience suggested that there is a dire need for professional supervision and more work needs to be done in this area.

In addition to this research experience, we also have experiences of both receiving and providing professional supervision in social work. As student social workers, both of us received fieldwork supervision when on placement from onsite supervisors and field liaison staff from universities. Receiving supervision while learning as a social work student is different from receiving supervision as a practitioner working in an organization. In his first job as a community social worker, the first author did not have a professional supervisor. He had a coordinator for reporting and administrative purposes. At the time, he was unaware that such a thing as professional supervision existed in employing agencies. After that, he worked as a fieldwork supervisor for social work students and visited placement agencies and read and corrected social work students' fieldwork reports. In his third assignment, he worked as a rehabilitation/placement officer for a non-government organization (NGO), and the main task was finding employment for visually disabled people. He was the only qualified social worker working in the NGO, though the manager was supportive, but not from the perspective of social work professional supervision. In hindsight, he would have greatly benefited from professional supervision in that role as he struggled to find and arrange employment for visually disabled people, though he was not lacking in his efforts. Later he had supervisors for his doctoral studies. Still he does not think it can be considered professional supervision in social work, though it may have similar elements depending upon the research subject. In a few universities, he has performed the role of field liaison for several students and worked with on- and off-site supervisors to facilitate students' learning and professional development. In addition, he was appointed mentor to colleagues at the initial stages of their academic careers. Outside his workplace, he has informally, as a professional friend, offered mentoring and support to several social work colleagues, who approached him, shared their experiences in confidence, and discussed their contexts and options. These experiences have helped him realize the significance of professional supervision in social work and motivated him to do this research and share it with you.

Similarly, the second author has significant professional supervision experience in corrections, child welfare and protection, and the university sector. He was privileged to have four social work student placements and three excellent supervisors as a student social worker. One student social work placement was difficult.

His initial supervision in the workplace was from non-social workers and was primarily aimed at administrative and job-related matters with an emphasis on refining and solving role ambiguities, role differentiation, and orientation. No discussion of ethics or professional values occurred. For 8 years, he operated as the sole worker in a small rural community without any formal supervision. Assessed as highly competent, effective, and innovative, the approach from management was "leave the good workers alone." He was fortunate to develop a peer-to-peer supervision arrangement with a professional in a different field who was also seeking professional stimulation, accountability, and the capacity for reflective and insightful and, at times, challenging professional interaction.

Over more than 40 years, he has supervised a wide range of people on a one-to-one basis, including direct staff reportees, other staff who did not report to him, students, trainees, staff involved in external contracted supervision services in settings such as a private prison, as well as health workers and child welfare staff. He has also undertaken group supervision with counseling and social work staff and has mentored and supervised managerial staff and experienced staff taking new roles as directors and leaders in social work agencies. He has also been the supervisor of multiple chief executive officers as chairman of a not-for-profit welfare-oriented organization for more than 20 years.

Rationale for and Significance of Professional Supervision in Social Work

Professional supervision in social work originated out of necessity. Given the complex nature of challenging work, often involving unique crises, whether it is extreme poverty and want, children and women in difficult circumstances, mental health, homelessness, chemical dependency, relationship issues, or unexpected life events, social work practitioners may need support from several perspectives. Some social work practitioners offer and receive professional supervision for thinking about and improving their practice and for the growth of the profession. Despite its inherent value, significance, and relevance, it has remained relatively neglected or inadequately attended to in the global context of the social work profession and practice. Social work is a broad, all-encompassing profession in terms of areas or sectors of practice such as health, hospitals, mental health, education, housing, child welfare, family, community development, NGOs, social security, and new and emerging fields of practice, for example, eco or green social work, and disasters. Relative to these broad fields of practice and expanding social work practice and practitioners, professional supervision is unable to match demand, both in terms of professional supervision in practice and also research and publications.

The availability of professional supervision assures practitioners that support is available to continue their practice with confidence. The support helps supervisees to clarify their questions, doubts, and uncertainties with experienced supervisors. It provides an excellent platform for supervisees and supervisors to reflect on practice issues and their work to address them in better or alternative ways. It helps to critically discuss how and where they have done well and reinforce good practices and how and where they have not done well and how they can correct and improve their practices. It facilitates reflective practice (Beddoe, 2010), which has emerged as an important method in many professions. Where possible, it helps to freely discuss organizational issues – whether it is work-relationship issues with a manager or supervisor, discriminatory practices, professional value conflicts, or workplace culture – and strategies to deal with them tactfully. It can, when necessary, even help with how to confront, take a stand, and fight for bringing change.

Due to demanding and intensive work, it is not unusual for social workers to experience burnout, which may lead to changing jobs or leaving the profession altogether. Professional supervision may help practitioners to constructively cope with burnout issues and continue to provide high-quality services. Based on their research, Chiller and Crisp (2012) have argued that professional supervision can help increase the retention of social workers in certain sectors where turnover is very high. Group supervision, depending upon how it is facilitated, can enhance peer sharing and learning. In some cases, such as managerial/administrative supervision, some social workers find it limiting, so external professional supervision offers a platform to discuss certain matters freely in confidence. In certain practice settings, such as mental health and registered or licensed social work practice systems, there is a minimum of hours of supervised practice required to gain a qualification to practice. In the case of performance and accountability issues, though this is not the sole purpose of professional supervision, it helps the practitioner to work around meeting these expectations. Thus, it contributes to appropriate, better quality, or new or improved services to people and communities. The process of supervision has the potential to be innovative in practice. As pointed out previously, while there is a significant need and demand for professional supervision, it has remained inadequately developed in the field and systemically. It is not available to all social work practitioners who need it across all sectors. In some sectors, such as child protection, disability, mental health, and aging, there is a growing demand for well-trained social workers. It is critical to organize systematic professional supervision in these growing areas. Overall, professional supervision in social work will benefit social workers and the people and communities they serve due to better- or high-quality services, employers by not losing experienced employees, and professional bodies by maintaining and enhancing professional standards.

Concept, Nature, Types, and the Main Features of Professional Supervision

As delineated above, although professional supervision in social work is broadly about professional attributes, agency of the practitioner and supervisor, people and communities, and organizations and institutions, the concept and nature of supervision vary depending upon the type of professional supervision. We have categorized professional supervision relating to student social workers, post-qualification practice supervision to seek license/accreditation to practice in certain settings and regions, line-management/ administration, group supervision, peer supervision, academic positions in the tertiary sector, independent supervision for practitioners, mentoring, and coaching. Although there is some clarity about these types or categories, in practice some people use them interchangeably, which may lead to confusion about their similarities and differences. We have tried to briefly clarify by delineating the purpose and motivation, the main features, and a few limitations of these types of supervision in Table 1.1.

Table 1.1 Types and main features of professional supervision

Types	Purpose/motivation	Main features	Some of the limitations
Student social workers	Learning social work practice Developing beginning minimum practice skills Relating theory to practice Internalizing social work values/ethics Acquiring tertiary qualification	Learning focus Student supervisor relationship Accountable to many players Prescribed curriculum	Mostly new Power differentials Very little flexibility
Supervised practice to seek license/registration/accreditation to practice as social workers in certain regions/settings	Enhance practice skills Discuss and reflect with supervisor Meet requirements of the licensing/accrediting agency License to practice	Practice focus Comply with licensing/accrediting requirements May include clinical practice skills Confirm whether I fit with social work and social work fit with me Prescribed by state agencies/professional bodies	Mandatory Power differentials Ends after completing supervised hours
Line-management/administration as part of employer organization	Employer prescribed Hierarchical Performance Employment Accountability Improving practice Better service outcomes	Hierarchical Performance driven Power Free discussion may or may not be possible	Power imbalance Professional matters may not be a priority Inhibited discussion
Group supervision	Discussion and learning in groups Improved practice Uniformity in practice standards Group socialization Economical	Supervisor/facilitator led Discussion in groups and learning Case/issue focused	May not discuss individual concerns One member may dominate Unconducive dynamics may emerge

(continued)

Table 1.1 (continued)

Types	Purpose/motivation	Main features	Some of the limitations
Peer supervision	Mutual sharing, support, and learning Reduce isolation Raise doubts, questions Confirming practice Just to debrief/talk	Voluntary Self-motivated and organized Discussion free from organizational constraints Trust and relationship Flexible Can be structured	May or may not be regular Some questions, issues may need further advice Can be very informal
Academic positions in the tertiary sector	Smooth transition from practice to academia Learning and teaching in the tertiary sector Research and publications Career advancement Academic socialization	Adapting to an academic culture Using practice experience in teaching/research Acquiring learning, teaching and research skills	Initially may be daunting Lack of a suitable supervisor/mentor Lack of the recognition of practice experience
Independent supervision/non-line-management	Enhancing practice Self-improvement Resolving organizational issues, value conflicts Free discussion without the manager's/employer's presence	Self-arranged, may or may not be supported by the employer Critical reflection on practice and improvement Free from organizational/manager's presence	Performance is not the sole focus Cooption may occur Focus may change to personal issues
Mentoring	Career advancement Personal growth and development Motivate and inspire Transfer knowledge Develop leadership Guide/advise/feedback Psycho-social support Overall wellbeing	Mentor with experience, expertise, and achievement Informal Agenda led by mentee Asymmetrical relationship Long term One to one Deep respect to mentor	Giver-receiver relationship Depends upon mentee's initiative May overwhelm mentee Cannot measure all outcomes Cultural differences

Types	Purpose/motivation	Main features	Some of the limitations
Coaching	Improving performance Enhancing skill Particular behavior change	Instructing Specific skills and goals Task focused Relatively short term Immediate feedback One to one or to group More accountability	Narrow/specific outcome Relatively short term The coach is not the performer

Source: Authors

Professional Supervision for Student Social Workers

As part of acquiring accredited social work qualifications, the Bachelor of Social Work (BSW) and Master of Social Work (MSW), student social workers are placed in government or non-government organizations or communities under the supervision of qualified social workers for a prescribed number of hours. These are generally known as field placements or workplace learning and organized by social work schools/departments in the tertiary sector. Some are undertaken concurrently with the BSW/MSW courses, some are in blocks, and some are a combination of both. For most students, this is the first experience of professional supervision in social work. It is an entry point for student social workers to the world of professional social work. These field placements are compulsory in almost all schools of social work. Generally, and preferably, professional supervision is provided by an onsite qualified social worker, and when this is not possible, an off-site supervisor is arranged on a paid or voluntary basis. A field liaison officer from the relevant social work school is also engaged in the field placements to ensure the placement is completed according to the course's curriculum requirements. The main purpose of the professional supervision of social work students is providing initial orientation to social work practice and the profession, developing beginning practice skills, relating theory to practice, and acquiring the qualification. Through this process, students internalize social work values and ethics, socialize in the profession, develop networks, and experience different expressions and fields of social work. Students mainly focus on learning under the guidance of supervisors and field liaison staff, according to the field education course curriculum. Although several learning options are provided, in many respects, there is little flexibility in these placements as practice competencies and ethical standards prescribed by the accreditation bodies need to be developed. The supervisee's status as a student has inherent power differentials while working with the supervisor and field liaison officer. As they are making progress toward acquiring the professional qualification, students are not treated as qualified practitioners. However, while it is a crucial part of professional supervision in social work, it is not the focus of this book.

Post-qualification Practice Supervision

After obtaining professionally accredited qualifications (BSW or MSW), many graduates begin practicing as social workers, as professional supervision is not required in many countries. Where licensing systems exist (e.g., in many states in the USA) and there are accreditation requirements for practice in certain settings such as mental health (e.g., in Australia), social workers must complete a prescribed number of hours of supervised practice under the supervision of a qualified and experienced social worker. This is generally known as post-qualifying supervised practice for obtaining a license or accreditation for practice. Depending upon the licensing system, it may also include clinical practice under supervision. The main purpose of this type of supervision is to sharpen practice skills, discuss and seek feedback from experienced supervisors, develop expertise in a particular area of practice according to ethical standards, and obtain a license or accreditation from the relevant licensing board or professional body. The overriding purpose is to maintain standards in practice to deliver better service to people and communities without causing any harm to them. It is also clearly linked to gaining employment. As these are mandatory requirements where they exist, this supervised practice must be completed. So, power differentials exist between the supervisee and supervisor, and the supervision ends after completing the prescribed hours. In some cases, if the supervision fee is paid by supervisees, there may be potential for cooption and ethical issues.

Supervision by the Line-Management/Administration

This is the most common type of supervision provided to many social workers where it exists. Professionally trained and experienced social workers, who are line-managers or administrative heads, provide professional supervision to social workers working under their management and administration with a view to achieving better practice and better service outcomes. Their more explicit role is administrative accountability, allocating work and supervising to ensure the work is completed according to the expected standards, both in terms of time and delivery of service. The focus is on the performance of supervisees. Offering professional social work supervision may or may not be the role of line-managers. Some line-managers can provide both line-management and professional supervision to social work supervisees to their mutual satisfaction. Integrating these roles in terms of surveillance and support is a good achievement both on the part of supervisees and supervisors. Often such integration may not be achieved due to several factors. First, it may not be the explicitly stated role of supervisors. Second, even if it is, managers may not have adequate time as they are often overwhelmed by administrative roles and supervision workload. Third, due to management and rational orientation, organizations often may not give time for such professional supervision and may not recognize it. Fourth, when such a role is expected and recognized by organizations, some supervisees may not feel comfortable to openly and freely discuss all practice needs and issues as they are line-managers or administrative heads with power and authority. For example, some supervisees may be unwilling to bring up and work on personal issues that may affect work performance or cause distress in the individual (e.g., increased alcohol use, the birth of a new child, or family members with health problems that may affect work performance) due to the fear of how one is perceived. It could affect the perception of performance, job security, relationship, competence or promotions, etc. There may be mandated legal requirements of supervisors through work, health, and safety, or agency requirements that complicate the supervisor/supervisee relationship. Fifth, in some organizations, this type of professional supervision may not be a priority due to resource constraints and/or a lack of commitment to professional social work standards.

A more complex scenario is when the line-manager or administrative head is not a professionally trained social worker and cannot understand, appreciate, and support the roles and working approaches of a social worker. The practice matter may also be concerning when social workers experience professional value conflicts (personal values may conflict with agency, professional, and community values; agency values may conflict with professional and community values; and occasionally professional values may conflict with community values), unprofessional practices, and processes and cannot raise them due to power and hierarchy dynamics. In organizations, professional social work supervision through line-management or administration has great potential if it is appropriately incorporated and resourced.

Group Supervision

Group supervision is another important alternative or a supplementary approach to professional supervision in social work. It may be used independently or in combination with any of the other eight supervision approaches. Under group supervision, the qualified and experienced supervisor has an important facilitative role to engage a group of supervisees (the Board of Behavioral Sciences (2022) recommends three to a maximum of eight supervisees) in the supervision process to present cases, raise questions, discuss practice issues, and enhance learning and support from the group members (who may be peers). It is not only economical but also may help increase uniformity in practice standards. It may not be an appropriate platform to discuss an individual social worker's issues and concerns, depending upon the group norms and expectations. It is important to ensure that all group members respect each other and one member does not dominate in the group supervision, including the facilitator. Unconducive group dynamics may emerge, and sometimes, inadvertently, diversion from the main point may occur in the discussion. The facilitator and all group members have a critical role in ensuring that professional social work supervision objectives are achieved as far as possible through group supervision.

Peer Supervision

We define peer supervision as a voluntary, self-motivated and organized, egalitarian, and flexible platform created by two or more professionals from the same or related professions to share respectfully, trustfully, non-judgmentally, and mutually their experiences and reflect on them to learn from and support each other. It is also referred to as peer consultation (see Bailey et al., 2014). Further, peer group supervision is defined and discussed in Chap. 4 as one of the models of professional supervision. Mutual trusting relationships are essential in peer supervision. Peer supervision can be organized on a one-to-one (dyadic) basis or in groups at a mutually agreed frequency within or outside the organization. Without organizational or hierarchical constraints, peers feel free to raise questions and doubts and confirm good practices. It helps to reduce the practitioner's isolation in rural and remote areas. Although it is flexible and has the potential to become very informal and casual, it can be organized in a structured and systematic manner (Bailey et al., 2014; Napan, 2021; Philips, 2021). The peers' commitment is necessary to make it regular. For some critical and complex issues, peer supervision may not suffice. However, peer supervision is significant – where professional supervision is not available or offered (Egan et al., 2017, 2018), this is the best alternative if it works.

Supervision in the Tertiary Sector

This type of supervision is traditionally not included in professional supervision in social work because it may not be perceived as social work practice in a narrow sense. Our experience suggests that it is as important as any other type of supervision discussed here. Professional supervision in the tertiary sector refers to experienced social work academics offering mentoring and support to social work practitioners entering teaching and research careers in universities, colleges, or similar educational institutions. Rich experience in practice notwithstanding, many practitioners find entering, settling, and developing an academic career daunting, at least initially. Professional supervisors and mentors need to be organized to guide and offer help and support to smoothly transition social workers from practice to academia. It may involve becoming familiar with academic culture and institutions, learning-teaching strategies, research, writing and publications, doctoral research, and submitting grant applications. Although theoretically recognized, it is not uncommon for some practice-based academics to feel that their practice experience is not valued in academic institutions, particularly when they find it challenging to progress and make an academic career. Professional supervisors and supervisees need to work together to prevent such situations and to prosper academically. As this type of professional supervision is closely connected to social work professional goals and commitments, professional bodies and other relevant institutions need to include it in their practice and supervision standards.

Independent Supervision

Under this type of supervision, qualified and experienced social workers offer professional supervision to social work practitioners to discuss the practice issues and needs identified by supervisees. The independent supervisors may or may not be in the employer organization of the supervisees. If they are located in the employer organization, they are certainly not direct line-managers or administrative heads. Some employer organizations may or may not support this type of external supervision with or without funding. Some organizations that do not support formal supervision may be of the view that supervision is a continuous process that fosters a culture of support and pro-social modeling of behavior and values that are acceptable. However, often these independent supervision sessions are sought by supervisees so that they can freely and openly discuss practice issues; organizational or management issues to seek advice, reflect and improve practice, and also navigate complex organizations or difficult managers or supervisors; and professional or ethical dilemmas. This type of supervision may also be organized to meet licensing and/or accreditation requirements. In some cases, supervisees even pay to attend such supervision sessions. Supervisors need to be careful that these supervision sessions do not draw attention to supervisees' personal issues. Sometimes, supervisors as mentors and supporters play a delicate role and must separate personal and professional issues and appropriately refer the supervisee to relevant resources to attend to personal issues. It is also important to prevent potential coopting tendencies. It is also critical to ensure responsibility for action taken on key issues and guard against any conflicts of interests.

Mentoring

Just as professional supervision is a popularly used phrase in professional social work practice, the term mentoring is widely employed in academic organizations and the corporate and business sectors and in some cultures as an alternative to supervision. Professional supervision can include elements of mentoring, depending upon how it is done, but mentoring does not capture all aspects of professional supervision in most contexts. We define mentoring as a mentee initiated and focused formal or informal arrangement in or outside the organization, in which a mentor, with experience, expertise, and achievement credentials, unselfishly motivates and inspires, guides, advises, provides feedback and psychosocial support, and transfers knowledge to mentees to advance their career and personal development (Ross-Sheriff & Orme, 2017; KSU, 2022) and remains as a well-wisher of the mentee, even after terminating the mentoring relationship. Mentoring is generally a long-term (1–2 years or more) process and is conducted on a one-to-one basis. Implicit in the relationship is a deep respect of the mentee to the mentor, who often assumes the role of a giver and the mentee is a receiver. So, in many respects, it is an asymmetrical relationship. Sometimes, the mentor's accomplishments can be overwhelming, and it may be difficult to measure mentoring outcomes. However, as illustrated below in some cultures, mentoring is a more preferred term than supervision.

For example, a large government agency working in child protection appointed two senior Aboriginal men to significant positions and organized an external supervisor, co-author of the book. The term professional supervision was not used, as it had pejorative connotations of power and control; the "white" man having knowledge that is "imparted" to the Indigenous man; and the consequent devaluing of Indigenous knowledges and privileging of white knowledges. Thus, the term "learning together" was adopted between the supervisees and the supervisor, and for formal correspondence and reference within the agency, the term "mentoring" was used as it was more culturally appropriate.

Coaching

Coaching is defined as a specially arranged and performance-driven activity between the coach and the coachee or coachees, who will together determine the required targets, tasks, time, goals, and skills, including behavior change, and the coachee will pursue/practice to achieve them under the instruction of the coach. Though the term is popular in sports, for professional practice purposes, coaching arrangements are done in highly specialized areas, with a short timeframe, regular practice and immediate feedback, and more accountability. Generally, the focus is narrow and specific and on outcomes (Ross-Sheriff & Orme, 2017; KSU, 2022). Professional supervision can include some elements of coaching, but coaching cannot be equated with professional supervision.

Some Basic Principles

It is critical to note a few basic principles that are common to any type of supervision discussed above. These were not stated earlier to avoid repetition. All supervisors and supervisees should follow certain ethical standards and values and principles relating to supervision. These are respect, confidentiality, integrity, reflective practice, realizing human potential, commitment to improving practice, and service to people and communities.

Mode of Supervision

The traditional mode of offering supervision has been in-person and face-to-face. With the advent of information and digital technology, it is gradually changing, and many supervisors and supervisees are having supervision by using teleconference or through the Internet. AASW (2014, p. 4) states that "Supervision may be accessed by a range of means including, but not limited to: face-to-face, online, telephone, video/web conferencing." Following the COVID-19 pandemic and shutdowns, the use of the Internet, zoom rooms, and similar online platforms for supervision meetings has become a norm. It is important to factor this mode of operation for supervision purposes as it opens new opportunities with its own strengths and limitations.

The Role of Professional Bodies

Social work professional bodies have a significant role in creating policies, programs, and standards for developing, implementing, and monitoring professional supervision systems in education, training, and practice, both in the interest of the profession and the public. Not all professional bodies perform all these functions as their status, role, acceptance and effectiveness differ in each country's context. It is also important to note that in some countries social work professional bodies do not exist, though social work is taught and practiced. Such countries may draw on international professional bodies' advisory standards and the statement of ethical principles (IASSW/IFSW, 2018, 2020). However, as an example, it may be useful to look at a few professional bodies' relevant policy documents to explore how they promote and practice professional supervision.

Two international professional bodies – the International Association of Schools of Social Work and the International Federation of Social Workers (IASSW and IFSW, 2020, p. 13) – have collaboratively developed the Global Standards for Social Work Education and Training to lift and maintain minimum social work education standards worldwide so that interested countries can adopt these standards according to their local contexts. This is a very important policy document for social work education, training, and practice. These standards have a separate section on social work in practice, which, among other things, states that social work schools should (a) develop a comprehensive practice education manual and make it available to field placement supervisors and instructors, (b) establish policies and procedures for students' practice placements and supervision, (c) appoint and orient qualified and experienced placement supervisors/instructors, and (d) provide ongoing support to them, including training and education. The two professional bodies also have collaboratively developed the Global Social Work Statement of Ethical Principles (2018), but the statement does not refer to the term supervisor or supervision.

The CSWE (2015, 2022) accreditation standards 2015 and the second draft 2022, under competency 1, ethical, and professional behavior, direct social workers to use supervision to guide professional judgment and behavior. Further, the standards specify that to offer supervision to both BSW and MSW students placed in agencies, the supervisor should have accredited qualifications and a minimum of 2 years' post-qualifying practice experience (B and M 3.3.6, p. 16). If the field placement is in the place of employment, a qualified employment supervisor can offer field supervision, provided it is different from the employment supervision (3.3.7, 17).

Similarly, the Australian Association of Social Workers (AASW, 2021), in its social work and education standards, includes professional development and supervision as one of the eight domains of practice standards (AASW, 2013) and one of the graduate attributes. The TEQSA (2017) guidance note on Academic Quality Assurance requires social work education providers to ensure quality supervision for students in field placements and to take precautions to prevent indifferent supervision. It also states that field educators should provide a minimum of 1.5 hours of formal, structured supervision of students during every 35 hours of placement, and at least half of it should be on a one-to-one basis (4.5.6). For students who undertake only one placement, due to recognition of prior learning, their supervisor should be onsite and a qualified social worker (4.7.2). If students are placed in their place of employment, it does not allow the employment supervisor to be the placement supervisor (4.1.7). The field educator remains the primary supervisor responsible for assessing learning outcomes (4.5.4). The supervisor should "have a minimum of 2 years of practice experience and be eligible for membership of either the AASW or the equivalent professional association" (4.8.2, p. 13).

Obviously, this type of professional supervision is only limited to student social workers discussed above under types of supervision. However, as summarized below, the social work codes of ethics cover professional supervision for all social work practitioners in a broad sense.

In the US National Association of Social Workers (NASW, 2021) Code of Ethics, under the preamble, supervision is included as one of the activities to address social justice, social change, and related issues. Under the purpose of the code, technologically assisted service includes supervision as one aspect of social work practice. The code emphasizes the importance of receiving supervision before trying interventions and approaches that are new to them to ensure competent services (1.04. b). When standards are not established or do not exist in an emerging area of practice, the code suggests, among other steps, seeking supervision to protect clients from harm (1.04. c). The code also has a separate clause, 3.01, for supervision and consultation, which states that it is the ethical responsibility of social workers to offer supervision only in their expert area of knowledge, skills, and competence (a); to set clear, apt, and culturally sensitive boundaries (b); and to "evaluate supervisees' performance in a manner that is fair and respectful." It also specifies that social workers who assume administration/management leadership roles have the responsibility to take reasonable steps to allocate adequate agency resources to provide suitable staff supervision (3.07. c).

Like the NASW, the AASW code of ethics (AASW, 2020) includes supervision as part of social work practice (p. 6) and professional integrity (p. 10). "Under professional competence, social workers have a responsibility to: utilise available supervision as well as other specialist consultation, such as mentoring, coaching and supervision; and take active steps to ensure that they receive appropriate supervision as a means of maintaining and extending practice competence" (4.4, p. 14). For example, as part of supervision, a specialist consultation may be needed in highly complex cases that may involve medical procedures and court litigation in child protection or family dispute matters. It also suggests undertaking supervision when certain decisions are made (5.2.10), professional boundaries are compromised (5.7.2), and self-disclosure is intended (5.7.6). It also states that social workers in management roles are "to arrange professional supervision for social work staff, including culturally safe supervision, where appropriate" (7.2.7, p. 25). The code prescribes professional supervision to social workers who work in fee-for-service settings. Social workers must ensure that they have appropriate supervision and oversight if they are commencing first time as fee-for-service sole operators (8.1.16). Those social workers who are in fee-for-service private practice need to take active steps to receive appropriate supervision to maintain and extend practice competence (8.1.17).

In addition, the AASW (2014) has developed supervision standards for supervisors and supervisees. By stating the aims, purpose, values, functions, and processes of social work supervision, six standards for supervisors and three for supervisees are developed. The main purpose is to enhance professional skills and competence and ongoing learning and retain social workers in organizations. Three stated values are respect for persons, social justice, and professional integrity, and three stated functions are education, support, and accountability. The six standards for supervisors relate to ethical supervisory relationship, contract and record-keeping, competency, managing a supervisory relationship, achieving the purpose and functions of supervision, and managing unethical behavior of supervisees. The three standards for supervisees are maintaining an ethical relationship, active participation, and establishing the supervisory process to meet their needs. For new social work graduates with less than 2 years' experience or for social workers entering a new field of practice or facing challenges, fortnightly 60 minutes supervision meetings are recommended. For social workers with more than 2 years' experience, monthly 60 minutes meetings are recommended. As stated above, in the eight practice standards (AASW, 2013), one standard (8) is specially developed for professional development and supervision. These separate supervision and practice standards reflect the importance the professional body, the AASW, attaches to supervision.

This importance is well reflected in the criteria and eligibility to become an Accredited Mental Health Social Worker (AMHSW) in Australia (AASW, 2022). Regarding supervision, one of the criteria states that "Applicants should be able to show that they have been formally supervised, in line with the AASW Supervision Standards," summarized above. During the post-qualifying social work practice experience, social workers must have fortnightly supervision for 60 minutes in the first 2 years. "Generally, supervisors should have a higher level of practice experience than their supervisees and should have some training in supervision." In this case, it may be noted that the supervisor may be other than a social worker in a specialized area of practice (e.g., a psychologist, medical practitioner, or mental health nurse). Similarly, where social work licensing systems exist, supervised practice requirements, among others, must be met to acquire the license. For example, in California, the Board of Behavioral Sciences (2022) states that to qualify to be a Licensed Clinical Social Worker (LCSW), a minimum of 104 weeks or 3000 hours of supervised practice must be completed. The Washington State Department of Health (2022a, b) states "that licensure candidates must complete a total of 4000 hours of postgraduate supervision experience within a minimum of 3 years under approved supervisors." Although such requirements differ from state to state, they indicate the significance of professional supervision in social work.

These and similar professional supervision requirements – whether as a student of the BSW or MSW, a post-qualified new social work practitioner, an experienced practitioner seeking license or accreditation, or an ethical requirement to improve practice through regular supervision by professional bodies or licensing boards – suggest that supervision is a critical professional social work engagement both for supervisees and supervisors. Professional social work associations and other relevant organizations have a critical role to play in the growth of the profession, practitioners, and their organizations, for the ultimate benefit of people/clients and communities.

Objectives of the Book

This book was conceptualized with a view of sharing social work practitioners' views about professional supervision and supervisors' experiences about offering supervision and expectations from supervisees and whether supervisors focus on character and qualities in the process of supervision. To present this analysis in a context, it also discusses changes and challenges in social work and welfare and the concepts, types, and models of supervision. The overriding objective and outcome the book aims to achieve is to promote the practice of professional supervision in social work not only in mandatory contexts such as while studying and seeking licensing or accreditation but also as a self-motivated voluntary activity with a focus on building character and qualities. However, achieving this outcome depends upon how the ideas presented in this book inspire social workers to practice professional supervision in their practice to enhance their professional growth and the quality of service they deliver to people and communities.

Research Methods Followed

The data presented in this book were generated by following a mixed-methods approach and partly drawn from an Australian Research Council Discovery grant project, "Virtuous practitioners: Empowering social workers," which was approved by the CSU's Human Research Ethics Committee. The primary qualitative data were collected by randomly selecting and conducting interviews with 15 social work supervisors. These supervisors worked in mental health, child protection, family and domestic violence, disability, counseling, management, and private practice settings. Four were from rural areas, six from private practice, six from the public sector, and three from non-government organizations. Their age ranged from 44 to 68 years and experience from 8 to 40 years. Most of them had professional supervision as part of their role.

In addition, 50 social work practitioners across Australia were interviewed. A few Chapters, 1, 2, 3, and 4, are mainly based on secondary data from books, book chapters, journal articles, and online resources. As both authors have supervision experience in terms of receiving and offering supervision, their reflections (by using the reflective method) and interpretations are included wherever relevant. Although the study was based in Australia, professional supervision issues discussed in the book are relevant globally and to many countries' local contexts.

Organization of the Book

This book is organized into 13 chapters. This first chapter introduces the book by clarifying the concept of professional supervision in social work and sharing the authors' motivations and rationale for writing this book. Then, it discusses the nature and types of supervision, the role of professional bodies, the book's objectives, the research methods followed, and the organization of the book.

As professional supervision occurs in the overall socioeconomic and political context of social work and welfare, and supervisees and supervisors need to be aware of this, the second chapter provides a broad overview of social work as a profession and its global expansion and raises the question of if and how it is responding to some challenges and opportunities. It discusses whether social work has met its mission and the politics surrounding it. The chapter points out some changes and challenges relating to colonization, neocolonization and decolonization, deprofessionalization, populism, nationalism and welfare chauvinism, digitalization, and online trends and the sustainable development goals, climate change, and disasters. It also briefly reflects on the implications of these challenges for supervision and raises fundamental questions for further reflection and action.

The third chapter introduces the contexts of organizations and practice settings in which most professional supervision is conducted. The organizations discussed are government organizations (GOs), non-government organizations (NGOs), not-for-profit and for-profit organizations, faith-based organizations, philanthropies/trusts/foundations, corporate social responsibility-oriented organizations, international NGOs, and multilateral organizations. Social work practice settings include social protection/security, health and hospitals, private practice/mental health, child welfare/protection, family/domestic violence, school social work, corrections, community, research/policy/advocacy, and rural and remote. As line-management versus non-line-management supervision is a critical issue, it looks at respective strengths and weaknesses. The chapter argues that professional supervision should be extended to nonclinical practice organizational contexts and settings such as community, social enterprise, and policy practice.

Drawing from the available literature, the fourth chapter familiarizes a range of models of professional supervision. We have categorized these models into purpose- and goal-based models, path-based models, and the integration of purpose- and path-based models. These three types of models have been summarized to show supervisees and supervisors the choice available for their supervision practice. Our analysis identifies seven purposes of supervision and argues that all the purposes and goals of supervision are not addressed and not achieved as the line-management supervision is dominated by administrative and management matters. Further, most of the models appear to have a clinical practice orientation.

The fifth chapter discusses some of the critical dilemmas and challenges identified by supervisors. These relate to line-management supervision versus non-line-management (external) supervision, supervision in private practice, supervision through phone and online (digital supervision), supervising social workers and non-social workers and new and experienced social workers, and the role of the professional bodies in supervision. It also looks at the issue of developing certain qualities or character in supervisees. The chapter exposes the issues of balancing surveillance and support and keeping human-centeredness in supervision and the need for the development of virtues and qualities.

The general process followed by supervisors and the essentials and content of professional supervision identified by them are discussed in Chap. 6. The analysis of interviews with supervisors showed that the beginning process they follow is wide-ranging. Some keep it open, flexible, informal, and conversational, whereas others follow a structured, contractual process. Further, it discusses 17 main elements or essentials and 10 core themes of professional supervision shared by supervisors. Both the essentials and contents of supervision seem to revolve around administration, education, and support functions of supervision, but these are mostly driven by supervisees and active listening and guiding by supervisors. It points out the prominence of reflective practice and the neglect of the ending process in the supervision.

The seventh chapter explores the expectations of supervisees and supervisors. Supervisors think that supervisees expect supervisors to make themselves available, support, respect, provide space for ventilating, have a plan/direction/advice, help solve problems, enhance learning, facilitate reflection, share alternative perspectives, and offer honest feedback, be accountable, and maintain continuity and counsel. On the other hand, supervisors expect supervisees to come prepared; take follow-up action; analyze issues from different perspectives; discuss ethical dilemmas; be critical, honest, and responsible; and have a proper focus. The chapter shows similarities and differences in supervisees' and supervisors' expectations to enhance professional supervision.

In Chap. 8, the core issues discussed in supervision are analyzed. The supervisors' narratives suggested these relate to organizational contexts, clients/practice, maintaining boundaries, personal issues, and the recognition of good work done.

Issues relating to developing competency, both in terms of skills and knowledge, and maintaining boundaries are discussed. The analysis suggests that the organizational issues were more challenging to practitioners than the issues they experienced in their practice with people/clients. While discussion of the issues in the supervision is important, the supervision should not be dominated by issues alone. Good work done in practice should also be discussed in supervision.

Different concepts and theories used by supervisors are analyzed in Chap. 9. Some of the concepts and theories discussed in the chapter are broad and educational, such as adult learning, Kolb's cycle, reflective practice, and systems theory, whereas some others are more therapeutic or clinical such as narrative therapy, family therapy, and the psychodynamic lens. Of the concepts used by supervisors, over half relate to social work clinical practice theories. Most of the supervisors seem to use these models in combination or by mixing other ideas, generally known as an eclectic approach. The chapter does not elaborate on any concept or theory but develops an understanding of what concepts and theories supervisors use to supervise supervisees.

The tenth chapter discusses how supervisors use practice wisdom in supervision. It delineates practice wisdom in three areas. First, it discusses how the supervisors' practice wisdom is inextricably linked to the supervisors' experience. It emphasizes the significance of sharing the relevant experience with supervisees, reflecting on it, sharing what has not worked with humility, and appropriately self-disclosing. Second, it identifies the supervisors' practice wisdom in some of their statements such as "we cannot be good at everything," "do not just jump in, think," and "if in doubt, throw them out." Third, it develops a list of supervision practice principles suggested by the supervisors. The invaluable wisdom shared by the supervisors is generally useful for both supervisors and supervisees.

Whether and how supervisors try to develop virtues/qualities in supervisees as part of the professional supervision is explored in Chap. 11. First, it discusses some social workers' qualities as perceived by supervisors. These include finding one's own answers/self-determination, strengths-based thinking, a non-judgmental approach, human rights, empowerment, honesty and accountability, patience, tolerance, understanding and care, compassion, good relationship/link to the wider world, shared learning, and similar. Through their narratives, the second part shows how supervisors develop some qualities such as strengths, honesty, reflection, good listening, decision-making, warmth, confidence, humor, and similar in supervisees. The chapter contends that there is scope for purposefully focusing on developing virtues/qualities of social workers both through education and training and through professional supervision.

The core subject of Chap. 12 is developing the "being" of supervisees. It discusses the supervisors' views about the personal and professional being of supervisees. It shows how most supervisors emphasize the significance of integrating the two as they cannot be separated. Further, analyzing the supervisors' narratives, it discusses developing the supervisee's being by role modeling, discussing supervisees' qualities, creating a safe environment, caring, looking into family value conflicts/influences, and using previous situations for comparisons. This beginning discussion suggests that there is a potential use of the professional supervision platform to holistically strengthen the being of the supervisee with a focus on developing virtues/qualities, and supervisors can play a crucial role in this.

The final chapter brings together the range of ideas explored in the book and argues for action for professional supervision. It asserts that as planned and purposeful development of virtues/qualities in supervisees does not occur, it is critical to purposefully focus on developing the virtues/qualities of social workers both through education and training and through professional supervision. Acknowledging the limitations of the study and suggesting a few ideas for further research, it highlights the main trends impacting the practice and the increasing need and demand for professional supervision across the sectors. Given the growing knowledge and skills in this field, the authors call for a coordinated action involving all stakeholders to enhance access to professional supervision for all who need it.

Conclusion and Summary

The main purpose of this chapter is to briefly introduce the book. Toward that end, it clarifies our conceptualization of professional supervision in professional social work and how our experience has motivated us to write this book. The analysis of the concept shows that professional supervision in social work revolves and reveals, and at times rebels, around professional attributes, agency of the practitioner and supervisor, people and communities, and organizational and institutional contexts. Practice experiences, challenges, and opportunities in each one of these and together make fertile ground for practitioners to discuss, reflect, and grow. Professional supervision is significant to all stakeholders from several perspectives as it facilitates care and quality of services to people and communities. As there is much confusion about different types of supervision, at the outset, it delineates nine different types of supervision with their respective purposes, features, and limitations in a summary form. As professional bodies are one of the important stakeholders in professional supervision, it is necessary to consider their role in it. The book uses a mixed-methods approach and aims to facilitate professional supervision in social work, focusing on building character and qualities. By briefly introducing each chapter, the final section shows how the book is organized. The next chapter discusses some of the changes and challenges in social work and welfare and their implications for professional supervision.

References

AASW. (2013). *Practice standards – 2013*. AASW.
AASW. (2014). Supervision standards – 2014. AASW.
AASW. (2020). *Australian Association of Social Workers Code of Ethics 2020*. AASW.

AASW. (2021). *Australian social work education and accreditation standards 2021*. AASW.
AASW. (2022). *Criteria and eligibility for AMHSW*. Accessed on 4 February 2022 from https://www.aasw.asn.au/membership-information/information-for-applying-for-the-accredited-mental-health-social-worker-credential
Bailey, R., Bell, K., Kalle, W., & Pawar, M. (2014). Restoring meaning to supervision through a peer consultation group in rural Australia. *Journal of Social Work Practice: Psychotherapeutic Approaches in Health, Welfare and the Community*. https://doi.org/10.1080/0265053 3.2014.896785
Beddoe, L. (2010). Surveillance and reflection: Professional supervision in 'the risk society'. *The British Journal of Social Work, 40*(4), 1279–1296. https://doi.org/10.1093/bjsw/bcq018
Board of Behavioural Sciences. (2022). *Licensed clinical social worker*. Accessed on 4 February 2022 from https://www.bbs.ca.gov/applicants/lcsw.html
Chiller, P., & Crisp, B. R. (2012). Professional supervision: A workforce retention strategy for social work? *Australian Social Work, 65*(2), 232–242. https://doi.org/10.108 0/0312407X.2011.625036
CSWE. (2015). *Education policy and accreditation standards for Baccalaureate and Master's social work programs*. Accessed on 2 February 2022 from https://www.cswe.org/Accreditation/Standards-and-Policies/2015-EPAS
CSWE. (2022). *Education policy and accreditation standards for Baccalaureate and Master's social work programs*. Accessed on 2 February 2022 from https://www.cswe.org/Accreditation/Information/2022-EPAS
Davys, A., & Beddoe, L. (2021). *Best practice in professional supervision: A guide for the helping professions* (2nd ed.). Jessica Kingsley Publishers.
Egan, R., Maidment, J., & Connolly, M. (2017). Trust, power and safety in the social work supervisory relationship: Results from Australian research. *Journal of Social Work Practice, 31*(3), 307–321. https://doi.org/10.1080/02650533.2016.1261279
Egan, R., Maidment, J., & Connolly, M. (2018). Supporting quality supervision: Insights for organisational practice. *International Social Work, 61*(3), 353–367.
Henrickson, M. (2022). *The origins of social care and social work: Creating a global future*. Policy Press.
IASSW, & IFSW. (2018). *Global social work statement of ethical principles*. Accessed on 2 February 2022 from https://www.iassw-aiets.org/archive/ethics-in-social-work-statement-of-principles/
IASSW, & IFSW. (2020). *Global standards for social work education and training*. Accessed on 2 February 2022 from https://www.iassw-aiets.org/featured/5867-announcement-of-the-updated-global-standards-for-social-work-education-and-training-the-new-chapter-in-social-work-profession/
KSU (Kent State University). (2022). *Know the difference between coaching and mentoring*. The Center for Corporate and Professional Development. Accessed on 14 June 2022 from https://www.kent.edu/yourtrainingpartner/know-difference-between-coaching-and-mentoring#:~:text=Coaching%20is%20more%20performance%20driven,holistic%20approach%20to%20career%20development
Napan, K. (2021). The spirit of peer supervision. In K. O'Donoghue & L. Engelbrecht (Eds.), *The Routledge international handbook of social work supervision* (pp. 272–283). Taylor and Francis.
NASW. (2021). *Code of Ethics of the National Association of Social Workers*. Accessed on 2 February 2022 from https://www.socialworkers.org/About/Ethics/Code-of-Ethics/Code-of-Ethics-English
Philips, K. M. (2021). Supervision of peer support workers. In K. O'Donoghue & L. Engelbrecht (Eds.), *The Routledge international handbook of social work supervision* (pp. 187–199). Taylor and Francis.
Ross-Sheriff, F., & Orme, J. (2017). Mentoring and coaching. In *Encyclopedia of social work*. Oxford University Press. https://doi.org/10.1093/acrefore/9780199975839.013.1146

TEQSA. (2017). *Guidance note: Academic quality assurance.* Accessed on 16 June 2022 from https://www.teqsa.gov.au/latest-news/publications/guidance-note-academic-quality-assurance

Tsui, M. (1997). The roots of social work supervision. *The Clinical Supervisor, 15*(2), 191–198. https://doi.org/10.1300/J001v15n02_14

Washington State Department of Health. (2022a). *Social worker and social worker associate: Postgraduate supervision hours.* Accessed on 4 February 2022 from https://www.doh.wa.gov/LicensesPermitsandCertificates/ProfessionsNewReneworUpdate/SocialWorker/PostgraduateSupervisionHours

Washington State Department of Health. (2022b). *Licensing information.* Accessed on 16 June 2022 from https://doh.wa.gov/licenses-permits-and-certificates/professions-new-renew-or-update/social-worker-and-social-worker-associate/licensing-information

Chapter 2
Changes and Challenges in Social Work: Implications for Professional Supervision

Introduction

Professional supervision needs to be cognizant of changes and challenges in social work and welfare as it cannot occur in isolation from them. Ongoing changes experienced through societal trends influence and shape the profession, affecting both supervisors and supervisees. Some of the issues experienced by practitioners and their desire for professional supervision may emanate from contemporary changes and challenges. Thus, it is useful to have a broad overview of social work as a profession and its global expansion and think about how it responds to some of the challenges and opportunities. Following this, this chapter discusses whether social work has met its mission and the politics surrounding it. Then, it broadly discusses changes and challenges relating to colonization, neocolonization, and decolonization; deprofessionalization; populism, nationalism, and welfare chauvinism; digitalization and online trends; and the sustainable development goals, climate change, and disasters. It also briefly reflects on the implications of these challenges for supervision. The chapter concludes with a summary.

Social Work as a Global Profession

In one sense, social work is a well-established, at least in some countries, growing and expanding global profession when one views the profession from the perspective of the seven attributes discussed in the first chapter. For quick reference, these attributes are: "a clearly defined and altruistic purpose; transmissible theoretical knowledge (which may be trans- or interdisciplinary); specialised skills or techniques; a commonly held values base and enforceable ethical code; a high degree of individual responsibility and autonomy in decision-making; self-governing

© The Author(s), under exclusive license to Springer Nature
Switzerland AG 2022
M. Pawar, A. W. (Bill) Anscombe, *Enlightening Professional Supervision in
Social Work*, https://doi.org/10.1007/978-3-031-18541-0_2

association, with a credentialling process, and accountability to others within the association; and public and political recognition as a distinct professional group (this includes prestige)" (Henrickson, 2022, p. 187). Three international professional bodies – the International Federation of Social Workers (IFSW), International Association of Schools of Social Work (IASSW), and the International Council on Social Welfare (ICSW) – have been in existence since the late 1920s and significantly contribute to the development of the profession.

Over the years, the concept and meaning of social work have evolved, and it is currently understood and defined as follows by the international professional bodies, IFSW/IASSW, and internationally agreed in their General Meeting and General Assembly, respectively (IFSW/IASSW, 2014).

> Social work is a practice-based profession and an academic discipline that promotes social change and development, social cohesion, and the empowerment and liberation of people. Principles of social justice, human rights, collective responsibility and respect for diversities are central to social work. Underpinned by theories of social work, social sciences, humanities and indigenous knowledges, social work engages people and structures to address life challenges and enhance wellbeing. The above definition may be amplified at national and/or regional levels.

The core element of enhancing wellbeing in the social work concept is closely connected to welfare, as welfare is a state or condition in which "people, communities and societies experience, a high degree of social wellbeing" (Midgley, 1995, p. 13). Acknowledging that the term welfare is misunderstood and misused, Midgley (1995, pp. 13–14) articulates the condition of welfare comprising the following three elements: "the degree to which social problems are managed; the extent to which needs are met; and the degree to which opportunities for advancement are provided." Social workers and their professional associations contribute to managing problems, meeting needs and rights, and creating and connecting to opportunities for facilitating or enhancing the social functioning of people and communities.

They have developed the "Global Social Work Statement of Ethical Principles" (translated into 10 languages, most from Europe), "the role of social work in social protection systems" (see https://www.ifsw.org/what-is-social-work/global-definition-of-social-work/), the global standards for social work education and training (see https://www.iassw-aiets.org/featured/5867-announcement-of-the-updated-global-standards-for-social-work-education-and-training-the-new-chapter-in-social-work-profession/), and the global agenda (see https://www.iassw-aiets.org/global-agenda/), among others. They also have regional branches and consultative status with UN bodies. The IFSW has 144 national level organizations as its members, and it represents over five million social workers (IFSW, 2022). Similarly, the IASSW has nearly 350 school members, about 200 individual members (https://www.iassw-aiets.org/our-members/#1580474856533-43de923d-7ab9), and 5 regional organizations (IASSW, 2021a). They together organize biennial international social work conferences. The IASSW (2021b) global directory of schools of social work census shows that in 2010 there were 2110 social work degree sites in 125 countries, and in 2020, there were 1384 programs from 114 countries. The decline in the number of social work programs during this period is perhaps due to a reduced response rate to the census or that some schools have closed. Our observation of an increase in social work schools in some countries suggests that the former is more likely the case than the latter. Given the global need and demand, social work is a growing and expanding profession, and these schools in over 125 countries train thousands of social workers ready for entry level practice. They all need professional supervision, which may or may not be available.

At the national level, several countries have professional associations and organizations (e.g., AASW, NASW, CSWE, NAPSWI) with their respective codes of ethics and accreditation standards. For example, the IFSW has listed codes of ethics from 20 member associations at the national level (most from Europe) and hopes to add more to the list (IFSW, 2022, https://www.ifsw.org/global-social-work-statement-of-ethical-principles/). According to the accreditation standards, professional bodies accredit courses offered by social work schools by following a rigorous process (e.g., the AASW in Australia and the CSWE in the USA accredit their respective social work programs). In addition, as stated in the first chapter, in some countries (the USA, New Zealand), social work licensing systems are implemented, and the "social worker" title is well protected in the industry.

Most importantly, many social work educators, practitioners, and researchers have contributed to the social work discipline through their publications in the form of reports, monographs, books, textbooks, journal articles, newsletters, and other forms. The Scimago website lists 57 journals in the subject category of social work, with most either published in the UK or the USA. There are many other social work journals that are not included in this list. All these suggest the development of the discipline in terms of knowledge, skills, and techniques over the years. Relevant resources from this knowledge base are useful for professional supervision.

Drawing strength and support from these developments, many professional bodies and thousands of social work practitioners dedicate their careers and lives to fighting for social justice, human rights, social change, and development. Whether they work in the public sector, private sector, NGOs, disaster contexts, or the volunteer sector, and with individuals, groups, communities, or organizations and institutions, their dedicated work directly or indirectly contributes to various degrees to human wellbeing, welfare, and social change and development.

The Promise and Politics of Social Work

The above presented synoptic picture of social work as a global profession reveals rugged terrain when we zoom in on portions of the profession. The questions we raise and observations we make are not new but are pertinent to professional supervision in social work, both to supervisors and supervisees. The promise of professional social work – poverty and human suffering alleviation and employment, social change and development, empowerment and liberation of people, human rights, social justice, respect for diversity and social cohesion, reducing inequalities – is highly political as this promise is very closely connected to the welfare state or any nation-state. Over the past century, has professional social work globally delivered on this promise? The analytical and scholarly response to this question is complex and beyond the scope of this book. However, in our analysis, that promise has not only been globally delivered so far, but it has also been diluted by being translated into practice.

Although poverty has significantly reduced globally, the social work profession cannot take full credit for this. And yet nearly one billion people are poor and about half of them are children and women (World Bank, 2021). Extreme hunger is prevalent both in developed and developing countries. Many people are unemployed. The nature and conditions of employment have changed (about two billion people are employed in the unorganized or the informal sector, UN, 2022). Most countries do not have access to reasonable social protection provisions. Inequality, mental health issues, domestic violence, and social disharmony have continued, if not increased. Human rights are violated and social justice is denied to many people. Many children, women, and the elderly live in vulnerable and poor conditions. Modern slavery and exploitation continue in different forms. While refugees and migrants have increased, gates to receive them have not only become narrower and in some cases also closed, but also have been electrified to shock and penalize those desperately seeking asylum. In some ways, the severe treatment of refugees and migrants has become a significant source of winning elections and gaining power to sustain injustice and human rights violations. Why has all this happened? Why does it continue to happen?

A few answers may be found in analyzing the evolution, construction, and transportation of professional social work worldwide. Although the roots of caring and sharing, particularly of vulnerable people, and community development in different cultures and nations are yet to be systematically explored, the beginning of professional social work we are familiar with is linked to Judo-Christian values and theology (dignity of life, family, love, compassion, and responsibility), the ills of industrialization (vagrants and destitute, exploited working poor class), Elizabethan poor laws and new poor laws (caring for needy and work for the able-bodied in work houses), the contributions of the Evangelical Reformers, enlightenment values (self-determination, autonomy, human rights, and liberty), volunteerism and colonization (Henrickson, 2022), and conflicts, wars, and their impact.

Through the experimentation and exchange of ideas about charity organizations (COs) and settlement houses (SHs) between the UK and its (former) colony America, the first social work training program was established in 1898 at Columbia University, New York City, and by 1917, 17 social work schools were established to train social workers to help the poor and needy in a professional manner beyond religious orientation and volunteerism (Henrickson, 2022). Two important publications – Mary Richmond's (1917) *Social Diagnosis* and Virginia Robinson's (1930) *A Changing Psychology in Social Case Work* – laid a crucial foundation for social work training and practice culture that seem to be globally dominating irrespective of their local relevance. Despite differences in their approaches (the former focuses on social evidence and environment and the latter on the psychic determinism as stressed in psychoanalysis (Oberndorf, 1932)), both focused on the significance of relationship and casework, what we now call working with individuals and clinical social work practice, which has dominated social work practice in the US, UK, Australia, Canada, New Zealand, and many other countries till today.

With the background of Judo-Christian values and liberal thoughts, the impacts of growing industrialization, international migration, World Wars I and II, and the Great Depression provided a sound ground for the proliferation of casework practice and making individuals responsible for their own conditions. This social work model was transported to most of the British colonies in Africa, South America, and Asia as a solution to social problems existing in those countries.

While independence movements were gradually gaining momentum in different countries against oppressive and divisive ruling policies of colonizers, the concept and practice of the welfare state were becoming popular in northern European countries (e.g., Germany, France, and the UK). As Henrickson (2022) noted, the Lutheran and Catholic churches took responsibility for relief activities and preventing poverty, and supported settlement houses. States recognized structural factors that caused social issues and introduced several welfare measures to protect workers and the elderly. Beveridge's reports entitled *Social Insurance and Allied Services* (1942) and *Full Employment in a Free Society* (1944) were particularly notable, having influenced post-war reconstruction conditions in the UK and her colonies. In essence, welfare states emerged and influenced colonies, which gained independence at different times and tried to emulate the idea of the welfare state in different forms and shapes with limited resources. Among others, social workers trained in the casework paradigm were employed by the state to implement a range of welfare services and programs.

Nearly 70 years ago, in 1953, Keith-Lucas (1953, p. 1076) had argued and articulated the political theory implicit in casework theory in the US context, which was essentially about the relationship between the individual and society or the nation-state. As access to welfare provisions has been reducing in terms of meeting eligibility criteria, that relationship has continued with more difficulties. This issue is further discussed in the section populism, nationalism, and welfare chauvinism.

> During the past twenty years literally millions of people in the United States have been brought into a new relationship with officials of their local, state, and national governments – namely, the relationship of client and social caseworker. Governmental social casework today affects the lives of more than five and a half million recipients of public assistance…
> People are impelled into a relationship with a social caseworker because they are in trouble. The caseworker is the medium through which the client may have to establish his right to enough money to avoid starvation, or with whom he must treat in matters as vital to his happiness and rights as separation from his wife, loss of custody of his children, commitment to an institution, sterilization, or a radical change in his manner of living.

This perhaps was the case in most countries where Western social work was transported. Thus, professional social work was criticized and questioned from several perspectives.

First, as social workers joined hands with the welfare state to implement its programs and services, the social work profession and social workers were perceived as controlling agents of the state engaged in band-aid work (Tomlinson, 1977) with a clinical practice focus, often treating symptoms by ignoring causes. So, professional social work has failed to meet its reform and social justice agenda. Social work's mixed agenda of control versus reform is a critical issue in the profession. Some argue that it is possible to work with the state and as an insider initiate change, whereas others question this position due to power and structural issues. Whether it was the power of the king and power of religious institutions, and collaboration and power sharing between them, or the power of the modern welfare state, the common focus has been on how to control, manage, and exploit the poor and make them responsible for their conditions (see Henrickson, 2022). Many conservative governments with liberal and market ideologies have amended eligibility criteria to receive welfare benefits, making it more difficult and humiliating for people who receive them. Many social workers working in such systems found themselves helpless but implemented them.

Second, the way Western professional social work has been transported and implemented in colonies and newly created independent nation-states has attracted serious concerns, including professional imperialism, neo-colonialism, and continuation of the hegemony by the West. As part of this broader hegemonic agenda, aid and scholarships were given, and aspiring scholars were lured to the UK and the USA to receive Western training, including the casework paradigm, and impart the same on their return. For example, most of the first author's social work educators were trained in the USA, and the curriculum they followed was US based.

Third, as a result, social work education recipients and practitioners began reflecting over the years on the relevance of the Western social work clinical training in developing country conditions with varied traditions and cultural practices. Although the political question of imperialism and hegemony was seldom raised, cultural relevance to the prevailing conditions was a practical question and issue. We think that professional social work is caught between its promise and global hegemonic politics.

Social work professional associations, educators, practitioners, and researchers are well aware of this critical issue and know that the need for the indigenization of social work curricula, training, and practice is over debated, discussed, and documented (Healy, 2014; Gray et al., 2008). Healy thinks that there may be complex reasons for not indigenizing the social work curricula but does not state what those reasons are. To us, they include the impact of colonization, the dominance of the Western social work model, and the available social work literature. Without understanding local needs and issues in a cultural context, insensitively imposing the Western curricula over a long period impacts the psyche of the local people and makes them feel that what they have is less or not important or useful and whatever was externally given from the West is desirable and best. That is the deep impact of colonization, imperialism, and hegemony. It sits contrary to the promise of the social work profession to liberate and empower people, but the profession has flown with the wind on imperialism, except that it allows to raise, write, and discuss this issue, but without any substantive action so far.

Despite debate, discussion, and publications on the indigenization issue, the dominant casework paradigm appears to have resisted the opportunities to do so.

For example, to enhance the relevance of social work education and training for developing countries, in the 1970s a few scholars from the mid-western universities in the USA came together to incorporate a social development perspective in the social work curriculum and established a professional body, namely, the International Consortium for Social Development (Hollister, 2015; Raymond & Cowger, 2012; Pawar & Androff, 2021). Although this initiative had some impact on their courses, at the national level, it appears it did not make any impact due to the dominance of the casework paradigm.

The re-emergence of social work in China was another opportunity to indigenize social work according to the country's context, but the Western social work model seems to have dominated either through the gates of Hong Kong or through direct exchange programs. Ku and Ho (2020, p. 12) confirm this as follows:

> Through a highly uneven global knowledge system, and aid programs in international development, the social work models of the United States and Britain have been exported to the Chinese universities and public sector. This happens within a network of status and power embedded in the hegemonic knowledge hierarchy with its powerful financial sponsorship. But, as some scholars are pointing out, social work that originated in the urban context of Western countries is substantially different from the socio-politically and culturally specific context of Chinese society (Cheung & Liu, 2004). Gray (2008) has critically argued that Western influences sometimes obstruct rather than help the development of social work in mainland China.

The third example is the three international professional bodies: IASSW, IFSW, and ICSW declared the global agenda for social work and social development in 2010. This agenda followed as the main theme in their international conferences (Pawar & Weil, 2021). Later, the UN declared the sustainable development goals in 2016. In some publications and statements on their websites notwithstanding, it is unclear whether the casework-dominated paradigm has provided any space for social development curriculum in the courses. It appears the forces of colonization and neocolonization still have a strong hold on most of the world.

Changes and Challenges

Colonization, Neocolonization, and Decolonization

Like the debate and discussion about indigenization, there is a lot written and published about colonization and decolonization, generally, and in the context of social work (Ibrahima & Mattaini, 2018; Sewpaul & Henrickson, 2019; McNabb, 2019; Yadav, 2019; Garrett, 2020; Mabvurira, 2018; Tatenda & Rumbidazi, 2020; Clarke, 2021). Colonization, neocolonization, and decolonization together have temporal, spatial, capital, political/people, impact, and action and reaction dimensions, and these are related in a complex way. Colonization gradually occurred over 500 years in the name of exploration, commerce, and trade and then occupation of the lands through different means, often forceful and violent, which has generated wealth, power, and space for the colonizers at the cost of significant suffering, lives, and losing lands, languages, knowledges, and cultures of the colonized. The oppression, suppression, subjugation, and repression and revolts against them by the colonized people are well documented, shared, and listened to with a deep sense of social injustice and violation of fundamental human rights. Despite gaining independence from countries, the impact and intervention continue in a neocolonial form. The trend of decolonization is emerging and building up as the collective consciousness of the colonized. It is a reaction to centuries of injustice. It has great potential to develop into a constructive action to rediscover their strengths, knowledge, culture, and identity and relate to the local and global, including the past colonizers.

As part of the colonization project/practice, referred to earlier, Western social work spread to the rest of the world. Although it was not the intention of social work schools and courses, they sit with the background of brutal colonization processes that ignored and ridiculed local knowledges and practices and imposed Western thought. Even when many countries have become politically independent, neocolonial practices and dominance continue. Perhaps, this is why the indigenization of social work has not occurred to the extent that is needed.

Can a decolonization and/or post-colonial approach help achieve indigenization and improve practice? How can the decolonization approach be employed in supervision? Acknowledging that "'decolonising' encompasses a multiplicity of viewpoints," Garrett (2020, p. 308) draws on Bhambra et al.'s (2018, p. 2, as cited in Garrett, 2020) explanation as follows:

> To broadly situate its political and methodological coordinates, 'decolonising' has two key referents. First, it is a way of thinking about the world which takes colonialism, empire and racism as its empirical and discursive objects of study; it re-situates these phenomena as key shaping forces of the contemporary world, in a context where their role has been systematically effaced from view. Second, it purports to offer alternative ways of thinking about the world and alternative forms of political praxis.

This explanation needs to be extended to a practice coordinate and the third referent, which connects thinking to doing and being (Pawar & Anscombe, 2015). From this perspective, decolonizing professional supervision in social work calls for a new way of thinking about the colonization process and alternative ways of practice with people. Depending upon the context, the subject itself may evoke emotions and trauma. Thus, decolonization informed practice might be needed as we are hesitant to use the phrase, "trauma informed practice" that is linked to the colonized practice and Western thought. In a cultural context, to begin with, appropriately acknowledging, admitting, apologizing, forgiving, peace building within and outside, and a balanced focus on "self" and "other" may be considered. Then, it is important to respect and understand local cultural practices and beliefs and use the ones that are not harmful to anyone. The social work definition stated above includes practice based on indigenous knowledges, among others. Thus, decolonization in social work must result not only in alternative ways of thinking but also alternative ways of action and practice that are rooted in local people and communities, and their culture, which also should contribute to global understanding.

The following initiatives may be considered examples of decolonization. In response to the 2012 Australian Social Work Education and Accreditation Standards (AASW, 2012), a group of scholars in consultation with schools of social work, under the leadership of Aboriginal academics, developed and published a teaching and learning framework, 2014, which they called Getting it Right: Creating partnership for change and integrating Aboriginal and Torres Strait Islander (ATSI) knowledges in social work education and practice. The framework looks at field education, governance, and leadership and the recruitment and retention of ATSI students and staff along with some strategies (see Bessarab et al., 2014).

By bringing together a group of scholars (from Bhutan, Cambodia, Laos, Mongolia, Myanmar, Nepal, Sri Lanka, Thailand, and Vietnam), Akimoto (2017) has initiated research on Buddhist social work and through the process of seminars, dialogue, and discussion tried to develop a working framework and definition of Buddhist social work (pp. 59–60). Similarly, some scholars have conducted seminars and workshops in India to discuss and spread the idea of "Bharatiyakaran"/ Indianization of social work. While this initiative appears to have great potential to indigenize and decolonize the social work curriculum in India (see Das et al., 2021), Kumar (2019) argues that the trend of "Bharatiyakaran"/Indianization of social work raises more contradictions and questions (see Pawar, 2019). On the one hand, like Judo-Christian social work, Buddhist social work and Bharatiya social work may be perceived as normal developments of the process of decolonization, but on the other hand, they pose the risk of perceiving them as populist/nationalist responses, which we discuss in the later section of the chapter.

Deprofessionalization

If the conceptualization of the social work profession is a Western, modern thought and a colonized practice, does decolonization of social work entail deprofessionalization? What is the agenda of deprofessionalization?

Deprofessionalization connotes social workers mechanically routinizing practice and losing their discretion to individualize and make decisions; a decline in employment of social workers, where they should be employed; and the employment of social workers in positions that do not need professional qualifications, or do not utilize, or underutilize social work knowledge and skills (see Healy & Meagher, 2004, pp. 244–246; Clark, 2005). Deprofessionalization has an element of loss of trust and confidence or an element of doubt by the public in social work professionals (Pippa, 2001) due to reasons including competency, quality, and accountability (see Clark, 2005) concerns, inappropriate decisions, and poor and unsuitable delivery of services. Deprofessionalization also refers to evolutionary progress or a state of the social work profession where resources, knowledge, and power are shared with people and communities, who give meaning to services (rather than calling them service users), in the spirit of democratization (Groulx, 1983, p. 39).

As the main subject matter of this book is professional supervision in social work, the discussion on deprofessionalization may appear strange. The thought and trend of deprofessionalization, in some respects, may shake the very foundation of professional supervision. Deprofessionalization is a real concern for those social workers and professional bodies who have struggled to establish it as a profession and enjoyed the status of social work as a profession. For some others who are against or do not support the professionalization (Healy & Meagher, 2004) due to their service or philosophical orientation such as democratization, it is a welcome development. Apart from this, in some cultures and countries, mainly in the global south, where social work has not yet gained the status of a profession and/or where it is confused and mixed with similar work done by volunteers, politicians, and community organizations and interest groups, the phenomenon of deprofessionalism already exists. For example, in the Indian context, years ago, when the first author introduced himself as a social worker to a community member, the person's response was to ask what political party I belonged to.

As deprofessionalization has many meanings, perspectives, and perceptions, for professional supervision in social work, it is critical to understand the process of deprofessionalization, the belief and attitude of deprofessionalism, and the pre-stages of professionalization, depending upon the context of supervisors and supervisees. The trend of deprofessionalization is not unique to the social work profession. It has been noted and discussed in other professions, such as nursing, medicine, education, and auditing. The purpose of stating that it is common with other professions is not to normalize the trend for social work, but to understand it and act and practice proactively and properly.

It appears that during the growth of welfare states globally, the number of social workers, social work training institutions, and professional bodies grew and attained professional status in some nation-sates and societies (e.g., the USA, UK, Canada, New Zealand, and Australia). Some governments recognized trained social workers and their professional bodies, some required social work qualifications for certain jobs, some established licensing and registration systems, and some protected the title of "social worker" in employment positions. The so-called welfare state came under considerable criticism, in our view prematurely, due to the resurfacing and rise of liberal ideology and conservative governments, which embraced a market philosophy and managerialism and privatization. While it does not have to be this situation, this ideological uprising has contributed to the deprofessionalization in social work as managerialism and privatization with profit, efficiency, effectiveness, accountability, evidence, and outputs and outcomes perspectives interfered with professional social work values and principles, autonomy, discretion, individualization and decision-making, and the employment of social workers.

"Professional" work of social workers under this paradigm of performance measurement and dictated and deterministic decision-making came under criticism from postmodern and post positivist perspectives and thereby contributed to the deprofessionalization of social work. Delivering services under managerialism and privatization parameters while adhering to social work values and principles has created a complex situation for some social work practitioners and the profession.

Forced decisions (e.g., child protection) and restricted services (e.g., mental health and ageing) have raised questions about the quality and adequacy of services and accountability to citizens. These practices appear to have contributed to the erosion of public trust in the professions and to some extent they might have contributed to the deprofessionalization of social work.

Another related factor is the need for multiprofessional and multidisciplinary teamwork to address wicked problems in a coordinated manner. In such multiprofessional and multidisciplinary teamwork, social work professional judgments frequently are undermined or ignored, and this can create a sense of deprofessionalization. This is often noticed in certain settings, such as medical, where a physician's viewpoint prevails; in law enforcement, the police prevail; and in the judicial setting, judges prevail. Through this process, latent deprofessionalization of social work can occur.

The need for professional social work services is so great both in terms of quality and quantity, particularly in some sectors such as ageing, mental health, and disability (at least in the Australian context), but the social work profession is unable to train an adequate number of social workers to meet this demand. Consequently, those services are delivered by other workers, trained or untrained. This phenomenon also appears to have created confusion about professional social work services and has contributed to the deprofessionalization of social work.

In addition to these external factors, within the social work profession, some believe that there is no need to professionalize social work, which we call deprofessionalism. They do not support registration and licensing, or similar systems. This belief and attitude seem to emanate from their commitment to service, where serving the needy is the humane thing to do. To them professionalism has an element of expert power, authority, and giver mentality. The service receiver is perceived as a non-expert, powerless, and a receiver. For example, Pippa (2001, 8–9) argues that old professions such as medicine and engineering are "characterized by elitism, paternalism, authoritarianism, having a mastery of knowledge (highly gate-kept and accessible by no one else), control, aloofness, detachment and distance." Social work practice that follows medical models in clinical practice may have these tendencies. Generally, it appears to create a situation of haves and have-nots and anti-egalitarianism. Social work values and principles are against such professionalized practice. To them deprofessionalization is a good thing as it democratizes the service in terms of sharing resources, knowledge, and power (see Groulx, 1983, p. 39) with people and communities.

In some countries and regions, although social work schools and professional bodies exist and social workers practice, perhaps due to historical, cultural, or political reasons, social work as a professional practice is not accepted and established, which we call pre-stages of professionalization. In some of those countries, social workers have been trying for years (e.g., in India) with governments and communities, but it is uncertain whether and when social work will be recognized as a professional practice as other interest groups and organizations have been engaged in similar work. They may have strong beliefs and attitudes toward deprofessionalism.

From a decolonization perspective, is there any need to professionalize social work like the West in the rest of the world?

For our book, it is pertinent to draw on Clark's (2005, 182, 185–190) contention that irrespective of professionalization, deprofessionalization, and deprofessionalism, social workers as individuals are ultimately responsible and accountable for their work, their success, and failures, which "are partly attributable to the moral and intellectual character of professionals as individuals and therefore it is important to attend to the improvement of professional character" along with the knowledge component. We will revisit this subject later in the book.

Populism, Nationalism, and Welfare Chauvinism

In several nation-states, the growing trend of populism, nationalism, and welfare chauvinism may be observed in different degrees and forms in terms of peoples' views, politics, policies, and programs particularly impacting and excluding certain groups such as migrants, refugees, and minority groups (Davies & Deole, 2017; Fenger, 2018; Ketola & Nordensvard, 2018; Edwards et al., 2020; Singh, 2021) and generally creating social tensions and divisions based on ethnicity and nativism. The fundamental bases and consequences of these trends may appear to be directly in conflict with social work values and goals of social justice, human rights, diversity and collective responsibility, service, equality, social cohesion, empowerment and liberation, and social change and development. If social workers are torn between these trends and their professional values, and justify these trends or part of them in some ways, how can one address and reconcile this problem in practice? To some, these phenomena may emerge as a challenging issue in professional supervision and practice. Thus, it may be useful to be familiar with these trends in the context of supervision.

Traditionally, populism had a positive connotation, suggesting a popular view of most people. It is part of the operation of democracy that allows for all voices, but the popular or majority voice prevails (Canovan, 2016; Ketola & Nordensvard, 2018). However, due to modernization and globalization processes and the way democratic systems function, and their impact on people's socioeconomic and cultural lives, populism is characterized by anti-elitism, anti-establishment, and anti-pluralism (see Muller, 2016). According to Mudde and Kaltwasser (2017), populism refers to a society separated into two opposing groups, "the pure people" and "the corrupt elites," and "us" and "them." Although populism and nationalism are connected, they differ in their operation and are sometimes mixed up and often confused. Nationalism has an important element of boundaries of the nation, especially at the time of a state's foundation, and it follows state institutions such as "national constitutions, censuses and maps and as required it tries to balance with societal, everyday representations of the nation" (see Singh, 2021, 254). In relation to welfare, Suszycki (2011, p. 56, as cited in Keskinen, 2016, p. 355) states welfare nationalism is a "commitment to the welfare-related national interest and ideas." Welfare and national identity are closely connected and welfare provisions are based on national membership, and the welfare state should be an important focus of politics and the economy. For example, migrants and refugees and minorities are considered and approached from the perspective of the nation-state political economy and not from that of them and us (see Keskinen, 2016, 355). "Welfare chauvinism refers to the idea that social benefits should be restricted to 'nationals'/natives or 'our own'" (Andersen & Bjorklund, 1990, p. 212, as cited in Fenger, 2018, p. 190) and non-natives like refugees and migrants should be excluded.

In contemporary societies and nation-states, the phenomena of populism, nationalism, and welfare chauvinism are prevalent, and this is generally dubbed as populist radical right (De Koster, et al., 2012; Ennser-Jedenastik, 2018; Fenger, 2018; Ketola & Nordensvard, 2018; Edwards et al., 2020), though it is observed in both right and left politics (Bonikowski et al., 2019). Leaders of many countries are drawing on this populist card and appearing to appease the masses by re-erecting racism, xenophobia, and discrimination and causing conditions to conflagrate violence against minorities, refugees, and migrants. It appears as social injustice, the violation of human rights, and social disharmony blatantly caused, silently watched, and ignored by populist leaders. What happens to social work values and principles? Clinical social work practice is necessary to help these victims fight their trauma, but it only treats the symptoms and not the cause. It is critical for social workers to understand what kind of social change and development has occurred over the years that has led to populist movements in many countries and how some leaders are using it to regain and retain power and what role the social work profession and social workers can play and what kind of fortitude and commitment they need to cultivate to counter this type of social change and development.

There may be several theses to explain this new and profound and perplexing social problem, but we will point out a few of them in summary form, hoping that you may explore them further. In some respects, it is the corrupt operation of the democratic and other political systems in which all types of elites come together to influence each other to take advantage of the system in their favor. Political donations and lobbying by powerful groups are examples. Over the years, people have watched this and lost faith in the system. They also have experienced the process of globalization and outsourcing of their jobs and unemployment and related issues. The production of goods and services by replacing, displacing, and misplacing labor has led to relative deprivation and growing inequality in a materially prosperous world. Simultaneously, under the influence of liberal ideology and conservativism, and market and managerialism, welfare provisions have been reduced, restricted, and highly means-tested by making it difficult to access them. Often the welfare state is blamed for overspending, including on non-natives, causing strains on limited resources. Over the years, this appears to have pent up people's frustration. Intra- and international migration and multiculturalism, with all their positive aspects, in some cases have led to the decline of self-identity and the search for a new identity. Who am I in this mad multicultural, digital, and globalized world? Where do I belong? There appears to be the perception of the loss of an individual and collective sense of identity, which may be due to a lack or loss of spiritual, ethnic, and native identity. Perhaps, is this the antithesis of multiculturalism? Further, there is a future risk that instead of identifying with and relating to human beings, some people may identify with digital objects. A lack of identity can confuse one's existence and cause harm to self and others. Rather than addressing these structural issues caused by governments and elites, some leaders appear to be using this overall complex situation to invoke anti-sentiments within and between groups by blaming governments and their policies; attacking the welfare state; and stopping, accusing, and penalizing migrants and refugees as if they (radical nationalists) are the people's voice, protecting the national interest and identity. Social workers must thoroughly analyze this disturbing situation to understand what kind of social changes and developments have occurred and what kind of social work practice is needed.

De Cleen and Speed (2020, p. 526) suggest that:

> Instead of taking welfare chauvinism at face value, there is a need for analyses to demonstrate the ways in which welfare chauvinism is performed in very simplified and rhetorically empty ways, ways which work to prevent it being held to account against the cold hard facts that more people have become ill or died because of these policies.

In the context of health, they have found that excluding non-natives from health benefits will harm natives. It is in the interest of the welfare of natives, and it is critical to extend health benefits to all.

Bonikowski et al. (2019) aptly suggest developing solutions to structural problems faced by people, but without legitimizing and supporting exclusionary ideologies, ideas, and practices and without compromising the rights and protections of minority groups.

> To be sure, there are myriad worrisome anti-pluralist and socially regressive aspects to the radical right, but the structural forces that have led to the rise of this form of politics are real, and they are felt viscerally by those voters who are most affected by rapid social change. Without addressing economic dislocation, perceptions of collective status loss, and widespread social and cultural insecurity – as well as the reality of political polarisation and ineffective governance – moralistic dismissals of voters attracted to ethno-nationalist populism are unlikely to reverse the contemporary tide of radical politics. At the same time, the challenge is to offer solutions to real grievances without legitimating exclusionary ideologies and infringing upon the rights and protections of minority groups. (Bonikowski et al., 2019, pp. 63–64)

Digitalization and Online Trends

The fourth industrial revolution, led by the fast growing and quickly changing innovations in information and digital technology, has contributed to social justice and injustice as it has both good and bad consequences (Mohan, 2018). The social work profession needs to recognize these proactively and promptly and act to achieve social justice and prevent injustice. How are social work professional bodies and practitioners responding to the phenomena of digitization and the online world?

The profession has introduced certain changes in the social work code of ethics. For example, eight provisions of section 8 of the IASSW/IFSW (2018) Global Social Work Statement of Ethical Principles relate to the ethical use of technology and social media. They confirm the application of all ethical principles in the digital context of social work practice. These provisions require social work practitioners to guard against threats posed to the principles of confidentiality, privacy, informed consent, inclusivity, and risks associated with the use of technology and asynchronous communication and difficulties in verifying identity. They also need to report in accordance with the statutory requirements to protect the person or others from the potential harm and danger and to licensing authorities if the matter of jurisdiction is a concern. Similar provisions are included in the NASW (2021) and the AASW (2020; 5.5.15 about data storing and records; 5.7.3 about professional boundaries) Code of Ethics. The broad scope of the use of digital technology in social work is well captured in the NASW code of ethics.

> … social workers need to be aware of the unique challenges that may arise in relation to the maintenance of confidentiality, informed consent, professional boundaries, professional competence, record-keeping, and other ethical considerations. In general, all ethical standards in this Code of Ethics are applicable to interactions, relationships, or communications, whether they occur in person or with the use of technology. For the purposes of this Code, "technology-assisted social work services" include any social work services that involve the use of computers, mobile or landline telephones, tablets, video technology, or other electronic or digital technologies; this includes the use of various electronic or digital platforms, such as the Internet, online social media, chat rooms, text messaging, email, and emerging digital applications. Technology-assisted social work services encompass all aspects of social work practice, including psychotherapy; individual, family, or group counselling; community organization; administration; advocacy; mediation; education; supervision; research; evaluation; and other social work services. Social workers should keep apprised of emerging technological developments that may be used in social work practice and how various ethical standards apply to them.

AASW (2014) supervision standards accept offering and receiving online supervision but suggest having strategies to ensure supervisory relationships and the quality of the supervision.

In addition to following these ethical requirements and taking precautions to prevent risks associated with the use of digital technology, social workers also need to address digital social justice issues relating to the digital divide and digital inequality on the one hand and digital injustice on the other.

Some people social workers work with still do not have access to digital technology devices or the digital literacy to use them. This may be due to economic reasons, a lack of digital infrastructure, and remote locations. Over two-fifths of the world population do not have access to the Internet (ITU World Telecommunication/ICT Indicators database, 2020, as cited in Ingram, 2021). In South Asia and sub-Saharan Africa, only about 20% of people have access to the Internet. In developed countries such as the USA, 12% do not have access to the Internet (World Bank, 2020; as cited in Ingram, 2021), and in Australia 9% of adults do not have a home internet connection (ACMA, 2022). The digitally divided world is creating socio-economic exclusion of some people and countries, thereby increasing inequalities.

Social workers need to fight for increased access to Internet and communication devices, as they can be used to raise awareness, knowledge, and skills development, enhance information freedom, and deliver telehealth services. Where they have been used properly, they have helped to address gender issues; increase economic activities and income, awareness, and advocacy; offer support; and reduce isolation.

Some of those who have access and use them are abused and exploited, leaving them vulnerable due to new working arrangements and a lack of adequate and appropriate laws. Digital communication technology has become an important means of emotional and financial abuse, bullying, creating isolation, excessive and addictive use, and hate, often severely impacting the victims, who may require innovative social work approaches to work with them. Some of those who have been working in the digital economy sectors such as Amazon, Uber, and similar companies do not have safe working conditions and employment security, and there are no relevant laws to protect them. A gig economy has redefined the relationship between the employer, employee, and contractor and led to short-term insecure positions. Further, the number of people working from home has increased without safe work conditions. It is important to consider helping this vulnerable group. As working in the digital sector requires a certain level of knowledge and skills, some of those who lose employment may be unable to upskill and catch-up and may remain unemployed. Social workers also need to think about ways of enabling and empowering them. Overall, the fourth revolution provides new opportunities and challenges for social work practitioners, educators, and researchers to deliver their services locally, nationally, and internationally, and it may be the subject of supervision, depending upon the context. It is critical to ensure that digital and online trends do not lead to neocolonial, hegemonic practices.

The Sustainable Development Goals, Climate Change, and Disasters

The 17 sustainable development goals (SDGs) – 2016–2030, agreed by the 192 nation-states, is a historic global achievement by the United Nations. These goals relate to reducing poverty, hunger, and inequalities; enhancing health, education, and gender equality; access to clean water and sanitation; affordable clean energy, work, and economic growth; industry innovation and infrastructure; sustainable cities and communities; promoting responsible consumption; climate action; life below water and on land; building peace, justice, and strong institutions; and developing partnerships to achieve the goals. Unlike the millennium development goals, which did not make adequate progress to address environmental issues (Pawar, 2017), of the 17 SDGs, more than half of them squarely focus on environmental issues. Competitive gross domestic product at the nation-state level and economic growth-focused development over the years have led to an ecological crisis, global warming, and climate change, which threaten the very survival of human beings. As discussed earlier, the international professional bodies, the IASSW, IFSW, and

ICSW, have a global agenda relating to social work and social development; this agenda incorporates these SDGs. In our own teaching to social work students, we have discussed climate change mitigation and adaptation strategies. Social workers can play a critical role in addressing both strategies. The methods of reducing global warming have become more of a political issue rather than an environmental issue. Globally, there is no consensus on climate change targets because the evidence consistently produced by the Intergovernmental Panel on Climate Change (IPCC, 2021) has been disregarded; nation-states tend to focus on their respective national borders and politicize these issue for purposes other than the environment. However, the environmental issues are global in nature and do not understand national borders. The political economy of environmental issues is dynamic, sensitive, and short-sighted and tends to focus on popular decisions to win the votes of people as we have discussed under populism. We have argued earlier that there are some critical and real issues the social work profession and social workers must consider and act on.

First, relating to values and principles, environmental justice has become an integral part of social and economic justice. So, environmental justice should be considered in all decisions, actions, and inactions. Second, although addressing environmental issues disrupts some economic systems (e.g., closing coal mines; petrol to electric vehicles), it also opens up new opportunities, generally known as the green economy. Social workers need to focus on these opportunities. Third, generally, those developed countries that contribute more to climate change are better resourced than those that bear the impact of climate change in developing poor countries, including land-locked and island states, which seem to contribute least to climate change. They are therefore morally and ethically responsible to contribute to climate change mitigation and adaptation strategies, programs, and provisions throughout the world, particularly to poor countries and vulnerable population groups in all countries that have been caught in the humanitarian crises (Pawar, 2021). Fourth, irrespective of developed and developing countries, climate change impacts vulnerable and disadvantaged groups most, and they have least resilience and capacity to cope with the impact. As frequent disasters and human toll are expected, necessary preparation and readiness are needed to respond to these crises. Finally, to prevent and cope with these climate crises, preparation and training is needed for social workers to work along with other professionals. To proactively respond to these changes and emerging issues, it is necessary to consider to what extent the casework dominated model in social work is useful and what new thrust needs to be incorporated into supervision and practice.

Implications for Professional Supervision in Social Work

Implications for professional supervision may be broadly discussed in terms of appreciating, analyzing, and acting. The evolution of social work practice and the profession over more than a hundred years has achieved a good deal by serving humanity. In some respects, it gives a deep sense of satisfaction to be part of this noble and selfless profession. Understanding and being aware of self and others with a focus on strengths, alleviating miseries, and empowering and enabling the powerless are complex task, and it is natural to encounter complex issues. Supervision helps to discuss it constructively, if not solve it every time. As a conscientious professional, it is necessary to raise critical questions about the profession. What is its mission? Why has it not achieved that mission? In light of socioeconomic and cultural changes, and societal evolution, are there any new directions, new strategies, and innovations needed?

Thinking about the promise and politics of social work and these changes and challenges should provide some insights for offering and receiving supervision. Some of the issues social workers experience and observe in their practice each day are perhaps due to these and similar developments. Sometimes, the way people and communities behave is probably due to these structural factors, which might have caused their anger, aggression, apathy, or withdrawal. Equally, the behavior of managers and bureaucrats and ethical conflicts may be linked to these changes and their impacts. These generally observed reactions, whether of people and communities or organizations, are only symptoms. In the supervision discussion, it is critical to pose the right questions and go beyond these symptoms and look at what is causing them with a view to counter them systematically and systemically. It is also important to take cognizance of positive changes and use them in practice. Sometimes, challenges and difficulties or new encounters are great opportunities for innovation in practice. The application of digital technology and its long-lasting influence on human behavior, relationships, and mental health are of profound concern and so is the crisis of human and cultural identity. Common to all these issues are environmental crises and consequent opportunities. How can social work prepare and respond to these challenges? Perhaps, it requires new thinking and visioning, building the being of the social worker. Do we need to act in the same way we have practiced for over 100 years as a profession, or do these social changes call for new ways of thinking, acting, and practicing?

Conclusion and Summary

Social work is a relatively well-established profession, at least in some countries, and it is a globally growing and expanding profession. Social workers do contribute to the welfare and wellbeing of people and communities. By looking at the promise and politics of social work, we have argued that the promise has not been globally met, and we attribute it to, among other things, the dominant casework model in social work and its colonization of the rest of the world. The chapter discusses changes and challenges relating to colonization, neocolonization, and decolonization; deprofessionalization; populism, nationalism, and welfare chauvinism; digitalization and online trends; and the sustainable development goals, climate change, and disasters. Through rapid developments over the years, at the cost of environment and ecological systems, have we, have governments appropriately managed social problems and met human needs, and have they created opportunities for human realization? Our analysis of the above discussed changes and challenges suggests profound implications for human existence, identity, and wellbeing. Does this provide a new perspective for professional supervision in social work? We hope this background information provides some insights and new vistas for discussion in professional supervision.

References

AASW. (2012). *Australian social work education and accreditation standards*. AASW.

AASW. (2014). *Supervision standards – 2014*. AASW.

AASW. (2020). *Australian Association of Social Workers Code of Ethics 2020*. AASW.

ACMA. (2022). *Communication and media in Australia: How we use the Internet*. Accessed on 14 February 2022 from https://www.acma.gov.au/publications/2021-12/report/communications-and-media-australia-how-we-use-internet#:~:text=Nearly%20all%20Australian%20adults%20(99,prior%20to%20COVID%2D19%20lockdowns

Akimoto, T. (2017). *How is Asian Buddhism involved in people's life: Exploring the Buddhist social work*. Shukutoku University, Asian Research Institute for International Social Work.

Andersen, J. G., & Bjorklund, T. (1990). Structural change and new cleavages: The progress parties in Denmark and Norway. *Acta Sociologica, 33*(3), 195–217.

Bessarab, D., Green, S., Jones, V., Stratton, K., Young, S., & Zubrzycki, J. (2014). Getting it right: Teaching and learning framework, 2014. Australian Government Office of Learning and Teaching.

Beveridge, W. H. (1942). *Social insurance and allied services*. His Majesty's Stationery Office.

Beveridge, W. H. (1944/2015). *Full employment in a free society*. Routledge.

Bhambra, G. K., Gebrial, D., & Nisancioglu, K. (2018). Introduction: Decolonising the university? In G. K. Bhambra, D. Gebrial, & K. Nisancioglu (Eds.), *Decolonising the university* (pp. 1–19). Pluto.

Bonikowski, B., Halikiopoulou, D., Kaufmann, E., & Rooduijn, M. (2019). Populism and nationalism in a comparative perspective: A scholarly exchange. *Nations and Nationalism, 25*(1), 58–81. https://doi.org/10.1111/nana.12480

Canovan, M. (2016). Trust the people! Populism and the two faces of democracy. *Political Studies, 47*(1), 2–16.

Cheung, M., & Liu, M. (2004). The self-concept of Chinese women and the indigenization of social work in China. *International Social Work, 47*, 109–127.

Clark, C. (2005). The deprofessionalisation thesis, accountability and professional character. *Social Work and Society, 3*(2), 182–190.

Clarke, K. (2021). Reimagining social work ancestry: Toward epistemic decolonization. *Affilia*. https://doi-org.ezproxy.csu.edu.au/10.1177/08861099211051326

Das, B. M., Kumar, M., Singh, D. P., & Shukla, S. (2021). *Indian social work*. Routledge.

Davies, L., & Deole, S. (2017). Immigration and the rise of far-right parties in Europe. *IFO- Institut/ Leibniz-Institut für Wirtschaftsforschung, 15*(4), 10–15. http://hdl.handle.net/10419/181254

De Cleen, B., & Speed, E. (2020). Getting the problem definition right: The radical right, populism, nativism and public health; comment on "a scoping review of populist radical right parties' influence on welfare policy and its implications for population health in Europe". *International Journal of Health Policy and Management, 10*(8), 523–527. https://doi.org/10.34172/ijhpm.2020.143

De Koster, W., Achterberg, P., & Van der Waal, J. (2012). The new right and the welfare state: The electoral relevance of welfare chauvinism and welfare populism in the Netherlands. *International Political Science Review, 34*(1), 3–20. https://doi.org/10.1177/0192512112455443

Edwards, T., Mendes, P., & Flynn, C. (2020). Is welfare chauvinism evident in Australia? Examining right-wing populist views towards Muslim refugees and Indigenous Australians. In C. Noble & G. Ottmann (Eds.), *The challenge of right-wing nationalist populism for social work: A human rights approach* (1st ed., pp. 151–167). Routledge.

Ennser-Jedenastik, L. (2018). Welfare chauvinism in populist radical right platforms: The role of redistributive justice principles. *Social Policy and Administration, 52*(1), 293–314. https://doi.org/10.1111/spol.12325

Fenger, M. (2018). The social policy agendas of populist radical right parties in comparative perspective. *Journal of International and Comparative Social Policy, 34*(3), 188–209. https://doi.org/10.1080/21699763.2018.1483255

Garrett, P. M. (2020). 'Disordering' the world: Frantz Fanon's contribution to social work's understanding of decolonisation. *Critical and Radical Social Work, 8*(3), 305–322. https://doi.org/10.1332/204986020X15945757040444

Gray, M. (2008). Some considerations on the debate on social work in China: Who speaks for whom? *International Journal of Social Welfare, 17*, 400–406.

Gray, M., Coates, J., & Yellow Bird, M. (Eds.). (2008). *Indigenous social work around the world: Towards culturally relevant education and practice.* Ashgate.

Groulx, L. (1983). Deprofessionalisation of social service: Demands of democracy or pretensions to a new power. *International Social Work, 26*(3), 38–44. https://doi-org.ezproxy.csu.edu.au/10.1177/002087288302600306

Healy, L. M. (2014). Global education for social work: Old debates and future directions for international social work. In C. Noble, H. Strauss, & B. Littlechild (Eds.), *Global social work: Crossing borders, blurring boundaries* (pp. 369–380). Sydney University Press.

Healy, K., & Meagher, G. (2004). The reprofessionalization of social work: Collaborative approaches for achieving professional recognition. *British Journal of Social Work, 34*, 243–260. https://doi.org/10.1093/bjsw/bch024

Henrickson, M. (2022). *The origins of social care and social work: Creating a global future.* Policy Press.

Hollister, D. (2015). "Honoring the pioneers." Remarks by David Hollister. In *The 19th ICSD International symposium*, Singapore, July 7–10, 2015.

IASSW. (2021a). *Our members (updated 30 September 2021).* Accessed on 11 February 2022 from https://www.iassw-aiets.org/our-members/#1580474856533-43de923d-7ab9

IASSW. (2021b). *Launch of the global directory of schools of social work census 2020.* Accessed on 12 February 2022 from https://www.iassw-aiets.org/featured/7152-launch-of-global-directory-of-schools-of-social-work-census-2020-2/

IASSW & IFSW. (2018). *Global social work statement of ethical principles.* Accessed on 2 February 2022 from https://www.iassw-aiets.org/archive/ethics-in-social-work-statement-of-principles/

Ibrahima, A. B., & Mattaini, M. A. (2018). Social work in Africa: Decolonising methodologies and approaches. *International Social Work, 62*(2), 799–813.

Ingram, G. (2021). *Bridging the global digital divide: A platform to advance digital development in low- and middle-income countries.* Brookings Global Working Paper # 157. Center for Sustainable Development at Brookings. Accessed on 21 June 2022 from https://www.brookings.edu/research/bridging-the-global-digital-divide-a-platform-to-advance-digital-development-in-low-and-middle-income-countries/

IFSW. (2022). *2021 end of year report.* The International federation of Social Workers (IFSW).

IFSW/IASSW. (2014). *Global definition of social work.* Accessed 18 June 2022 from https://www.ifsw.org/what-is-social-work/global-definition-of-social-work/

IPCC. (2021). In V. Masson-Delmotte, P. Zhai, A. Pirani, S. L. Connors, C. Péan, S. Berger, N. Caud, Y. Chen, L. Goldfarb, M. I. Gomis, M. Huang, K. Leitzell, E. Lonnoy, J. B. R. Matthews, T. K. Maycock, T. Waterfield, O. Yelekçi, R. Yu, & B. Zhou (Eds.), *Climate change 2021: The physical science basis. Contribution of working group I to the sixth assessment report of the intergovernmental panel on climate change.* Cambridge University Press.

ITU World Telecommunication/ICT Indicators database. (2020). *World Telecommunication/ICT Indicators Database 2021 (25th edition/December 2021).* Accessed on 8 July 2022 from https://www.itu.int/en/ITU-D/Statistics/Pages/publications/wtid.aspx

Keith-Lucas, A. (1953). The political theory implicit in social casework theory. *The American Political Science Review, 47*(4), 1076–1091. https://doi.org/10.2307/1951126

Keskinen, S. (2016). From welfare nationalism to welfare chauvinism: Economic rhetoric, the welfare state and changing asylum policies in Finland. *Critical Social Policy, 36*(3), 352–370. https://doi.org/10.1177/0261018315624170

Ketola, M., & Nordensvard, J. (2018). Reviewing the relationship between social policy and the contemporary populist radical right: Welfare chauvinism, welfare nation state and social citizenship. *Journal of International and Comparative Social Policy, 34*(3), 172–187. https://doi.org/10.1080/21699763.2018.1521863

Ku, H. B., & Ho, D. K. (2020). The predicament of social work development and the emergence of social work action/practice research in China. *Action Research, 18*(1), 7–18. https://doi.org/10.1177/1476750320902902

Kumar, A. (2019). Ideas old and new: Bharatiyakaran/Indianisation of social work. *The International Journal of Community and Social Development, 1*(3), 254–263. https://doi.org/10.1177/2516602619878353

Mabvurira, V. (2018). Making sense of African thought in social work practice in Zimbabwe: Towards professional decolonisation. *International Social Work, 63*(4), 419–430. https://doi.org/10.1177/0020872818797997

McNabb, D. (2019). A treaty-based framework for mainstream social work education in Aotearoa New Zealand: Educators talk about their practice. *Aotearoa New Zealand social work, 31*(4), 4–17.

Midgley, J. (1995). *Social development: The developmental perspective in social welfare.* SAGE.

Mohan, B. (2018). *The future of social work: Sevan pillars of practice.* SAGE.

Mudde, C., & Kaltwasser, C. R. (2017). *Populism: A very short introduction.* Oxford University Press.

Muller, J. W. (2016). *What is populism?* University of Pennsylvania Press.

NASW. (2021). *Code of Ethics of the National Association of Social Workers.* Accessed on 2 February 2022 from https://www.socialworkers.org/About/Ethics/Code-of-Ethics/Code-of-Ethics-English

Oberndorf, C. P. (1932). A changing psychology in social case work: By Virginia P. Robinson. (The University of North Carolina Press, Chapel Hill, N.C., 1930, p. 204.). *International Journal of Psychoanalysis, 13*, 243–244.

Pawar, M. (2017). Social development: Progress so far. In J. Midgley & M. Pawar (Eds.), *Future directions in social development* (pp. 41–57). Palgrave Macmillan.

Pawar, M. (2019). Further comment on ideas old and new: Bharatiyakaran/Indianisation of social work. *The International Journal of Community and Social Development, 1*(3), 264–266. https://doi.org/10.1177/2516602619876500

Pawar, M. (2021). Opinion: Action needed on World Humanitarian Day. *Charles Sturt University Media,* 18 August 2021. https://news.csu.edu.au/opinion/action-needed-on-un-world-humanitarian-day

Pawar, M., & Androff, D. (2021). International Consortium for Social Development: Members' views and future directions. *The International Journal of Community and Social Development, 3*(2), 98–125.

Pawar, M., & Anscombe, A. W. (2015). *Reflective social work practice: Thinking, doing and being.* Cambridge University Press.

Pawar, M., & Weil, M. (2021). Global community practice. In *Encyclopedia of social work.* Oxford University Press. https://doi.org/10.1093/acrefore/9780199975839.013.930

Pippa, G. (2001). Changing culture and deprofessionalisation. *Nursing Management, 7*(9), 8–9. https://doi.org/10.7748/nm.7.9.8.s3

Raymond, F., & Cowger, C. C. (2012). International Consortium for Social Development. In L. M. Healy & R. J. Link (Eds.), *Handbook of international social work: Human rights, development and the global profession* (pp. 292–296). Oxford University Press.

Richmond, M. (1917). *Social diagnosis*. Russell Sage Foundation.

Robinson, V. P. (1930). *A changing psychology in social case work*. University of North Carolina Press.

Sewpaul, V., & Henrickson, M. (2019). The (r)evolution and decolonization of social work ethics: The Global Social Work Statement of Ethical Principles. *International Social Work, 62*(6), 1469–1481.

Singh, P. (2021). Populism, nationalism, and nationalist populism. *Studies in Comparative International Development, 56*(2), 250–269.

Suszycki, A. (2011). Welfare nationalism: Conceptual and theoretical considerations. In A. Suszycki (Ed.), *Welfare citizenship and welfare nationalism* (NordWel Studies in Historical Welfare State Research II) (pp. 51–77). University of Helsinki.

Tatenda, M., & Rumbidazi, N. (2020). Radical transformation, decolonisation, and their implications for social work. *African Journal of Peace and Conflict Studies (formerly Ubuntu: Journal of Conflict and Social Transformation), 9*(3), 9–25.

Tomlinson, J. (1977). *Is band-aid social work enough?* Wobbly Press.

UN. (2022). *World Day of Social Justice 20 February: 2022 theme: Achieving social justice through formal employment.* Accessed on 22 February 2022 from https://www.un.org/en/observances/social-justice-day

World Bank. (2020). *World development indicators*. World Bank.

World Bank. (2021). *Poverty: Overview.* Accessed on 22 February 2022 from https://www.worldbank.org/en/topic/poverty/overview#1

Yadav, R. (2019). *Decolonised and developmental social work: A model from Nepal*. Routledge.

Chapter 3
Contexts of Supervision: Organizations and Practice Settings

Introduction

In our interviews with practitioners, a few social workers commented that their work with people, clients, families, and communities was enjoyable and fulfilling. However, their real issue was with the organization in which they worked. That issue may be management, administration, resources, a supervisor, the volume of work, the prescriptiveness of the work, models and theories and approaches to the work, the frequency and depth and time-consuming nature of accountability for the work performed, and sometimes the poor alignment of work outcomes and performance measured work outcomes. Or it may relate to the values of the organization and professional social work. Whatever it is, their remarks showed that organizations play a critical role in social work practice and if social workers have issues with the organization, it needs to be understood and addressed. As discussed in Chap. 1 (see Fig. 1.1), organizations and institutions are inextricably linked to most professional supervision in social work and supervisees and supervisors. The delivery of most social welfare policies, programs, and services flows from organizations, and most social work practitioners work in those organizations. Thus, both formal and informal organizational cultures are critical for social work practitioners, as they are impacted by them. Equally, supervisors, particularly non-line-management supervisors, must understand the organizational culture as they offer supervisory inputs. Similarly, there is a variety of practice settings such as health, hospitals, schools, criminal justice, corrections, defense forces, and community, and the culture and nature of supervision in these settings varies.

Formal organizational culture may be understood in terms of the organization's vision, purpose and mission, values, strategic goals and plans, targets, administrative and management structures, policies and procedures, authorities and delegations, budget and resource allocations, communication channels, employee safety and support, and provision and opportunities for staff development. Informal

© The Author(s), under exclusive license to Springer Nature
Switzerland AG 2022
M. Pawar, A. W. (Bill) Anscombe, *Enlightening Professional Supervision in Social Work*, https://doi.org/10.1007/978-3-031-18541-0_3

organizational culture is how different people with different values, beliefs, backgrounds, and attitudes come together, relate to and interact with each other (at informal get-togethers, lunchtimes, and meetings), and create their own small group environment to interpret and make sense of the formal organization and lead a social life in the workplace context.

This chapter recognizes the significance of the contexts of organizations and the practice settings in professional supervision in social work and briefly introduces different types of organizations and practice settings. These are mainly government and non-government organizations (GOs, NGOs). Within NGOs, there are not-for-profit and for-profit organizations, faith-based organizations, and philanthropies/trusts/foundations, corporate social responsibility-oriented organizations, international NGOs, and multilateral organizations. Some of the practice settings discussed are social protection/security, health and hospitals, private practice/mental health, child welfare/protection, family/domestic violence, school social work, industrial social work, corrections, community, research/policy/advocacy, and rural and remote. Across all these types of organizations and settings, the supervisor's context matters for supervisees, whether the professional social work supervisor is a line-manager or non-line-manager. The supervision can occur in all contexts, and often the former can face stress and tension due to the need to manage and balance the roles of support and surveillance. The non-line-manager also faces some challenges, but some circumstances necessitate such supervision. This chapter discusses the strengths and weaknesses of both supervision approaches and concludes with a brief summary.

Organizational Context

Government Organizations

Generally, government organizations are one of the major employers of social workers, though this may not be the case in some countries where governments do not require the social work qualification for certain welfare-oriented positions. Government organizations may be categorized under three levels of government. These are the federal or central level, the state level, and the council or local government level. For example, Services Australia (previously Centrelink) is one of the major Australian government organizations that deliver services relating to social security, Medicare, and child support across Australia. At the state level, although the names of the government organizations (or departments) slightly vary, they organize and deliver services relating to child welfare and protection, families, education, health, and corrections. Local governments play an important role in implementing both federal and state government policies and programs.

The main features of the GOs and NGOs can be seen in Table 3.1. One of the common characteristics of government organizations is that they are often large and so is their area of coverage, with some having responsibility for the entire country

Table 3.1 The organizational context of government and non-government organizations

Feature	GOs	NGOs
Values and commitment	Generic	Specific and generally high
Size	Large	Small
Basis	Legislative	People and their commitment
Structure	Hierarchical/bureaucratic	Less hierarchical/ bureaucratic
Delegation/authority	Top to bottom	Top to bottom (less pronounced)
Budget/finance	Allocated and relatively stable	Planned and raised – unstable
Communication	Top to bottom	Both ways with ease
Changes/amendments	Difficult and time-consuming	Short time frame with ease
Computer networks	Large and complicated	Relatively small
Political environment	Very sensitive	Somewhat sensitive
Accountability	Often to the minister	Often to the board, donors, consumers
Risks/mistakes/ innovations	Low	High
New management	Changed nature of GOs and their relationship NGOs	Changed nature of NGOs and their relationship GOs

Source: Authors

and others for states or territories. They employ hundreds of employees. Social work practitioners perform critical functions and deliver important services to people at the grassroots level, so they are the face of the organization for many people, even though they may represent a very small part of the whole organization. Secondly, these organizations are created through legislation, thus have a legislative mandate, and should implement services according to the relevant legal provisions and procedures (Ozanne & Rose, 2013). Thirdly, they have a large vertical and horizontal hierarchical bureaucratic and administrative structure (see Matheson, 1996; Gardner, 2006). Fourthly, this organizational structural arrangement has an inbuilt power, authority, and delegation that is usually exercised from the top to lower levels. Fifth, this also defines communication channels and protocols for employees. As demanded by the top, bottom-to-top communication occurs for compliance, reporting, and accountability purposes. Sixth, due to legal, structural, and authority aspects of these organizations, they are rightly perceived and described as rigid or less flexible in their operations. Seventh, although there are mechanisms to seek feedback and improve, it is challenging for social workers to provide feedback due to fear of the structure. Even after providing feedback, it is difficult to make changes in the immediate future. Any suggested changes, if accepted, may take a long time to implement. If there are any shortcomings and flaws in the operation, it can impact many people. Eighth, most of them also use an extensive computer technology network, which may sometimes frustrate some users, particularly if they do not have the necessary knowledge and skills to do so. Ninth, government organizations and their work are accountable to a government minister, and the external political environment and changes in politics and governments can significantly influence the organization's budget, resources, and operations. Such changes may significantly impact service delivery, but peoples' reactions are often absorbed by social work practitioners, who may experience work stress and self-care issues. Tenth, generally government administrative systems tend to avoid mistakes and risks and focus on procedures, conformity, and standards (Keeling, 2019). Finally, the application of management principles in government organizations, generally known as new managerialism, has changed the nature of organizations in terms of limited resource allocation, performance measurement, evidence-based outcomes and outputs, and devaluing and replacing other professional roles. Such changes have posed problems for some social workers. One of the issues for GOs is that many programs are designed from the top-down and often for political ends. The idea of client "codesign" of programs and policies is limited. This is especially true for some areas of social work where the "expert" designs the social program with limited or no input from those most affected by the program or policy. Often the criterion is "system efficiency" rather than client effectiveness. For the professional supervisor, it is an important question whether one's supervision is primarily for the worker or ultimately for the service users as a group.

Although councils and shires are government organizations at the local level and are generally known as local governments, they are relatively small compared to federal and state governments and their jurisdiction. There is also great variation among councils in terms of size, resources, and plans and strategies. They receive grants from the state and federal governments to deliver several social services. Some social workers work in community and social development divisions to consult, plan, and deliver services to communities. In addition to some of the above organizational dynamics, sometimes social workers may need to work with mayors and councilors, depending upon the issues and demands made by them. While there are positives and problems associated with this type of locally politicized work, it may be difficult to balance professional work with politics and that may create value conflicts, work stress, and pressures.

Generally, it is important and useful for supervisors and supervisees to know this and similar government organizational contexts. It may help them relate to and discuss some of the practice issues considering the contexts of government organizations at different levels. However, in light of Gardner's (2006, pp. 50–51) remarks and experiences, as noted below, it is important and useful to have a balanced view about, and positive outlook toward, government organizations with the hope of bringing change by being an insider (Pawar, 2021; Giloba & Weiss-Gal, 2022).

> We tend to think of bureaucracies as large, inflexible, and unyielding organizations that are likely to be a constant struggle to work in. It is important to balance this picture (which is undoubtedly often true), with acknowledging that bureaucracies can also be open to change, respond to pressure, and allow freedom to operate. My own experience of working in bureaucracies reflects this mixture: I have experienced many of the frustrations, from realizing that you cannot move a piece of furniture without filling in a form to endless wrestling with rules about program guidelines that did not quite fit the situation of particular clients. However, I have also experienced times within bureaucracies where new ideas were welcomed, I had considerable freedom to operate within broad role guidelines and I could influence program development. (Gardner, 2006, pp. 50–51)

Non-government Organizations (NGOs)

NGOs, also known as voluntary organizations, are another broad category of organizations that have significantly increased in the past and where many social workers choose to work at different levels. As social work practitioners, it can include face-to-face work with people and communities and middle and top administrative and managerial roles such as coordinators, program directors, chief executive officers, and similar positions, depending upon the social workers' experience and choice of roles. The main features of the NGOs contrasting with GOs are listed in Table 3.1. The nature and type of NGOs significantly vary in terms of their values, plans, strategies, functions, and size. Their size ranges from very small, medium, to very large organizations. That is, one, two, to three staff members working for a small community organization to hundreds of staff members covering a large area with many offices or branches. Thus, their organizational context significantly varies, which has implications for professional supervision in social work. Riddle and Robinson (1995, p. 26) state that the NGO

> Can be used to describe small locally based, and loosely established voluntary and largely grassroots types of associations, as well as large national, and even transnational voluntary associations with formal constitutions, employing hundreds of staff.

Most NGOs are known for their distinct values and commitments, but these can vary from one organization to another to the extent of contradicting or conflicting with other NGOs (Korten, 1995). For professional social workers, sometimes this can be a source of conflict and discomfort if the NGO's values conflict with their professional and personal values.

NGOs perform a range of roles from simple charity to the delivery of government services or building organizations and institutions for health and education. In a developing country context, Heyzer (1995, p. 8) has identified the following three roles for NGOs, but they can be equally applicable to developed country contexts.

1. To support and empower local communities at the grassroots, which is essential for achieving sustainable development
2. To develop greater political influence through networking within and across national boundaries
3. To participate in shaping the direction of the development agenda

NGOs provide a great opportunity for social workers to engage in grassroots mobilization, community organization, and advocacy. However, performing such roles may be relatively difficult in GOs.

Compared to GOs, most NGOs are less hierarchical and less bureaucratic; but this may not apply to large, national level NGOs. Although delegation and authority are top to bottom, it is less pronounced than GOs. Communication can occur both ways – top to bottom to top – with ease. Regarding budgeting and finance, some NGOs can be more vulnerable due to their inability to raise required funds and resources to undertake necessary operations, and sometimes this leads to competition among NGOs for limited resources. This vulnerable financial context of the organization can create work pressure on social workers and sometimes may threaten their employment. In NGOs, it may be relatively easy to bring changes in a short time due to flexibility in the process. They are also less likely to have complex computer networks. Depending upon the type of NGO, the political environment may or may not matter to them. As generally, NGOs are relatively free from legal and procedural requirements; they can take more risks, afford to commit mistakes, and be experimental and innovative to address the needs and issues of people and communities. They are accountable to their board, donors, and consumers. However, the application of new management principles in GOs and NGOs has changed their nature of functioning and the relationship between them. Under the influence of privatization, competition, and market ideologies, many NGOs have become "government non-government organizations" and deliver government services as per the contractual obligations (Carson & Kerr, 2017). Despite this development and impact on some NGOs, we believe that due to their organizational context discussed above, most NGOs can achieve what Korten (1995, p. 98) has observed about them.

> Their small size, independence and focused value commitments give them a capacity for social and institutional innovation seldom found in either government or business. They serve as forums for the definition, testing and propagation of ideas and values in ways that are difficult or impossible for the other two sectors. Their commitment to integrative values, over political or economic values, gives them a natural orientation to the perceived needs of politically and economically disenfranchised elements of the population that are not met through the normal political processes of government or the economic process of the market.

This NGO perspective and their roles may appeal to some social workers. They may choose to work with NGOs, at least for some part of their career and be able to receive and offer professional supervision while keeping this broad organizational context in mind. The value commitment of NGOs might need to be elevated in professional supervision above any requirement for accountability.

As stated above, NGOs are a broad umbrella of organizations, and it is useful to look at some important categories or types of NGOs for clarity and further understanding of the organizational context. Some of the NGOs we have considered are not-for-profit and for-profit NGOs, faith-based NGOs, social enterprises, philanthropy and trusts, and corporate-supported organizations as part of corporate social responsibility, international NGOs, and multilateral organizations.

Not-for-Profit NGOs

As the name suggests, the main motive of not-for-profit NGOs is service to people and communities and not making a profit and/or, if a profit is made, not using it for their own purpose. As discussed above, their values, roles, size, and area of focus significantly vary. Ozanne and Rose (2013, p. 4) note that not-for-profit NGOs have a variety of structures and raise funds from various sources, including donations, government grants, and grants from philanthropies and trusts. Any surplus or profit is used for the organization's objectives rather than sharing it with board members or employees. As discussed above, fully depending on external funding can be problematic if it is not available or if it is conditioned to use in a particular way and for a specific purpose. This can impact the context of the work and workers (Cortis & Blaxland, 2020).

For-Profit NGOs

For-profit NGOs are similar to NGOs except that they openly make clear their intention to make profit from their work. If a profit is made, it is shared among the owners or shareholders, according to the agreed norms and rules. Following the introduction of a competitive tendering process by the Australian government, for-profit NGOs have increased in Australia. According to Ozanne and Rose (2013, p. 5), like not-for-profit NGOs, "For-profit NGOs can range from small companies where two or three social workers have joined together to provide fee-for-service counseling and consultancy services, through to large multinational companies that exist to provide contract services to governments in a range of areas, including human services, health and transport." The drive to make a profit can influence the organizational context and work culture as workers may be asked to produce or deliver more services with relatively less support. Further, the quality of service may be compromised, impacting service recipients and conflicting with professional values. This may also lead to performance targets and supervision with little flexibility. Thus, the Productivity Commission's (2017, p. 6) report includes this statement, "Some participants stated that for-profit providers should be excluded from delivering human services arguing, among other things, that providers incentivised by profit are not suited to offer high-quality services to vulnerable people." However, the Commission has recommended not to discriminate based on organizational type in tendering and contracting government services (Productivity Commission, 2017, p. 46). Supervisors and supervisees must consider whether the primary motivation for professional supervision is profit, de-risking reputational risk to the organization, meeting contractual obligations, improving service efficiency, or enhancing client outcomes.

Faith-Based Organizations

Faith-based organizations, which are also considered charities, are NGOs and are mostly not-for-profit. If profit accrues, it is used for social services or the purpose for which the charity has been established. Their faith, commitment, and service flow from their religion or whatever similar aspect of life they believe in. One of their main purposes is the advancement of religion, but this is not the whole and sole purpose. According to Knight and Gilchrist (2015, p. 3), "35% of charities with the purpose of advancing religion also have other purposes: advancing education (24%), relief of poverty, sickness or the needs of the aged (18%), childcare services (4%), and a wide range of other charitable objectives (16%)." Further, they found that most faith-based charities in Australia were smaller (annual revenue is less than

$250,000) and only 12% were large (annual revenue of more than $1m). Although some have other purposes and may not require employees and service receivers to follow the faith they are advancing, the context of most faith-based organizations is dominated by the faith they are advancing. Social workers who dovetail well with a faith-based organization may not find any issues working with such organizations. Whereas, social workers who have concerns about certain practices emanating from a particular faith and whose professional values conflict may find it challenging to work in this organizational context. To prevent such issues, some faith-based organizations recruit only those who belong to their faith. Beyond their faith and religion, many faith-based organizations submit tenders to governments and compete to obtain grants to deliver services to communities. This may be making their organizational context complex as they may need to integrate or balance their purpose of advancing religion with serving diverse population groups that may or may not belong to their faith. How (comfortably) social workers practice in this organizational context and whether they have concerns are important issues for discussion in their professional supervision. Professional supervisors and supervisees and faith-based organizations may have significant differences in understanding the basis of faith. These differences may be theological or practical. In addition, the supervisor will need to be mindful of the characteristics of any particular faith-based organization. For example, a professional supervisor may not be able to offer a full range of options to the supervisee if the organization has faith-based prohibitions. This becomes problematic when the faith-based organization accepts government money under a contractual obligation. The professional supervisor and supervisee may find themselves in a position where altering the contractual obligation by providing a full suite of services would infringe the faith-based organization's reason for existing.

Social Enterprises

Social enterprises are NGOs and can include for-profit and not-for-profit objectives and faith-based organizations. An alternative term, social entrepreneurship, is often used interchangeably to discuss this subject. Luke and Chu's (2013, p. 764) case studies-based conceptual analysis clarifies that "social enterprise reveals a focus on the purpose of social businesses, while social entrepreneurship reveals an emphasis on the processes underlying innovative and entrepreneurial activity for social purposes." Social enterprise or social entrepreneurship ventures can be understood as "organisations that: are led by an economic, social, cultural, or environmental mission consistent with a public or community benefit; trade to fulfil their mission; derive a substantial portion of their income from trade; and reinvest the majority of their profit/surplus in the fulfilment of their mission" (Barraket et al., 2016, p. 3). Their size significantly varies, from very small to large enterprises, reaching out internationally.

Although social work knowledge and skills are relevant to building social enterprises (Nandan et al., 2019; Pawar, 2019b), many social work practitioners are not engaged in them. To some social workers, the field seems relatively new, but their interest and involvement are likely to grow in coming years as social enterprises are increasing in number (Barraket et al., 2016), and some of them are popular as they help address the needs of vulnerable groups in innovative ways. The organizational context of social enterprises, on the one hand, includes inventing and identifying a locally relevant social enterprise and engaging disadvantaged groups in them to produce goods and services and, on the other hand, marketing those goods and services to earn a reasonable income for those who have engaged them. Integrating and applying social work and business knowledge and skills with a social purpose requires multidisciplinary engagement and professional supervision. Innovative supervision in this organizational context requires further exploration.

Philanthropies/Trusts/Foundations

Philanthropies, trusts, and foundations may be loosely considered as another type of NGO. They may be established by corporate bodies, industrialists, businesspersons, and any individuals with the resources to do so. Their size and coverage vary significantly, from local to international. They set specific aims and priority areas and allocate grants to individuals, organizations, institutions, associations, and cultural groups. Some also directly engage with communities and enter into private-public partnership projects. Social workers work in various capacities for philanthropies, trusts, and foundations, from entry to middle to senior management positions, and gain good experience. Their work may involve seeking and assessing grant applications, field visits, and monitoring, following-up on progress reports, and liaising with relevant officials within and outside the organization. The work culture and organizational context are quite different, and it may be difficult to find professional supervision. In relatively small philanthropies, trusts, and foundations, the organizational context can quickly change when the head of the organization changes, as can the operating styles and thrust of work. Sometimes such changes can cause stress and confusion for social workers, who may decide to leave work. Professional practice and supervision in this organizational context are important and must be well developed (McClendon et al., 2016).

Corporate Social Responsibility-Oriented Organizations

According to Carson and Kerr (2017, p. 160), "corporate social responsibility (CSR) is a concept that involves businesses proclaiming that their conduct is ethical and socially responsible, rather than being concerned only with maximizing profit. Key elements identified for a successful CSR partnership are shared values and trusting relationships between the business, its suppliers and its customers, value creation for all parties and staff engagement." In some countries (e.g., India), eligible corporates must allocate a minimum percentage of their profit to CSR activities. This has significantly increased CSR-related work in training, partnerships, and projects. CSR is also demonstrated through philanthropies, trusts, foundations, and social enterprises.

In addition to corporate social responsibility, there is an increasing emphasis on environmental and social responsibility and good governance (ESG), which may mean that corporates are seeking to partner with agencies that can further the corporate's environmental, social, and governance agendas. The shift from focusing on shareholder profitability to including ESG requirements offers both opportunities and pitfalls for professional supervision. It could mean that some corporates, recognizing the need for effectiveness in social services, provide funding and expertise to the social sector at no cost. However, it also could mean the corporates become increasingly interested in the social sector to offset their ESG responsibilities and seek greater control of their ESG spending.

There is a great variation in the nature of their work as some directly engage with communities, some partner with GOs and NGOs, and some provide funds. Social workers engage in CSR-related work in different capacities, from consultants to project coordinators and directors. There are potential tensions between corporate culture and approaches and professional social work culture and approaches. A desire to see immediate outputs and outcomes and a larger impact with company interest on the one hand and following community participation and engagement processes without discernible changes on the other can cause stress and tension. In such an organizational context, providing and receiving professional supervision is critical.

International NGOs

International NGOs are generally large and operate in multiple countries with regional offices. New and smaller INGOs may operate in a few countries. Some may be rooted in or linked to faith-based organizations, philanthropies, and foundations. They focus their work on a specific area, such as health, education, poverty, environment, human rights, advocacy, disability, children, women, humanitarian, and relief work, and some cover multiple areas according to their mission and objectives. Locally, they collaborate with both GOs and NGOs. Many social work practitioners work in them at different levels, depending upon their experience, and many new social workers aspire to work in them. The organizational context of INGOs is different from other organizations with their accountability mechanisms and ways of operation. Very big ones almost work like government organizations, though they have more flexibility. The mission and vision of the INGO, funding capacity and priorities, management and administrative leadership styles (Zook, 2015), stakeholders, and people from different professional backgrounds and different countries make the organizational context. Cross-cultural competencies, language, and cultural awareness are highly relevant. At the practice level, it is common to frequently encounter new situations and contexts. Feelings of loneliness, a sense of loss, and cultural shock are not uncommon, at least initially. Often workers must work independently in demanding situations with or without professional supervision. Providing and receiving professional supervision in INGOs is highly relevant and very much needed, but it may not be readily available. It is critical to be clear about the purpose of supervision: whether to enhance service delivery, support the individual worker, or assist the functioning of the international NGO, or a combination of these. There also needs to be an appropriate fit between the professional supervisor and the supervisee.

Multilateral Organizations

Multilateral organizations are mostly government organizations constituted by multiple nation-states to address their common needs and issues, broadly peace, security, and development. Some examples of multilateral organizations are United Nations agencies such as the United Nations Children's Fund (UNICEF), the World Health Organization (WHO), International Labour Organization (ILO), United Nations Development Programme (UNDP), UN Research Institute for Social Development (UNRISD), and the World Bank. Other similar organizations include the Organization for Economic Cooperation and Development (OECD), the European Union (EU), and BRICS (Brazil, Russia, India, China and South Africa). A small number of social workers opt for careers in these organizations; some also take consultancy and internships where such opportunities are available. The positions may not directly relate to social work qualifications, but social work knowledge and skills are applicable in some contexts. The organizational context of multilateral organizations is similar to government organizations. Although social workers may be engaged in small departments or heading divisions, navigating this type of complex organization; working with staff members with multicultural backgrounds, international transfers, and assignments; and having an international perspective constitute the organizational context. Professional supervision may or may not be available in this organizational context, but in our view, it is important to organize it. However, it may be complex and challenging from many perspectives (language, culture, engagement of multiple partners, etc.).

Social Work Practice Settings

As part of the organizational context, the nature of social work practice where social workers work, what is generally called a practice setting, is equally important in professional supervision in social work. We briefly discuss ten practice settings below, though social workers work in many other settings, and this list is far from exhaustive.

Social Protection and Security

According to government welfare policies and programs, social workers help deliver a range of social protection, security provisions, and benefits such as unemployment allowances, pensions for the elderly, youth allowances, support for mothers and children, and crisis payments for domestic violence victims, to name a few. As discussed above, depending upon the national context, different departments or agencies carry out the work under a bureaucratic structure by carefully assessing eligibility criteria and completing records as required by the established procedures. In Australia, such an agency is called Services Australia, where 681 social workers are employed in 216 locations (Commonwealth of Australia, 2021). They provide short-term or brief counseling to deal with personal or family problems and needs, domestic violence, emergencies and disasters, information about government payments, and other relevant services and help in meeting income security obligations and referrals to support services (Department of Human Services, 2016; Services Australia, 2022). They also join emergency response teams during disasters. They work face-to-face and increasingly online through smart centers, reaching out to people beyond the local area, which comes with challenges. As in other public sector settings, social workers must balance their role between advocacy for the people they work with and administrative compliance for their organization (Mendes & Hargreaves, 2018; Commonwealth of Australia, 2021). Most social workers are supervised by senior social workers, who are also their line-managers.

Health and Hospitals

This is one of the well-established and traditional settings in which social workers have been working from the beginning of the profession. This setting can include GOs, NGOs, for-profit, not-for-profit organizations, and some may be supported by faith-based organizations, philanthropies, or foundations. These are complex organizations (Bawden & McDermott, 2018), where multidisciplinary professionals, doctors, psychiatrists, nurses, social workers, and other allied health professionals constantly engage in demanding work.

Mental health is a specialized area of clinical practice within the health setting, and many social workers are engaged in it. Dedicated mental health hospitals and separate psychiatric wards are common in large hospitals. The move from an institutional to community focus, recovery thrust, and multidisciplinary contributions with the relative dominance of psychiatrists further add to this context. Sometimes, legal aspects, clinical versus social perspectives, and tight budgets (Petrakis & Sheehan, 2018) can complicate the context. Generally, large hospitals have a separate social work department, where social workers work under the supervision of a senior social worker or the department head. Small hospitals usually have a social worker but without a designated department, and sometimes they are supervised by nursing or medical staff. In this complex setting, social workers deal with issues relating to social work assessments, support for patients and family members, contributing to discharge decisions, rehabilitation support, therapies, emergency, crisis and grief, community health, advocacy for patients, and health policy (AASW, 2015). Professional supervision in health can often raise the issue of generalist supervision versus specialist supervision. Supervisors and supervisees need to consider the specialist knowledge required in the particular health field. It is an important question as to what level of knowledge a professional supervisor needs to supervise a specialist oncology social worker or social worker specifically working in genetic counseling or infertility and a range of other specializations. While offering opportunities to serve suffering patients and their loved ones and gain invaluable experience and knowledge, from the organizational perspective, there are many challenges in health and hospital settings. These include helping patients navigate the hospital system; paperwork; convincing multidisciplinary professionals about the merits of the social worker's assessments and decisions, particularly when there are differing views; the dominance of the medical profession; supervision of social workers by nursing or allied health staff; value conflicts; heavy work or caseloads; and a lack of opportunities to pause and reflect.

Private Practice

Social workers in private practice work in a number of areas, including mental health, law, organizational change, forensic social work, workers' compensation, and specialist reports to courts, tribunals, and insurance companies. Private practice is gaining momentum in some countries such as Australia and the USA. For example, in Australia, over 2000 accredited mental health social workers (AMHSW) help people enhance their mental health, and about 40% serve in rural and remote areas. Most of them (more than 75%) have more than 10 years of experience. On behalf of the Commonwealth Government, AASW assesses and accredits mental health social workers who register with Medicare Australia and offer services through a number of Commonwealth funded schemes and other agencies (AASW, 2019). In relation to the private practice, there are sole operators at the individual level who operate their private practice in one or multiple medical centers or in their own dedicated offices. Some social workers individually or together offer services by forming their own company and employing or providing space for other social work practitioners and allied health workers to operate. They often receive referrals from medical practitioners and other relevant agencies. The use of digital media to offer these services is becoming common. They create an organizational context for practice that needs to ensure quality practice and viability by earning an income or making a profit. Disciplined record-keeping, adhering to the regulatory regime, continuous training and updating, and maintaining accreditation are required. The issue of negligence insurance is also a consideration as well as accountability for performance. If qualified, some of them also offer supervision to social workers.

Child Welfare and Protection

Child welfare and protection work is mainly undertaken by state level GOs, though some services are contracted to NGOs. Often governments purchase services, and NGOs provide services such as foster care assessments, out-of-home care, family finding, supported accommodation, family and domestic violence refuges, and family support services. Social work in these settings typically integrates elements of a legal setting due to mandatory requirements, legal responsibilities and guardianship for children, and work with judicial systems, police, lawyers, prosecution staff, courts, and judges. It also includes significant social aspects relating to preventive and supportive work with children and families and their communities and coordination and monitoring of services. The organization and the nature of work involved make it a complex, demanding, and stressful setting. Historically, it carries the stigma of removing children from families with associated racial connotations. Working with multidisciplinary staff members, some involuntary clients, balancing care and control, legal judgment and professional social work judgment, particularly if there are differences, and ethical issues, are normal features of this setting. Writing reports according to legal and procedural requirements, meeting deadlines, and responding to questions by impacted families and the court can cause stress. Like other organizations, child welfare and protection agencies are impacted by managerialism that focuses on risks, accountability, contracting services, workload, and performance (Tilbury, 2018). Politically, it is a sensitive setting if there are incidents such as serious injuries or deaths. Due to the nature of the work, a high turnover of workers is not uncommon, despite a few supportive measures. Some organizations offer line-management supervision, case discussion seminars and workshops, and peer or group supervision. Social workers work at different levels of the organization, practicing with people, clients, and communities to administrative and managerial responsibilities at higher levels.

Family/Domestic Violence

This also makes a complex setting as many agencies such as women's refuges and other services for the homeless, mental health providers, police, legal services, drug and alcohol services, and services for men are engaged in addressing the issue. The organizational context includes both GOs and NGOs. Often working with women, children, and men in crises and coordinating with a range of agencies to ensure their safety and security on the one hand, and confidence building, enabling, and empowering women toward self-reliance on the other, are norms in this setting. Limits to confidentiality, human rights issues, and ethical dilemmas are common. It is important to be aware of professional boundaries and their interconnections. Case management, well-trained staff, and the timely delivery of needed services are real challenges, as are mobilizing adequate resources to match the growing demand for services, advocacy, preventive community work, and effective multi-agency collaboration (see Chung, 2018). As in other settings, attention to burnout and self-care is needed in this setting.

School Social Work

School social work is an established field of practice and setting in some countries, such as the USA, the UK, and Australia (Oliaro, 2018; AASW, 2020), whereas it is still emerging in other countries. While students are the focus of social workers' practice, the school environment consisting of the principal, teachers, psychologists, administrative staff, and the broader school community makes this context complex. The level of resources depends upon whether it is a public school, private/independent school, or government education department employing social workers to cover several schools (Barrett, 2014, as cited in Oliaro, 2018). Meeting confidentiality and informed consent requirements and working with a range of stakeholders (teachers, parents, the student's peers, and relevant community agencies) are critical. Their line-manager is the principal for reporting and accountability purposes, though they cannot be professional supervisors unless they are qualified. The school setting provides an excellent opportunity to prevent likely issues and work early to support students. However, it also has challenges relating to a low numbers of social workers, high case/workloads, increased administrative work, reactive support rather than proactive, a lack of community engagement and role clarity, logistical issues, and inadequate funding (see Lee, 2012). Being set in an educational context, the focus is often upon educational outcomes rather than social outcomes. Without sophisticated tools, it may be difficult to identify how social outcomes contribute to better learning and educational outcomes. These details about the setting may help supervisors and supervisees to plan for their supervision.

If school social work is generally construed as social work in educational settings, most tertiary institutions and universities have student support services in which social workers are employed to help students who seek services. It has some similarities with school social work except that the age and needs of the students are different. The university organizational context and this practice setting, as it also focuses on students, are also relevant for professional supervision.

Corrections

The correction setting involves both government and private organizations due to the privatization of some aspects of corrections work, and in some cases, NGOs are engaged in the process. It also includes the juvenile justice system. It may be broadly categorized into institutional corrections and community corrections; each setting is different, though interconnected. Taken together, it is a broad setting in which social workers work in a range of positions, including contracted work, not necessarily designated as "social worker." For example, some social workers work under titles such as directors, welfare officers, probation and parole officers and case managers. The setting has a socio-legal and "involuntary clients" context. Adhering to and implementing legal requirements and procedures with a strict and inflexible regime on the one hand and focusing on care and rehabilitation on the other make the setting delicate and challenging. All those who work in these positions may not be qualified social workers, and working with those colleagues is important. Similarly, the line-manager may not be a qualified social worker, and administrative reporting requirements must be completed. Depending upon the position and roles, work with other agencies such as the courts, police, community agencies, government welfare departments, and families is required. The setting has contradictory approaches, punitive versus positively corrective, toward the reformation and rehabilitation of people (see Lipsey & Cullen, 2007, as cited in Trotter, 2018). Given the emphasis on safety and security, the professional supervisor must be aware that any documentation taken into or emanating from a prison is subject to security checks. Importantly, notions of empowerment can be perceived as dangerous in a control and command environment where the primary orientation is security. As the setting is mostly preoccupied with meeting statutory requirements, there may not be any regular practice of professional supervision.

Community

The community is a critical setting in which to practice an important method of social work practice, community organization, and development. To some it is known as an indirect setting, as direct clinical work with individuals is not expected. Communities can include a traditional geographically located community, online communities, communities of interest that are disconnected from particular locations, mutual interest groups from multiple locations, trade unions, business and management organizations, churches and other religious organizations, community centers, and social media communities. The platform to work with any of these communities may be based in any of the organizations, GOs to NGOs discussed above. So, the social worker's organization and type of community chosen for practice make the setting. For example, if we consider the traditional geographically located community, the community setting may be a particular council or shire area, a suburb, neighborhood, or an organization engaged in community work. The community's demographic profile, a particular area of practice within the community (e.g., social awareness about a particular cause, developing groups, community consultation, social enterprise, etc.), community leaders, politics, and the community power structure are crucial aspects of the community context. As this differs from one community to another, social workers learn more about the community context as they begin their work. It mainly involves working with groups, planning, advocacy, decision-makers, local authorities, and resource mobilization for programs and projects determined by community members. The community context also requires work with other professionals and workers relevant to the task. Considerations for the professional supervisor in the community setting may include a very clear understanding of politics, clear lines of accountability and responsibility, and clear communication approaches. Experienced community organizers are ideal supervisors to guide social workers. The new forms of evolving communities may require new approaches and strategies.

Research Leading to Advocacy and Policy

Social work research is another area of social work practice, and social workers may engage in relevant research projects in any of the organizations and settings discussed above. Like the community setting, it involves indirect practice and work with other researchers, agencies, and stakeholders. The setting demands complying with the funder's requirements, reporting progress to senior officials, and completing research projects on time. Like community work, it involves working with groups, multidisciplinary professionals, planning, advocacy, decision-makers, local authority, and legislators. Policy practice, which includes advocacy, is emerging as an important area of practice (Gal & Weiss-Gal, 2013, 2017; Pawar, 2019a). This setting has challenges, as the focus areas can be diverse, including service users' participation in research, using codesign approaches to engage impacted people, clients, and communities in policies, programs, and where advocacy is critical. Policy formulation, implementation, evaluation and change are seamless processes with inbuilt hurdles. Line-managers may not be professional supervisors, and professional supervision may not be readily available in this setting. As per the specific area of work, specialized supervision may be needed.

Rural and Remote

The rural and remote social work practice setting offers unique opportunities and challenges. Parameters of rural and remote differ from one country to another, but they are certainly non-urban. In the Australian context, rural is fewer than 25,000 people with reduced access to services, and remote is less than 5000 people with very restricted access to services (Roufeil & Battye, 2008, as cited in Wendt, 2018). From the social work practice perspective, rural and remote areas are generally among the most neglected globally. All the above and more practice areas are needed in rural areas. Reaching out to the most needy, vulnerable, and isolated populations groups is personally and professionally rewarding and challenging. The organizational context may include GOs and NGOs, often located at a distance. The setting has a generalist practice, community, and network approach due to the rural remote context (see Cheers et al., 2007; Pugh & Cheers, 2010). Some of the unique features of the setting are rural and remote peoples' and communities' expectations to attend to wide-ranging needs and issues; the blurring of the lines between formal and informal interactions, personal and professional life, and work-life balance (Maidment, 2012); a small team or lone work; and limited local referrals (Cheers et al., 2005). In this setting, social workers generally experience ethical issues, distance and isolation, a lack of anonymity and privacy, slow community acceptance, and relatively poor infrastructure, including accommodation. Appropriate supervision may not be available, though increasingly it may be accessed through online services if the digital infrastructure is in place.

Line-Management Versus Non-line-Management Professional Supervision in Organizational and Practice Settings

The wide-ranging organizational contexts and practice settings discussed above show that professional supervision is not limited to clinical practice, working with individuals and groups, or therapeutic work. There is an unexplored scope for professional supervision in all these organizational contexts and practice settings. The nine types of supervision discussed in Chap. 1 – social work students, post-qualification licensing/registration, line-management/administration, group, peer, tertiary sector, independent supervision, and mentoring and coaching – may be considered in these contexts. Of these nine, most are optional as these may or may not be organized depending upon opportunities. However, it is reasonable to assume that line-management/administrative supervision exists and is practiced in most of these contexts and settings. As professional supervision in social work is essentially a reflective learning process, it is important to ask whether the organizational contexts and practice settings discussed above offer planned learning opportunities for supervisees and supervisors through line-management and administrative supervision. Most social workers in all these settings have line-managers. Do they supervise them from the enabling, empowering, and strengthening perspective whether or not organizations have that kind of perspective?

In the child and family social work setting in the UK, by analyzing 34 supervision case discussions, Wilkins et al. (2017, p. 942) found that although supervisors believed in the reflective, supportive, and analytical aspects of professional supervision, their discussions primarily focused on management oversight. This perhaps happens because organizations "focus too much on 'what and when' things happen and not enough on 'how and why'." This finding cannot be generalized in all organizational contexts and practice settings as some supervisees have good supervision experience from line-managers who can integrate management oversight and professional learning and strengthening. However, this seems to be an exception rather than a norm, as most supervisors are busy and preoccupied with performance indicators and outputs due to the management-oriented organizational culture. Further, supervisees may not feel confident discussing issues with line-managers due to a power imbalance or a lack of professional background in social work. One way of approaching this challenging supervision context is organizing an independent external supervisor, within or outside the organization, who is other than the line-manager. While prima facie, non-line-management supervision appears a good solution because of free and frank discussion and dedicated time for supervision, a closer look at this approach reveals a few issues and limitations. It may be useful to look at the strengths and limitations of both approaches to supervision.

Line-managers have full knowledge of the organization, delegated authority to initiate change, and clear accountability. If they are well qualified and have time, they are in the best position to offer both types of supervision and may advocate better. On the other hand, under a non-line-management supervisor, supervision can occur according to the choice of the supervisee. Both can develop a non-power-based egalitarian relationship, share information freely, and dedicate specific time for supervision. In terms of limitations, line-managers may not have adequate time, may not be qualified for professional supervision, and potentially may abuse their power and authority. Supervisees may be fearful or uncomfortable about the arrangement and thus may not disclose all information, whether it is about conflicting values or performance. It becomes more problematic when they do not have a good relationship with the line-manager. External supervisors also face limitations – as they do not have full information about the organization, they cannot directly check and intervene, and they only receive the supervisee's version of any issue. In addition, dealing with confidential information may be problematic; there may be potential cooption, disconnection from management, and inconsistency between supervisee and organizational goals.

Both approaches to supervision are necessary as some settings demand such arrangements (King et al., 2017). The analysis helps to enhance strengths and work on limitations to improve the quality of supervision. On this matter, Davys and Beddoe (2021, pp. 96–99) have listed several disadvantages of external supervision and raised questions for external supervisors, line-managers, and supervisees to consider so that supervision can be improved.

For external supervisors, Davys and Beddoe (2021, p. 99) suggest considering and reflecting on the following questions:

> What can you do to support the full professional learning of your supervisee? Could you influence your supervisee's organization? How can you ensure you get good information? How do you influence in both directions and should you? What arrangements are in place for you to provide feedback to your supervisee's manager?

For line-managers who have accessed external supervision for their staff, they ask to consider and reflect on the following questions:

> How do you negotiate the lines of accountability and feedback on supervision issues and process? What arrangements do you have to liaise with the supervisor if you have concerns about your practitioner's work performance? What agreements are in place if the supervisor has concerns about the practitioner and/or the work context?

For supervisees with external supervisors, they ask to consider and reflect on the following questions:

What should you do to ensure that your supervision is accountable to your manager/workplace? What are the boundaries of confidentiality that you consider to be important?

Most line-managers are busy and preoccupied with administrative and managerial aspects of their job (King et al., 2017), and many may not be qualified supervisors. Professional supervision is not limited to clinical and casework or therapeutic practice, and most supervisees may prefer a non-line-management supervisor or self-managed supervision (King et al., 2017). The reflective questions raised by Davys and Beddoe (2021, p. 99) are critical to addressing limitations and enhancing the quality of professional supervision in social work. Given the wide-ranging organizational contexts and practice settings, it is important to extend and expand professional supervision in social work from clinical practice to a range of non-clinical practice settings discussed above.

Conclusion and Summary

This chapter recognizes that the contexts of organizations and practice settings significantly influence professional supervision in social work. It has summarized the organizational context of GOs and NGOs and a range of other organizations. It also has discussed the context of ten practice settings relating to social security/protection, health and hospitals, mental health and private practice, child welfare/protection, family, domestic violence, school social work, corrections, community, research/policy/advocacy, and rural and remote. The list is not exhaustive as many other practice settings may be included. It has discussed the general features of these settings to aid supervisors and supervisees. As professional supervision in social work appears to be mostly limited to clinical practice, case management, and therapeutic work, the chapter argues that such supervision needs to be extended to non-clinical practice organizational contexts and practice settings such as community, social enterprise, and policy practice. As most line-managers may not be available to provide professional supervision, it has discussed the option of non-line-management supervision, some of its strengths and limitations, and ways of reducing limitations to enhance the quality of supervision. The next chapter will discuss models of professional supervision in social work.

References

AASW. (2015). *Scope of social work practice: Social work in health*. AASW. Retrieved on 7 March 2022 from https://www.aasw.asn.au/document/item/8306

AASW. (2019). *Accredited mental health social workers*. Accessed on 15 March 2022 from https://www.aasw.asn.au/information-for-the-community/mental-health-social-workers

AASW. (2020). *Scope of social work practice: School social work*. AASW. Accessed on 8 March 2022 from https://www.aasw.asn.au/document/item/8308

Barraket, J., Mason, C., & Blain, B. (2016, June). *Finding Australia's social enterprise sector 2016: Final report*. Social Traders and the Centre for Social Impact Swinburne Melbourne. Retrieved from http://apo.org.au/system/files/64444/apo-nid64444-48516.pdf

Barrett, C. (2014). *School social work in the state of Victoria: 65 years of student wellbeing and learning support* (Unpublished PhD thesis). Melbourne University Melbourne.

Bawden, G., & McDermott, F. (2018). Social work in healthcare settings. In M. Alston, S. McCurdy, & J. McKinnon (Eds.), *Social work: Fields of practice*. Oxford University Press.

Carson, E., & Kerr, L. (2017). *Australian social policy and human services* (2nd ed.). Cambridge University Press.

Cheers, B., Darracott, R., & Lonne, B. (2005). Domains of rural social work practice. *Rural Society, 15*(3), 234–251.

Cheers, B., Darracott, R., & Lonne, B. (2007). *Social care practice in rural communities*. The Federation Press.

Chung, D. (2018). Social work in the domestic violence sector. In M. Alston, S. McCurdy, & J. McKinnon (Eds.), *Social work: Fields of practice*. Oxford University Press.

Commonwealth of Australia. (2021). *Services Australia annual report, 2020–21*. Commonwealth of Australia.

Cortis, N., & Blaxland, M. (2020). *The profile and pulse of the sector: Findings from the 2019 Australian Community Sector Survey*. ACOSS.

Davys, A., & Beddoe, L. (2021). *Best practice in professional supervision: A guide for the helping professions* (2nd ed.). Jessica Kingsley Publishers.

Department of Human Services (DHS). (2016). *Social work services*. Australian Government.

Gal, J., & Weiss-Gal, I. (2013). *Social workers affecting social policy: An international perspective*. The Policy Press.

Gal, J., & Weiss-Gal, I. (2017). *Where academia and policy meet: A cross-national perspective on the involvement of social work academics in social policy*. Policy Press.

Gardner, F. (2006). *Working in human service organisations*. Oxford University Press.

Giloba, C., & Weiss-Gal, I. (2022). Change from within: Community social workers as local policy actors. *The British Journal of Social Work, 52*, 3540–3558. https://doi.org/10.1093/bjsw/bcab263

Heyzer, N. (1995). Toward new government. NGO relations for sustainable and people-centred development. In N. Heyzer, J. V. Riker, & A. B. Quizon (Eds.), *Government-NGO relations in Asia: Prospects and challenges for people-centred development*. Macmillan and Asian and Pacific Development Centre.

Keeling, D. (2019). *Management in government*. Routledge.

King, S., Carson, E., & Papatraianou, L. H. (2017). Self-managed supervision. *Australian Social Work, 70*(1), 4–16.

Knight, P. A., & Gilchrist, D. J. (2015). *Australia's faith-based charities 2013: A summary of data from the Australian Charities 2013 report*. Australian Charities and Not-for-profits Commission, Melbourne. https://www.acnc.gov.au/tools/reports/faith-based-charities-australia-2013

Korten, D. C. (1995). *Getting to the 21st century: Voluntary and the global agenda*. Kumarian Press.

Lee, J. S. (2012). School social work in Australia. *Australian Social Work, 65*(50), 552–570.

Lipsey, M., & Cullen, F. (2007). The effectiveness of correctional rehabilitation: A review of systematic reviews. *Annual Review of Law and Social Science, 3*, 297–320.

Luke, B., & Chu, V. (2013). Social enterprise versus social entrepreneurship: An examination of the "why" and "how" in pursuing social change. *International Small Business Journal, 31*(7), 764–784.

Maidment, J. (2012). Introduction. In J. Maidment & U. Bay (Eds.), *Social work in rural Australia: Enabling practice* (pp. 3–18). Allen and Unwin.

Matheson, C. (1996). Organisational structures in the Australian public service. *Australian Journal of Public Administration, 57*(3), 15–27.

McClendon, J., Kagotho, N., & Lane, S. R. (2016). Preparing social work students for leadership in human service organizations through student philanthropy. *Human Service Organizations: Management, Leadership & Governance, 40*(5), 500–507.

Mendes, P., & Hargreaves, D. (2018). Social work in the field of income maintenance and employment. In M. Alston, S. McCurdy, & J. McKinnon (Eds.), *Social work: Fields of practice* (3rd ed., pp. 165–179). Oxford University Press.

Nandan, M., Tricia, B., Bent-Goodley, T. B., Mandayam, G., & Singh, A. (2019). Social entrepreneurship, social intrapreneurship, social innovation, and social value creation: An overview and implications for social work. In M. Nandan, T. B. Bent-Goodley, & G. Mandayam (Eds.), *Social entrepreneurship and intrapreneurship and social value creation: Relevance for contemporary social work practice.* NASW Press.

Oliaro, L. (2018). Social work in educational settings. In M. Alston, S. McCurdy, & J. McKinnon (Eds.), *Social work: Fields of practice.* Oxford University Press.

Ozanne, E., & Rose, D. (2013). *The organizational context of human service practice.* Palgrave Macmillan.

Pawar, M. (2019a). Social work and social policy practice: Imperatives for political engagement. *The International Journal of Community and Social Development, 1*(1), 15–27. https://doi.org/10.1177/2516602619833219

Pawar, M. (2019b). Community development, empowerment and social entrepreneurship by "Thankyou". In M. Nandan, T. B. Bent-Goodley, & G. Mandayam (Eds.), *Social entrepreneurship and intrapreneurship and social value creation: Relevance for contemporary social work practice.* NASW Press.

Pawar, M. (2021). "A promised land": Lessons for community organising at multiple levels. *International Journal of Community and Social Development, 3*(1), 10–29.

Petrakis, M., & Sheehan, R. (2018). Social work practice in mental health settings. In M. Alston, S. McCurdy, & J. McKinnon (Eds.), *Social work: Fields of practice.* Oxford University Press.

Productivity Commission. (2017). *Introducing competition and informed user choice into human services: Reforms to human services.* Report no. 85. Commonwealth of Australia. Accessed on 4 March 2022 from https://www.pc.gov.au/inquiries/completed/human-services/reforms/report

Pugh, R., & Cheers, B. (2010). *Rural social work: An international perspective.* The Policy Press.

Riddell, R. C., & Robinson, M. (1995). *Non-governmental organisations and rural poverty alleviation.* Clarendon Press.

Roufeil, L., & Battye, K. (2008). *Effective regional, rural and remote family relationships service delivery.* Australian Family Relationship Clearinghouse Briefing No.10. AFRC.

Services Australia. (2022). *How we help.* Accessed on 5 March 2022 from https://www.servicesaustralia.gov.au/how-our-social-work-services-can-help?context=22461

Tilbury, C. (2018). Social work in child protection settings. In M. Alston, S. McCurdy, & J. McKinnon (Eds.), *Social work: Fields of practice.* Oxford University Press.

Trotter, C. (2018). Criminal Justice: Extending the social work focus. In M. Alston, S. McCurdy, & J. McKinnon (Eds.), *Social work: Fields of practice.* Oxford University Press.

Wendt, S. (2018). Social work in regional, rural and remote Australia. In M. Alston, S. McCurdy, & J. McKinnon (Eds.), *Social work: Fields of practice.* Oxford University Press.

Wilkins, D., Forrester, D., & Grant, L. (2017). What happens in child and family social work supervision? *Child and Family Social Work, 22*(2), 942–951.

Zook, G. A. (2015). *Leadership understandings of organizational effectiveness: an exploration within the context of faith-based international nongovernment organizations.* PhD thesis, Eastern University. Accessed on 5 March 2022 from https://www.proquest.com/docview/1787578650?parentSessionId=CH%2BWjHqg3l6ZEnrLmYYTS%2F%2BsJXsZp7Ecj4%2FcYN9c5og%3D&pq-origsite=primo&accountid=10344

Chapter 4
Models of Professional Supervision in Social Work

Introduction

The title of this chapter, "Models of professional supervision in social work," raises expectations that professional supervision in social work is explained and discussed in terms of research variables and relationships between them to explain, verify, predict, falsify, and suggest future experimentation. At the outset, we would like to reduce or change that expectation by clarifying that the term model in this chapter is used in a loose sense to describe how supervision in social work is organized and conducted and how several authors have conceptualized it. The literature on models of social work supervision has emerged over more than 70 years (Bruce & Austin, 2000; White & Russell, 1995; Sewell, 2018); and some authors have tried to summarize and theorize it with some logic, order, and categorization (e.g., see Tsui & Ho, 1998; Tsui, 2005; O'Donoghue et al., 2018; Shulman, 2020a, b; Harris & Slattery, 2021). We aim to familiarize you with some of their conceptualizations of supervision models in summary form. By reviewing some models of social work supervision, we have developed three broad categories of supervision models. The first is purpose- and goal-based models, the second is path-based models, and the third is the integration of the first and second, that is, purpose- and path-based models. As the nomenclature of the categories indicates, the first category focuses on the purposes and goals of the social work supervision in terms of what needs to be or should be achieved in social work supervision. These broadly revolve around administration and management, education, support, and quality service delivery. The second category of path-based supervision models looks at different ways of achieving the purposes and goals. For example, these include line-management and non-line-management supervision models, a contract model of supervision, a model of supervision in private practice, digital and online supervision models, casework, clinical practice and therapy-oriented supervision models, a reflective learning model of supervision, peer group supervision models, group supervision models, a model of systemic supervision, a portfolio model of supervision, an appreciative supervision model, a cultural competency supervision model, a critical conversations model of supervision, and feminist supervision models. It appears that by responding to the prevailing contexts and their impacts on all stakeholders – people and communities, organizations, managers, and social work practitioners – different paths of supervision have emerged in the quest to achieve the purpose and goals of supervision. The third category of models attempts to integrate both the purposes and paths of supervision models. What follows is a summary of several models of supervision under the three categories along with brief comments on them. If any model interests you, we recommend going to the sources to find more details about them.

Purpose- and Goal-Based Models

Many scholars have emphasized the purpose and goals of professional supervision in social work in terms of functions, activities, and tasks of supervision (Erera & Lazar, 1994; Fox, 1983; Gitterman, 1972; Kadushin, 1985; Morrison, 2005; Kadushin & Harkness, 2014; Lowy, 1983; Shulman, 2020a, b; Harris, 2020; Harris & Slattery, 2021), and some also refer to it as structural-functional models (Tsui, 2005, p. 20). They all emphasize what needs to be achieved through the supervision process. They list up to six items as the purpose and goals of supervision – administration, education, job management, professional impact, support, and service delivery. To that list, we would like to add one more instrumental purpose relating to completing mandatory requirements prescribed by professional bodies or licensing agencies and tertiary institutions to acquire professional qualifications (BSW and MSW). These seven are discussed in brief below.

First, the purpose of supervision is to achieve the administrative and management goals of the organization. This is the traditional role of many supervisors. Kadushin and Harkness (2014, p. 28) have identified 12 administrative tasks of supervisors. These are "staff recruitment, inducting and placing, explaining supervision, work planning, assignment, delegation, monitoring, reviewing and evaluating work, administrative buffering, and acting as a channel of communication, an advocate, a change agent and community liaison." On similar lines, Harris and Slattery (2021, p. 363) include 14 tasks in their supervision model, PASE (practice, administration, support, and education). While performing these and similar tasks, the supervisor helps the supervisee to understand policies, programs, procedures, and processes to be followed while working in the organization and ensures that the supervisee performs according to the agency's set standards and expectations. The position therefore has elements of authority and surveillance. The role of the supervisee is to understand and follow these agency policies and procedures and demonstrate how they are meeting these standards and expectations.

Second, the purpose and goal of supervision are educational, which may include a range of tasks and activities. For example, Harris and Slattery (2021) list 14 tasks and activities. The role of the supervisor is to share knowledge and resources, provide leads to engage in a range of relevant activities, and help the supervisee develop further professional competencies and skills in a required area of practice according to the needs of each supervisee (Kadushin & Harkness, 2014; Harris & Slattery, 2021). The role of the supervisee is to acquire this knowledge, sharpen practice skills, and meet the administrative and managerial expectations. To Gitterman (1972), this helps to achieve the professional development of frontline staff, and for Lowy (1983), it was a learning model. Shulman (2020a) reinterprets it as supervision of direct practice covering assessment, intervention, and evaluation of client interventions and continued learning.

Third, according to Shulman's (2020a, b) delineation, the purpose of supervision is job management, which includes the supervisor guiding the supervisee in work-related issues such as record keeping, handling phone calls and missed sessions, timeliness, report writing, caseload management, and the resolution of ethical issues (e.g., managed-care requirements, insurance reimbursements). In some respects, it has the element of the first and second purposes discussed above.

The fourth purpose of supervision is to make a professional impact (Shulman, 2020a, p. 3). According to Shulman, the professional impact means, in the context of client-oriented activities, the supervisor guiding the supervisee to deal with other professionals such as psychiatrists, psychologists, teachers, and other allied health workers and influencing policies and procedures and political systems to improve interventions and outcomes for clients.

The fifth purpose of supervision is to provide support to the supervisee. As social work practitioners often work with complex crises and stressful situations, supervisors are expected to emphatically listen, demonstrate care to deal with stress and possible burnout, and provide support to enhance the confidence and optimism of the worker. Fox (1983, pp. 43–44) has well-articulated this supervisor's role as follows:

1. Consciously sustain and stimulate a climate of trust, respect, interest, and support.
2. Handle painful material openly, objectively, and directly.
3. State honestly when you cannot help or do not know how to proceed.
4. Empathize; seek to clarify perceptions and understand workers' feelings, attitudes, and behavior; recognize discouragement, tension, and anxiety.
5. Recognize and reinforce achievement and reflect on success as well as failure.

Likewise, Harris and Slattery (2021) have identified 16 supportive tasks and activities. The role of supervisees is to share in confidence with the supervisor what is happening to them as a professional practitioner and use the advice. This supportive role of the supervisor is expected to enhance job satisfaction, motivation, and retention (Kadushin, 1985; Kadushin & Harkness, 2014; Shulman, 1993).

Although Kadushin's (1985) supervision functions did not include the sixth purpose and goal, Gitterman (1972) suggested that the purpose of the organization-oriented model was to ensure the result of human service delivery, that is, better outcomes for clients. Later Kadushin and Harkness (2014, p. 9) included that "the ultimate objective of social work supervision is to provide efficient, effective and appropriate social work services to clients" (see also Henderson, 2009). This sixth goal, to realize better outcomes for clients and communities, is also confirmed as supervision of practice in the review undertaken by O'Donoghue et al. (2018). It is also well captured in Morrison's (2005, as cited in Wilkins et al., 2017, p. 942) 4 × 4 × 4 model.

Adapting Kolb's (1984) experiential learning cycle and building on the traditional purposes and functions of supervision discussed above (Turner-Daly & Jack, 2017), Morrison's 4 × 4 × 4 model in the child welfare context configures the purposes and goals of supervision. The first four represent the four functions of management, mediation, development, and personal support. The second four are the four activities of experience, reflection, analysis, and action planning. Finally, the third four recognize the needs of four stakeholders, the child (client/people), the worker, the organization, and partners, though Wilkins et al. (p. 942) state that "notably, parents are not considered key stakeholders." It essentially captures the core purposes of education, administration, and support (see Wilkins et al., 2017). It was used to develop training programs for child welfare workers in the UK. Turner-Daly and Jack (2017) observe that Morrison's model facilitates reflective supervision, a non-stigmatizing way of addressing performance issues, pragmatically dealing with power relationships, and positive outcomes for all stakeholders (Turner-Daly & Jack, 2017, p. 37).

Although in the literature we have not come across the seventh purpose of supervision, we thought it was important to acknowledge it as an instrumental purpose of supervision. Following the post social work qualification, some social workers complete the mandatory supervised practice under a qualified supervisor to gain a license and register as a clinical practitioner. Thus, the purpose of this type of supervision, in addition to the above six, is to seek a license or meet the requirements to practice as mental health social worker. Similarly, all student social workers complete compulsory supervised field education. Again, in addition to the above goals, the purpose of workplace education supervision is to help students socialize into the profession and complete their professional qualifications.

Purpose- and goals-based models capture the essence of professional supervision in social work. However, it may not be feasible to achieve all these purposes and goals in all organizations and practice contexts unless a conscious effort and appropriate arrangements in terms of resource allocations are made to achieve them. Some of the common problems in attending to these goals and achieving them are that most qualified supervisors are overwhelmed with administrative tasks and do not find adequate time for professional supervision, though they are aware of what they need and want to do (Wilkins, 2016; Wilkins et al., 2017; Turner-Daly & Jack, 2017). As managerialism has been followed in many organizations, supervisors with only management expertise are not qualified to offer professional supervision. Consequently, educational and support goals are often neglected. In the social work private practice context, it is not clear how the administrative goal, the way it was originally conceived, can be applied. Perhaps, in the 1980s, private practice was not the mainstream activity. These purposes and goals of supervision were conceptualized mostly in the context of casework or clinical practice, but social work is much broader than casework practice. Perhaps, a revision is needed to expand the purpose of professional social work supervision to other contexts such as community development and policy practice.

Path-Based Models

As stated in the introduction, in response to prevailing socioeconomic and political conditions and their impact on organizations and the social work profession and practices, several supervision paths have been followed, what we call path-based models, to achieve the purpose and goals of supervision. We introduce some of these models below. Please note that as they deal with the same subject matter, part of the content may overlap with other models and a few models may be combined.

A Line-Management Supervision Model

As discussed in the previous chapter, a line-management supervision model is an ideal type of supervision if it works for the qualified supervisor and the supervisee. Under this model, the line-manager provides administrative, educational, professional impact, job management, and supportive (sometimes supervision related to accreditation/regulation/license) inputs to the supervisee to achieve the best outputs and outcomes for people and communities, the organization, and the supervisee and supervisor. They may use any of the relevant models for learning and support. Many organizations working in child protection, social protection, hospitals, and similar use this model with different degrees of success. Line-management supervision has many strengths and limitations, which are discussed in Chaps. 3 and 5, respectively.

A Non-line-Management Supervision Model

Although line-management supervision is ideal in many respects, in practice many supervisors cannot do justice to the purposes and goals of supervision, even if they want to, due to the administrative workload and disciplinary differences, personal attributes, and hegemonic power issues involving hierarchic organizational structures. Under the influence of managerialism, some staff members without social work qualifications have become line-managers who cannot provide professional supervision to social workers. As discussed earlier, some supervisees have reservations about having professional supervision from line-managers due to the dynamics of power and authority. The growth of private practice has also created a demand for non-line-management or external supervision. These and similar reasons have created a path for the non-line-management supervision model.

There are a few approaches to organizing non-line-management supervision. One approach may be for the supervisee and line-manager to agree and organize a non-line-management supervisor within the organization mutually. Another way is to agree and organize an *external* non-line-management supervisor in consultation. The third way is the line-manager allows the supervisee to make an external supervision arrangement according to their choice. In these three methods, the line-manager/organization takes responsibility for organizing and bearing the cost of supervision. In a fourth approach, the line-manager or the organization, without consulting the supervisee, appoints or contracts an external qualified person to undertake professional supervision in the organization. In a fifth scenario, the line-manager gives consent to organize the external supervision but does not organize it or bear the cost. The last approach to organizing non-line-management supervision is for supervisees to organize and pay for it, with or without the consent of the line-manager and organization. Please note that these are six methods or approaches to organizing the external supervisor. External supervisors can use other suitable models to offer professional supervision to social workers.

Like line-management supervision, the non-line-management supervision model has some strengths and limitations and ethical concerns, which are discussed in Chaps. 3 and 5.

A Mixed Model of Line and Non-line-Management Supervision

Under this model, the purposes and goals of supervision are split between line and non-line-managers. The former takes responsibility for administrative supervision, and the latter assumes responsibility for professional supervision. This approach may help build the strengths and reduce the limitations of both approaches. However, it is important to keep safe and constructive communication among all the parties involved. In view of administrative and management pressures, organizations may be better off delegating professional supervision to external entities to develop and support staff members. A few organizations in child welfare and protection and corrections follow this model. The second author was engaged in providing non-line-management supervision in different capacities. In addition to line-management supervision, some practitioners are self-managing non-line-management supervision within and outside the organization, which provides further insights into the phenomenon of supervision.

A Contract Model of Supervision

The purpose of the contract model of supervision is to make the professional supervision process clear, systematic, certain, productive, accountable, and assessable (Morrell, 2008). The contract is a mutually agreed flexible document between the supervisor and supervisee or between the supervisor and organization (Morrell, 2008), and it is mostly up to them in terms of its content, what to include and exclude, unless the organization has a prescribed format to complete the document. Fox (2008, p. 39) has suggested the following seven questions to guide the preparation of the contract so that the needs of the supervisee and the knowledge and skills of the supervisor may be matched.

> What do you expect from each other? What can we give to each other? Are our goals the same? Can we achieve them? How can we achieve them? What constraints exist? How will we know when we have achieved the goals?

Further, Fox (2008, p. 40) suggests that the supervision goals need to be clear; specific; explicit; feasible in terms of opportunity, capacity, and resources; seen in the light of constraints related to the tasks formulated; modifiable over time; measurable; and prioritized. Beddoe (2017) also recommends a supervision contract with additional clauses such as mechanisms for feedback, boundaries, and confidentiality (see also Cohen, 1987). Depending upon the organizational context, a two-stage contract may be involved: one with the organization and another with the supervisee or supervisees in the case of group supervision.

Before drawing up the contract, it may be helpful to develop a list of considerations when people are beginning to undertake supervision, for example, context; the purposes of the supervision; boundaries of supervision (what is in and what is out); external or line-supervision; whether a particular theoretical position is being adopted; power issues in supervision; is the supervisee's "being" part of the supervision?; will the contract be formal or informal?; the nature of confidentiality; who is funding the supervision (and who should be funding it?)?; record-keeping; agenda setting; is the supervision subject to a trial period?; what is the duration of the supervision?; and what legal accountabilities (if any) are applicable?

When contracts include details as outlined above, there is greater certainty about the time and commitment involved in supervision. It also adds to the seriousness of the process – it makes it more formal, inflexible, and limited by what is stated in the contract. To make it work, both parties need to respect it. It may be noted that the contract is not supervision; it is just a means to guide the supervision process.

A Model of Supervision in Private Practice

As some social workers enter private practice and are self-employed, the AASW (2016) states that most of them "may not have the same day to day access to colleagues, managers and others to discuss challenging issues, therefore, it is imperative that self-employed social workers engage in regular supervision" (AASW, 2016). Depending upon their need, many social workers in private practice approach qualified social work supervisors and organize professional supervision at a mutually agreed frequency and duration on a voluntary or fee-for-service basis. They follow their own agenda and contract as required and seek the necessary input and advice from supervisors. Supervisors may come from GOs and NGOs or private practice, though private practice supervisees may not be located in any formal organization. However, they must also follow the required administrative procedures relating to professional body requirements, case notes, and record-keeping, referrals, and Medicare provisions. It is important to consider legal issues and issues of professional negligence, including the need for professional negligence insurance. This is relatively new, and the self-organized supervision model needs to be researched and well developed.

Digital/Online Supervision Models

Digital or online supervision models are not strictly supervision models as they only suggest the mode of organizing the supervision between the supervisor and supervisee and group members. The digital or online method of organizing supervision was gradually gaining momentum, but its use accelerated during the COVID-19 pandemic. As discussed earlier, it includes phone; teleconference; emails; social media; online platforms such as Zoom, Google Meet, and Microsoft Teams; recorded supervision video analysis (see Antczak et al., 2019); and feedback. Sometimes, these can be asynchronous. However, this method of supervision is recognized by social work professional bodies.

These methods of meeting have environmental and resource benefits as they save travel costs and time. Supervision can be extended to rural and remote places, provided the necessary digital infrastructure is available and accessible. Recorded versions may be replayed for reflection. However, users need to be digitally literate and have the resources to access the technology. A short attention span may limit on-screen interactions (Sherbersky et al., 2021). While sessions can be recorded, confidentiality and ethical issues and further training need to be carefully considered (see Mishna et al., 2021).

Casework, Clinical Practice, and Therapy-Oriented Supervision Models

Generally, these models focus on the supervisor and supervisee employing knowledge and skills of casework, clinical practice, and therapy to offer and receive supervision and to analyze the supervisory inputs, processes, and outcomes. It may be noted that there is a difference between the social worker-client interactions and relationship and the supervisor-supervisee interactions and relationship, and one should not apply the same dynamics to the two different contexts. In the supervision context, supervisees acquiring knowledge and skills for professional practice is referred to as the developmental model or approach, and supervisees understanding and integrating their personal and professional selves is referred to as the growth model of supervision (Stoltenberg et al., 1994; Tsui, 2005; Baker et al., 2002; Shulman, 2020b). Some supervision models tend to use social work concepts and phrases such as interaction, process, intervention, relationship, thoughts and feelings, the use of authority, strengths-based, transference and countertransference, and parallels (Latting, 1986; Williams, 1988; Tosone, 1998; Hawkins & Shohet, 2000; Lewis, 2001; Munson, 2002; Ingram, 2013; Hair, 2014; Kadushin & Harkness, 2014; Shulman, 2020b). Perhaps, as supervisors and supervisees are familiar with these concepts and theories and use them in their practice, they may find them relevant in discussing administrative, educational, support, and practice issues and interactional processes between the supervisor and supervisee.

Tsui (2005) has discussed these as "practice theory as a guide to supervision model, and the case work model," and Shulman (2020a) calls them "models of social work supervision." Tsui justifies such an approach to supervision because similar knowledge and skills (empathy, listening, non-verbal communication, observing, and the use of authority) are useful in supervision. The meeting between the supervisor and supervisee has a similar format and helps them build on what they are familiar with and relate to it (Liddle & Saba, 1983; Storm & Heath, 1985; Olsen & Stern, 1990).

Undoubtedly, the knowledge and skills of casework clinical practice and therapy are useful in professional social work supervision. Still, it is important to guard against creating a situation where the supervisee feels like a client, and the supervisor-supervisee role boundaries are compromised, and supervisees begin sharing personal issues, expecting counseling from the supervisor. Often these boundaries are delicate, and it is critical to draw a line between them. Ingram's (2013) model of balancing emotions in supervision may be useful.

A Reflective Learning Model of Supervision

Based on years of supervising experience, the reflective learning model of supervision (RLMS) was developed and published in 2001 (Davys & Beddoe, 2021, p. 120). It essentially draws from Dewey's (1998) reflective learning, Schon's (1983) reflective practice, and Kolb's (1984) experiential learning (as cited in Davys & Beddoe, 2021). The RLMS model has six steps that are rooted in Kolb's experiential learning theory that begins with concrete experience and then moves to reflection, abstract conceptualization, and active experimentation. The four-stage RLMS has six steps as per the following sequence:

Step 1: Beginnings include preparation by demonstrating respect, regard and trust, warmth, and beginning according to the cultural context. The second part of the beginning is agenda setting for the session often led by the supervisee. The supervisor may also contribute to the agenda.

Step 2: Event. Here the supervisee as per the agenda focuses on the issue or experience. While looking at the details of the issue, the supervisee clarifies the goal to be achieved by discussing the identified issue or experience. The supervisee may share the context of the issue or experience and narrate the story.

Step 3: Exploration. In the second stage of the RLMS, the supervisor explores what kind of impact the event, experience, or issue had on the supervisee. The impact is explored in terms of feelings, beliefs, attitudes, behavior, assumptions, and intuitions. The supervisor helps to explore what could be different, what is known, and what needs to be known. Second, the implications are explored in terms of professional practice, standards, theory and values, relationship dynamics, authority, organizational context, and policies. This process can also help identify areas for improvement. Appropriately, the supervisor's knowledge and wisdom may be shared. The supervisor's primary role is to explore, listen, clarify, and assist the supervisee in thinking about solutions.

Step 4: Experimentation. In this stage, the supervisee reexamines solutions and tries to test them. It helps to consider the understanding gained in the supervision, strategies to implement, limitations, resources, and contingency plan. Recording and review of the work also should occur.

Step 5: Evaluation. This is the final stage of the model that helps the supervisee assess whether the goal relating to the issue, event, or experience was achieved and whether the supervision session objective was met. Consider also whether additional issues have come up during the session that need to be discussed in the next session.

Step 6: Conclusion. The supervision session should be concluded as per the agenda and follow-up action items identified for the next session. It also should help supervisors to reflect on their listening and support provided, things to do differently, and new learnings (Davys & Beddoe, 2021, pp. 101–122).

Overall, the authors of the model (Davys & Beddoe, 2021, p. 121) argue that "with its emphasis on supervisee-led agenda, supervisee-directed goals, and supervisee-focused learning, the model supports a supervision relationship based on mutuality, and accommodates multiple meanings and understandings." About Step 4, which is the third stage of the model, experimentation, I wondered how testing was possible in the supervision session, particularly when the authors state that, "The reflective learning model of supervision promotes a way of thinking rather than a blueprint for doing" (p. 101).

Peer Group Supervision Models

The practice of peer supervision has an important place in professional supervision in social work as it fills certain gaps in supervision that other models may not (Sandu & Unguru, 2013; Bailey et al., 2014; Golia & McGovern, 2015; Ingram, 2015; Egan et al., 2017, 2018; King et al., 2017). Golia and McGovern (2015, pp. 635–636) define peer supervision as:

any facilitated, planned or ad hoc interactions with colleagues of similar experience levels, particularly clinical social workers, psychologists and other mental health counsellors-in-training, in both dyadic and group contexts, for the purposes of clinical training, professional development, and mutual aid and affinity. (Billow & Mendelsohn, 1987; Godden, 2010; Hare & Frankena, 1972; Kadushin & Harkness, 2002; Schreiber & Frank, 1983; Tsui, 2005, as cited in Golia & McGovern, 2015)

This definition mainly applies to the clinical practice context but can also be extended to non-clinical practice contexts. In most cases, peer groups do not have a formally appointed supervisor or facilitator. Often practitioners within or outside the organization voluntarily and formally or informally come together according to a mutually decided frequency and time; share their experiences on an egalitarian basis, with due respect to confidentiality and ethical requirements; and learn from each other. With the organization's support, the peer group supervision process may be formalized, and different members of the group may voluntarily assume responsibilities on a rotating basis to set the agenda; identify and present cases, topics, or issues; raise questions; and facilitate discussion to enhance reflection, learning, thinking of solutions, and professional development. At the informal level, it may even occur during tea and lunch breaks.

When formal supervision is not available or accessible, peer group supervision is the only option for many practitioners. Egan et al. (2017, 2018) found that peer supervision was used by 17.9 percent of social workers who participated in their survey. Thus, they observed that it was the most useful alternative process. Even when organizational supervision was available, many practitioners self-managed further supervision within and outside the organization to seek advice, guidance, and support (see Bailey et al., 2014; King et al., 2017). The absence of power and hierarchy, egalitarian relationships, self-motivation, and discipline, better belongingness, and group affinity and learning in a non-threatening environment are some of the heartening features of peer group supervision. Too much informality, casualness, and an unstructured agenda may mean the learning and practice agenda is not met and the session may turn out to be a social event, which may have some value for stressed social workers. When professional supervision is unavailable or not affordable for some organizations and practitioners, there is some merit in strengthening peer group supervision with appropriate training.

Group Supervision Models

Group supervision is another path to achieving the objectives of professional supervision in social work. Sometimes it is used as a substitute for or supplement to individual supervision (Kadushin & Harkness, 2014; Newgent et al., 2004). It requires an experienced group facilitator (who may be a line-manager or a non-line-manager, internal or external to the organization) and group members. The group size can vary, but the recommended size is 8–12 members (Muskat, 2013). The group supervision process ranges from informal to formal structures with specific roles and responsibilities. For example, see the model of systemic supervision discussed below. Like dyadic supervision, it is recommended for the group to have clear objectives, tasks, presentation of cases or role-plays, pauses and reflective methods, participation and discussion, norms, and evaluation mechanisms in consultation with the organization.

Although the group should develop its own norms, Kadushin and Harkness (2014, pp. 287–288) recommend the following:

- To allow everyone to have his or her say without undue interruption
- To listen carefully and attentively to what others are saying
- To respond to what others have said
- To keep one's contribution and response reasonably relevant to the focus of what is being discussed
- To keep in mind that group membership requires a measure of deindividuation – some setting aside of one's own preferences in order to maintain the integrity of the group
- To share material and experiences that might contribute to more effective professional practice

The above points also call for observing the nature of the group in terms of being open or close-ended and group dynamics, decision-making, and the leadership or facilitator role. Group supervision is not a substitute for individual supervision. When many social workers have similar issues or when discussion of a particular issue or case would benefit all practitioners or when reasonably uniform and consistent standards are expected in processes and decisions, the group supervision model may be an appropriate avenue. Some of the merits of group supervision are that it is economical, it saves time, and it enhances group sharing and group learning experiences, group interaction, and emotional support and offers opportunities to confirm doubts and solutions. Its limitations are individualization is not possible, it may appear competitive for group members, group norms may create pressure on individual members, tangential discussion may occur, and members may not be able to discuss individual cases or raise ethical and confidentiality issues. If the group has young and inexperienced and experienced members, the facilitator needs to carefully balance the content and discussion (Munson, 2002; Tsui, 2005; Kadushin & Harkness, 2014; Magnussen, 2018).

A Model of Systemic Supervision

The model of systemic supervision developed by Dugmore et al. (2018, p. 400) in a local authority children's social work service statutory setting in the UK "aimed to promote team resilience, reflexivity, and relationship-based practice alongside a robust stance on risk" and to achieve "potentially transformative as opposed to procedural and transactional practice" (p. 403). It uses Patridge's (2010, as cited in Dugmore et al., 2018) four construction aspects of the supervision process that focus on organizational development, primary participative research, learning to transgress, and adult learning. It also tried to address the organization's vision of "a shared language, systemic principle, a shift from one-to-one to group supervision, shared ownership of cases, increased morale and mutual support" (p. 403). Although the program developed through this model covered staff members at all levels in the organization, most time and resources were allocated to senior practitioners who supervised social workers so that they could play an important role in implementing the model on a continuing basis. The model was conceptualized and implemented in five stages.

In the first stage, a day workshop was organized for all practitioners and managers to introduce the supervision project, propose changes, and help them reflect on positive and negative views about the changes. We assume that the workshop was facilitated by an external consultant or supervisor.

The second stage, organizational immersion, aimed to provide an orientation to the systemic theory and principles and develop a shared framework and language for practice. It covered ideas relating to "an appreciative stance, systemic questioning, reflecting processes, cultural genogram and the life cycle, domains of risk and uncertainty, reflexive use of self and relationship and power issues relating to gender, race and class" (pp. 404–405). It involved two whole-day workshops for 20 participants per cohort and a 2-day follow-up workshop after 3 months until all relevant staff members in the organization were covered.

The third stage was designed to facilitate organizational development and culture by offering a specific program to the senior management team to orient them to the systemic approach. In addition, external consultants or supervisors provided ongoing consultation and support to senior management and practitioners.

In the fourth stage, monthly structured supervision meetings involving an external consultant or supervisor, senior practitioner or supervisor within the organization, and social work practitioner were held for 12 months. The meetings followed the supervisor assigned structured roles in terms of a presenter presenting a case or an issue. The consultant raises questions from several perspectives (appreciative strengths, resilience) and social worker practitioners as observers engage in reflective conversation by observing the dialogue between the consultant and the presenter, but without the participation of the consultant and presenter. The presenter shares observations of reflective conversations as sought by the consultant, and finally all members of the supervision group step out of the allocated roles and the whole group reflects on the process. The entire process is facilitated by a systemic supervisor or mentor. To sustain this supervision model, consultants provide mentoring and support to supervisors of teams for a further 6 months.

In the fifth stage, to build capacity and create systemic champions, supervisors and practitioners are chosen to provide further training and clinical expertise internally. Dugmore et al. (2018, p. 411) state that as they focused more on Stage 4, this stage is still evolving and its "aim is to work with a self-identifying group of Champions from across the workforce in a consultative way to construct the next stages to support the new way of working."

Overall, the model of systemic supervision is about group supervision that focuses on the whole organization. It is resource intensive both in terms of time and training, and it is challenging to get all staff members unless it is mandatory. It does not have one-to-one supervision, though consultants can mentor supervisors. The mentoring approach to supervisors can confuse the supervision focus or overlap between the two. The proponents of the model claim its applicability in health and education settings.

Portfolio Model of Supervision

The portfolio supervision model was conceptualized by O'Donoghue (2015), who tracked the evolution of social work supervision since the 1970s and looked at the broad socioeconomic and political changes (discussed in Chap. 2) and their impact on organizations. O'Donoghue also looked at how some organizations have moved from traditional supervision to only managerial supervision, the growth of private practice, licensing and registration systems, the role of professional bodies, the emergence of external supervision and consultancy and tensions relating to its recognition, and prevailing multiple approaches to supervision. The portfolio model of supervision tries to capture the complex and blurred phenomena of professional supervision in social work, with O'Donoghue referring to it as "An evolving paradigm of social work supervision" (p. 143).

The portfolio model of supervision has four important elements, as discussed below. First, the employing organization is responsible for providing professional supervision to social workers. To meet this responsibility, it has the option to provide professional supervision through traditional line-management supervision, which is a mix of administrative and professional supervision. If it cannot provide professional supervision for reasons such as the impact of new managerialism, it can sanction and approve external supervision within or external to the organization. In this case, the line-manager provides administrative supervision, and the external supervisor, within or outside the organization, provides professional supervision.

Second, professional bodies and relevant statutory agencies are responsible for mandating professional supervision to social workers. This requirement is clearly reflected in social work codes of ethics, supervision standards (discussed in Chap. 1), and licensing and registration systems. For example, these standards clearly specify the minimum hours of supervision required for certain areas of practice, such as mental health social worker or clinical social worker.

The third aspect is the supervisor and supervisee. The supervisor can be a line-manager integrating both roles and only administrative supervision for accountability purposes. In the case of the latter, the organization has the responsibility to arrange and approve a non-line-management professional supervisor, who may be internal or external to the organization. The social worker as a supervisee, as part of the professional responsibility, needs to receive supervision from the line-manager, non-line-manager, or a mix of both. O'Donoghue (2015, pp. 142–143) states:

> In a portfolio model, however, there is a developing emphasis towards it being the individual social worker's professional responsibility and ethical obligation to participate in professional supervision, and the organization's duty to sanction and approve the types of supervision delivered, as well as to provide management supervision.

The fourth element of the model includes societal forces that have influenced traditional models of supervision and the portfolio model of supervision. That is how neoliberalism and new managerialism have impacted organizational structures in terms of anyone with management knowledge and skills becoming the manager, disregarding professional knowledge and skills. Consequently, professional bodies have reasserted the professional supervision role through ethics and standards, licensing and registration systems, and private practice.

O'Donoghue (2015, p. 142) describes the portfolio model as an emerging professional construction of supervision.

> Supervision may occur through a traditional internal hierarchical arrangement or an external professional arrangement which focuses on all of the areas and objectives, or a mix of internal and external arrangements, which focus on particular areas and objectives. The assigned or designated supervisors may be a line manager, colleague or external consultant/contractor or a combination of these where there is a mixed arrangement. (See also O'Donoghue, 2010, p. 309)

This model assumes that in all country contexts there are well-established professional bodies, which assert the need for professional supervision, but some may not, and in some countries, such bodies do not exist. It appears to be more driven by clinical practice. Further, it is a model for the arrangement of supervision rather than the content of supervision and learning.

An Appreciative Supervision Model

By adapting the models developed by Rich (1993) and Van Kessel and Haan (1993), Cojocaru (2010) developed the appreciative supervision model that focuses on "discovering, understanding and implying positive situations" (p. 77). Cojocaru also uses the concept of parallel process (modeling) in supervision, which stems from the phenomena of transfer and counter-transfer developed in psychoanalysis. The model has many elements of the strengths perspective and environmental approach that looks at structural factors rather than solely concentrating on the individual. Cojocaru (2010, pp. 77–78) describes the model in four stages.

The first is the knowledge stage, in which both supervisor and supervisee recollect past successes relating to similar cases and situations. In this stage, the suggested questions to delve into for supervisees are:

What do you appreciate most about your client? What do you appreciate most about the client's family? What successes has your client had since you've started working with him/her? How do you explain these successes? Who else contributed to this success?

Questions for supervisors are:

What do you appreciate most in yourself as a case manager for the client's situation? What were your successes in connection with your client's situation? What have you felt best about in the relationship with your client? What is the most important thing you have contributed to changing your client's situation? What is the most important thing the organization has contributed to changing your client's situation? Which of the work procedures have been most useful to you? Which of your qualities have you used in order to change your client's situation?

The second stage is called the vision stage, in which the supervisor and the supervisee negotiate to develop a joint vision by formulating challenging

phrases during different phases of work with clients. Cojocaru suggests the following phrases as examples.the client knows well his/her situation and resources, and copes with the situation; the client appreciates the support received form the organization; the supervised social worker acts in cooperation with the client in order to change the situation; the supervised social worker is receptive to all the client's successes and appreciates them;
the supervised social worker appreciates his/her client's successes;
the supervisor is open, available and interested in the work of the supervised social worker;
the supervisor recognizes the efforts, successes and qualities of the supervised social worker;
the client is the individual most interested in changing his/her own situation etc.

The third stage is a program stage in which clear plans are developed to realize the vision developed in the second stage. To develop the plan, the following questions are suggested:

What can we do to help the client know his/her resources in his/her situation and overcome it? What do we do to make this client appreciate the support he/she is getting from the organization? What practices should we promote to make the social worker act in cooperation with his client? What must be done so that the supervisor recognizes the efforts, successes and qualities of the supervised social worker? What can the social worker do so that the client knows the social worker appreciates him/her? etc.

In the fourth stage, the action stage, plans developed in the third stage are applied by regularly meeting the client/people as per the desired frequency. By remaining flexible, the social worker helps the client/people to identify their resources and successes. By appreciating their experiences, the social worker helps them to develop a vision and an action plan within their environment.

The author's experiment with this model in the child welfare context suggests that the appreciative supervision model helps achieve better outcomes than problem-centered supervision, though the experiment is limited to casework/clinical/therapy practice. It may be adapted in other supervision contexts. In our view, the first stage may be difficult for a new social worker without any positive experience. However, the questions posed are useful to prompt discussion in a positive way.

A Cultural Competency Supervision Model

Cross-cultural competencies are needed while practicing with clients and in professional supervision in social work. Although these skills are relevant across all models, it is discussed as a specific model due to its significance and relevance. Different values, beliefs, and practices, diverse people, prejudice, and discrimination based on ethnicity, race, class, gender, age, place of origin, religion/faith, mental/physical disability, and immigrant status are not uncommon. We have observed the tendency to easily ignore the cross-cultural relevance and the use of skills and the dynamics of a dominant culture imposing on other cultures, knowingly or unknowingly (Noble & Irwin, 2009; Suet Lin et al., 2010; Lusk et al., 2017). If supervisors, supervisees, organizations, and people and communities are from different cultures and have to work together, there is the potential for various complexities, cultural tensions, and challenges (see Yan, 2008).

Shulman (2020a, p. 13, b) suggests four strategies to create a safe cultural space for supervisors and supervisees. They should (1) "recognise the existence of the issue; (2) acknowledge the difficulty in discussing such sensitive areas; (3) explore what makes it hard, as well as what would make it easier and safer; and (4) be prepared to be honest about the ongoing process of learning about others and ourselves" (see also Shulman, 2016). Similarly, Hair and O'Donogue (2009, p. 83) suggest supervisors

> … take a social constructionist lens to practice self-examination about culture and identity, engage with supervisees in the ongoing process of dialogic co-constructions of culture, and use their self-aware privilege and position to help advocate for within-group members who wish to configure social work supervision according to their culturally shaped meanings.

Likewise, Lusk et al. (2017) support creating knowledge of different cultures and culturally competent supervisors. Tsui (2005) has tried to integrate this model in his comprehensive model of social work supervision discussed in the next section.

A Critical Conversations Model of Supervision

Critical conversations are understood as "conversations in which power dynamics in social context are illuminated and examined in the moment *and* subsequently reflected upon to foster development of critical consciousness and reflection" (Kang & O'Neill, 2018, p. 188). Originally designed for social work classrooms (see Kang & O'Neill, 2018), O'Neill and Fariña (2018) have expanded the application of the critical conversations model to professional supervision in social work. Although well trained in professional social work, some social workers may unconsciously or consciously carry on their implicit privileges, biases, microaggression, and hidden discriminatory attitudes and be unwilling or unprepared to confront them as these are deeply internalized and normalized in them (see O'Neill & Fariña, 2018). The model illuminates and examines structural factors and power dynamics to raise critical consciousness through reflection about hidden racial and social injustices, prejudices, power and privilege, inequities, and their impact, in order to initiate action and change in supervisors and supervisees to ultimately benefit the client/people.

Within the context of structural and power dynamics, O'Neil and Fariña (2018, p. 304) suggest to recognize, reflect, name, discuss, and act, and toward that end, consider the following four questions and six steps for constructing critical conversations for supervisors and supervisees.

How does the content and context affect interaction in the moment?
What power dynamics do you notice?
What assumptions might be taken for granted?
What larger societal and structural power dynamics are implicated and active in current interaction?

The first step involves recognizing interpersonal dynamics relating to power, privilege, and oppression and deciding to engage in a critical conversation. The supervisor may decide to invite a critical dialogue. The second step calls for constructing the critical conversation by "tuning in to one's own internal experience in the moment related to intersecting social identities and locations in relation to the supervisee/supervisor and client(s) or issues in focus" (p. 305). In the third step, the supervisor and the supervisee "build scaffold and develop understanding" by allocating dedicated time to critically discuss differences and sameness regarding race, gender, microaggression, bias, and class. They also look at interpersonal dynamics. "Dive into conversation" is the fourth step in which the supervisor models:

1. Actively noticing what is occurring in the immediate interactions
2. Critically reflecting on these observations
3. Naming the power dynamics involved in the interactions and connecting these to larger forces of power, privilege and oppression
4. Discussing the elements in the material being addressed and the process of the conversation and "linking them to the larger structural dynamics of power" (Kang & O'Neill, 2018, p. 190, as cited in O'Neill & Fariña, 2018, p. 306)

As this is likely to be a difficult conversation, in the fifth step, named "transition forward," the supervisor appreciates the supervisee's contribution to the conversation and acknowledges the learning and growth that has occurred through the critical conversation. It may also involve plans to disrupt the "perpetuation of structural forces of oppression" and continue further conversations depending upon the need. The last step involves reflecting after the session. Some suggested questions for that purpose are: How am I feeling? What do I hope the supervisee/supervisor learned? What went well and not so well? What might I do differently? How can I best debrief the conversation?

Overall, the model helps supervisors and supervisees have critical conversations about sameness, differences, intersectionality, power and privilege, and how these impact them, including the people they work with. From a critical social work perspective, it is an important model, and though it is based in clinical social work, it has the potential to be used in other practice contexts.

Feminist Supervision Models

Understanding the perspective of patriarchy, feminist scholars argue that the arrangement of traditional supervision in social work is problematic due the hierarchy, power, and authority vested in the supervisor and that arrangement leads to unequal and inegalitarian relationships, interactions, and processes for the supervisee (Nelson et al., 2006; Hess et al., 2008; Falender, 2009). They offer alternatives to address this issue so that supervisors and supervisees may collaborate on an egalitarian basis and openly discuss privilege and oppression rooted in gender race and class (Prouty, 2001; Szymanski, 2003, 2005; Nelson et al., 2006; Falender, 2009; Arczynski & Morrow, 2017). One of the conceptualizations of the feminist supervision model is by Szymanski (2003), who suggests the following four steps. The first step involves forming a collaborative, non-authoritarian, respectful relationship between the supervisor and supervisee to reduce the hierarchy and power gap and foster the supervisee's growth and autonomy with due regard to professional boundaries. The second step involves undertaking a power analysis by the supervisor and supervisee to recognize and explicitly address power dynamics and differentials to minimize the influence of power in relationships. The third step calls for examining how diversity and social context in terms of racism, sexism, privilege, and similar intersecting identities influence wellness and the supervisory relationship. In the fourth step, the supervisor shares models of empowerment, promotion of feminist issues, and social change by engaging in feminist advocacy and activism (Szymanski, 2003, 2005; Arczynski & Morrow, 2017; McKibben et al., 2019).

The feminist approach to supervision has many merits and dovetails well with social work values and principles. A study has shown that feminist-oriented egalitarian relationships will lead to reduced non-disclosure on the part of supervisee (McKibben et al., 2019) and thereby better quality discussion, learning, and growth. However, practicing the feminist supervision model is complex and can cause tension as it calls for greater awareness and action and non-threatening and non-discriminatory reinterpretation of hierarchy, power, and privilege on the part of the supervisor, not only in words but also in deeds (Arczynski & Morrow, 2017; McKibben et al., 2019; Falender, 2009).

The Integration of Purpose and Path-Based Models

The integration of supervision models is not new. For example, Shulman (2020a, p. 7) states that "Most models have addressed the importance of integrating the personal and professional selves." Gitterman (1972) preferred the integration of organization-oriented and worker-centered model. Likewise, many models may be used in combination if they serve the purpose of supervision. As an example, we have presented the conceptualization of two integrative models, which try to bring together purpose- and path-based models based on an extensive literature review.

A Comprehensive Model of Social Work Supervision

By reviewing the available literature on social work supervision, Tsui and Ho (1998) and Tsui (2005) have conceptualized this model that tries to show the relevance of relating the four parties/stakeholders to their cultural contexts to make the purpose, path, and process of supervision meaningful. The model may be described in terms of six dimensions: the four stakeholders, their culture, the purpose (functions and tasks) of supervision, streams of relationship, the supervisory process, and outcomes.

The Four Stakeholders

As presented in the comprehensive model of social work supervision (Tsui & Ho, 1998, p. 197; Tsui, 2005, p. 40), the four stakeholders in the supervision are the agency/organization, the supervisor, the supervisee, and the client/people. They are closely interrelated to implement policies and programs of the agency and achieve the outputs and outcomes for the agency and the client/people.

The Cultural Context

According to the authors, the cultural dimension is an important contribution of the model. For supervision, it is important to recognize the culture of the agency, culture of the supervisor, culture of supervisee, and culture of the client and sensitively act proactively and respectfully by considering the cultural aspects and differences of each of these stakeholders. In many respects, all four cultural aspects may merge in unison when there are no differences, or there is a consensus about policies and objectives, values, beliefs, and the process of resolving issues and meeting needs and achieving the outputs and outcomes. It is also possible that there may be significant differences in these four cultures that may cause a lot of stress, or there may be the domination of one culture over the other (see Yan, 2008; Shulman, 2020b). For example, the agency may be committed to the welfare of the child, but there may be significant differences among the supervisor, supervisee, and the family/parents in how to achieve this due to cultural differences. Thus, the cultural context needs to be heeded and sensitively addressed.

The Purpose/Goals of Supervision

The model suggests that from the agency perspective, there are three main functions and tasks of supervision. The supervision should be able to help achieve administrative/managerial accountability in terms of the job performance of the supervisee, provide educational support in terms of enhancing the knowledge and skills of the supervisee, and offer (moral) support to the supervisee to facilitate quality practice.

Streams of Relationships

In the cultural context, the supervision should help develop and maintain not only the professional relationship between the supervisor and supervisee but also the relationship between supervisor and the agency, supervisee and the agency, supervisee and the client, and the client and the agency. These professional relationships are interconnected to achieve the objectives, procedures, processes, and targets of the agency and the best outcomes for the client.

Supervisory Process

Within a cultural context, the supervisory process includes the supervisor and supervisee mutually developing and agreeing to the supervision process and accordingly implementing it. It may be the details of the contract, format and the stage, agenda setting for meetings to cover the tasks and functions, the frequency and mode of meetings, presenting issues and sharing resources, reviewing progress, and seeking feedback. In a way, the supervisory relationship and process are connected. Perhaps, the better the supervisory process, the better the relationship.

Supervisory Outcome

The whole purpose of supervision is to better prepare the supervisee to work with and achieve better outcomes for clients. In Tsui's (2005, p. 43) words, "Effective client outcomes are, of course, the ultimate objective of social work supervision. ... supervision eventually works for the clients, not only for the workers."

Overall, the comprehensive model attempts to integrate both the purpose and paths of supervision, though it remains a proposed model. It mainly has a clinical practice focus. Although, on a couple of occasions, professional bodies are mentioned in the explanation of the model, the model does not provide an explicit place for professional bodies, which have assumed a critical role in the private and clinical practice domain and almost replaced the agency in some situations. The purpose and tasks do not include seeing better outcomes for the client, though under client social work, intervention, and outcome are indicated. Depending upon the nature of private practice, the agency, worker, and client remain accountable; we do not think accountability can change or be reduced.

Evidence-Informed Model of Social Work Supervision

This is a heuristic model proposed by O'Donoghue et al. (2018) by reviewing 130 peer-reviewed and research-based articles on the supervision of practicing social workers published from 1958 to 2015. Their model suggests including five dimensions in social work supervision as follows:

First, the construction and understanding of supervision should be based on the prevailing context that considers social, cultural, organizational, and professional aspects. Both the supervisor and supervisee should clarify their respective roles and responsibilities, approve of the supervision, and focus on education, support, and practice issues. Relational and reflective processes are critical in supervision.

Second, the practitioner focused supervision should create a safe space for supervisees to share their practice experiences and concerns without any fear. Supervisors need to demonstrate warmth, caring, and emotional support on the one hand and provide professional development inputs on the other. Supervisors may role model according to professional ethical standards.

Third, supervision focuses on forming and developing a supervisory relationship or alliance with due respect to cultural aspects. This purposeful relationship should be characterized by trust, support, honesty, openness, and the ability to collaboratively navigate power relations.

Fourth, the supervision interaction process should have a clear plan or structure in terms of beginning, content input, and ending. It should engage supervisees in reflective and problem-solving processes with cultural sensitivities.

Fifth, the final dimension focuses on supervision leading to improving practice in terms of delivering quality services to people and communities. It may include an emphasis on clinical and evidence-based practice and using research evidence to achieve better outcomes. Five questions for consideration are as follows:

(a) What are the best outcomes for this client in this situation?
(b) What research and other knowledge have you considered in relation to the client and their situation?
(c) How does it inform your understanding of the situation?
(d) How might it inform and assist your interventions?
(e) How will you evaluate and monitor progress toward the client's outcomes? (O'Donoghue et al., 2018, p. 352)

The proponents of the model claim that their analysis may contribute to the curriculum for supervisor education and training and help supervisors apply supervision knowledge and skills in international and intercultural contexts. Although the analysis and construction of the model have some merit, it remains a proposed model based on peer-reviewed articles and is yet to be tested by supervisors. It also appears to overlap with other models presented here as it tries to integrate the purpose and path of supervision. It contradicts what we have found in practice: many practitioners found the organization an issue, not the practice. Though well researched, the conceptualization, on the one hand, appears too simplistic and obvious as the supervision has to be context specific, practitioner focused, and relationship-based with a focus on supporting the supervisee and solving problems to see better outcomes for people, and on the other, it confirms with evidence that these are the fundamentals of supervision in social work.

Conclusion and Summary

This chapter has summarized three categories of supervision models: purpose- and goal-based models, path-based models, and the integration of purpose- and path-based models. Although we have discussed seven different purposes, administrative, educational, and supportive functions remain the most prominent, and the other purposes can be linked to these three main functions of supervision. To achieve the purpose of supervision, we have discussed 16 different models, but some of them, such as the contract model or digital model, are just means or methods of organizing the supervision, not the actual supervision. The models that integrate the purpose and paths of supervision appear comprehensive, but they are based on a review of the literature. Irrespective of what model or models are used, they have to be contextually relevant and specific, practitioner focused, and relationship-based with a thrust on supporting the wellbeing and professional and personal development of the supervisee and solving problems to see better outcomes for people and communities.

It may be noted that there is some overlap between these models, and they can be used in different permutations and combinations. The list of models appears long, but it is neither inclusive nor exhaustive of all models. We have not specifically covered any models relating to the supervision of students during their field placements. We might have missed some other important supervision models. We also have not delved deep into adult learning, reflective practice, and other support aspects relating to anxiety, stress, and burnout, which are critical in practicing supervision. One important limitation of these models is that most of them have narrowly focused on the clinical practice context. Undoubtedly, it is a crucial area of practice, but social work is much broader than that as social workers engage in community organization and development, policy practice, welfare administration, research training, and education. Thus, the practice of supervision needs to be systematically extended to these areas. Overall, the review of models of supervision in professional social work shows that the subject of supervision has grown in significance and application. Despite such growth and the development of a range of supervision models, appropriate and timely supervision is not available to all social workers. This suggests that there is tremendous scope for further refining, researching, expanding, and using these models. In the next chapter, we will discuss some critical dilemmas in professional supervision.

References

AASW. (2016). *Self-employment/private practice*. Accessed on 28 June 2022 from https://www.aasw.asn.au/document/item/4573

Antczak, H. B., Mackrill, T., Steensbaek, S., & Ebsen, F. (2019). What works in video-based youth statutory caseworker supervision - caseworker and supervisor perspectives. *Social Work Education, 38*(8), 1025–1040.

Arczynski, A., & Morrow, S. L. (2017). The complexities of power in feminist multicultural psychotherapy supervision. *Journal of Counseling Psychology, 64,* 192–205. https://doi.org/10.1037/cou0000179

Baker, S. B., Exum, H. A., & Tyler, R. E. (2002). The developmental process of clinical supervisors in training: An investigation of the supervisor complexity model. *Counselor Education and Supervision, 42*(1), 15–30.

Bailey, R., Bell, K., Kalle, W., & Pawar, M. (2014). Restoring meaning to supervision through a peer consultation Group in Rural Australia. *Journal of Social Work Practice: Psychotherapeutic Approaches in Health, Welfare and the Community.* https://doi.org/10.1080/0265053 3.2014.896785

Beddoe, L. (2017). Harmful supervision: A commentary. *The Clinical Supervisor, 36*(1), 88–101. https://doi.org/10.1080/07325223.2017.1295894

Billow, R. M., & Mendelsohn, R. (1987). The peer supervisory group for psychoanalytic therapists. *Group, 11*(1), 35–46.

Bruce, E. J., & Austin, M. J. (2000). Social work supervision: Assessing the past and mapping the future. *The Clinical Supervisor, 19*(2), 85–107.

Cohen, B. (1987, May–June). The ethics of social work supervision revisited. *Social Work, 32*(3), 194–196.

Cojocaru, S. (2010). Appreciative supervision in social work. New opportunities for changing the social work practice. *Revista de cercetare [i interven]ie social, 29*(1), 72–91.

Davys, A., & Beddoe, L. (2021). *Best practice in professional supervision: A guide for the helping professions* (2nd ed.). Jessica Kingsley Publishers.

Dewey, J. (1998). Analysis of reflective thinking. How we think (1933). In L. A. Hickman & T. M. Alexandra (Eds.), *The essential dewey* (Ethics, logic, psychology) (Vol. 2). Indiana University Press.

Dugmore, P., Partridge, K., Sethi, I., & Krupa-Flasinska, M. (2018). Systemic supervision in statutory social work in the UK: Systemic rucksacks and bells that ring. *European Journal of Social Work, 21*(3), 400–414. https://doi.org/10.1080/13691457.2018.1446914

Egan, R., Maidment, J., & Connolly, M. (2017). Trust, power and safety in the social work supervisory relationship: Results from Australian research. *Journal of Social Work Practice, 31*(3), 307–321. https://doi.org/10.1080/02650533.2016.1261279

Egan, R., Maidment, J., & Connolly, M. (2018). Supporting quality supervision: Insights for organisational practice. *International Social Work, 61*(3), 353–367.

Erera, I. P., & Lazar, A. (1994). The administrative and educational functions in supervision: Indications of incompatibility. *The Clinical Supervisor, 12*(2), 39–56.

Falender, C. A. (2009). Relationship and accountability: Tensions in feminist supervision. *Women & Therapy, 33,* 22–41. https://doi.org/10.1080/02703140903404697

Fox, R. (1983). Contracting in supervision: A goal oriented process. *The Clinical Supervisor, 1*(1), 37–49. https://doi.org/10.1300/J001v01n01_05

Fox, R. (2008). Contracting in supervision: A goal oriented process. *The Clinical Supervisor, 1*(1), 37–49. https://doi.org/10.1300/J001v01n01_05. (online publication).

Gitterman, A. (1972). Comparison of educational models and their influences on supervision. In F. W. Kaslow et al. (Eds.), *Issues in human services* (pp. 18–38). Jossey-Bass.

Godden, J. (2010). *Paper on supervision in social work, with particular reference to supervision practice in multi-disciplinary teams.* Birmingham.

Golia, G. M., & McGovern, A. R. (2015). If you save me, I'll save you: The power of peer supervision in clinical training and professional development. *British Journal of Social Work, 45*(2), 634–650. https://doi.org/10.1093/bjsw/bct138

Hair, H. (2014). Power relations in supervision: Preferred practices according to social workers. *Families in Society: The Journal of Contemporary Social Services, 95*(2), 107–114. https://doi.org/10.1606/1044-3894.2014.95.14

Hair, H. J., & O'Donoghue, K. (2009). Culturally relevant, socially just social work supervision: Becoming visible through a social constructionist lens. *Journal of Ethnic & Cultural Diversity in Social Work, 18*(1–2), 70–88. https://doi.org/10.1080/15313200902874979

Hare, R. T., & Frankena, S. T. (1972). Peer group supervision. *American Journal of Orthopsychiatry, 42*(3), 527–529.

Harris, T. (2020). *Successful supervision and leadership: Ensuing high-performance outcomes using the PASE model*. Routledge.

Harris, T., & Slattery, M. (2021). The PASE supervision model. In K. O'Donoghue & L. Engelbrecht (Eds.), *The Routledge international handbook of social work supervision*. Taylor & Francis Group.

Hawkins, P., & Shohet, R. (2000). *Supervision in helping professions*. Open University Press.

Henderson, P. (2009). *The new handbook of administrative supervision in counselling*. Routledge.

Hess, S. A., Knox, S., Schultz, J. M., Hill, C. E., Sloan, L., Brandt, S., et al. (2008). Predoctoral interns' nondisclosure in supervision. *Psychotherapy Research, 18*, 400–411. https://doi.org/10.1080/10503300701697505

Ingram, R. (2013). Emotions, social work practice, and supervision: An uneasy alliance? *Journal of Social Work Practice, 27*(1), 5–19.

Ingram, R. (2015). Exploring emotions within formal and informal forums: Messages from social work practitioners. *The British Journal of Social Work, 45*(3), 896–913. https://doi.org/10.1093/bjsw/bct166

Kadushin, A. (1985). *Supervision in social work* (2nd ed.). Columbia University Press.

Kadushin, A., & Harkness, D. (2002). *Supervision in social work* (4th ed.). Columbia University Press.

Kadushin, A., & Harkness, D. (2014). *Supervision in social work* (5th ed.). Columbia University Press.

Kang, H. K., & O'Neill, P. (2018). Teaching note: Constructing critical conversations: Building the scaffold for reflection and action. *Journal of Social Work Education, 54*(1), 187–193. https://doi.org/10.1080/10437797.2017.1341857

King, S., Carson, E., & Papatraianou, L. H. (2017). Self-managed supervision. *Australian Social Work, 70*(1), 4–16.

Kolb, D. A. (1984). *Experiential learning: Experiences as the source of learning and development*. Prentice Hall.

Latting, J. E. (1986). Adaptive supervision: A theoretical model for social workers. *Administration in Social Work, 10*(1), 15–23.

Lewis, W. (2001). Transference in analysis and supervision. In S. Gill (Ed.), *The supervisory alliance: Facilitating the psychotherapist's learning experience* (pp. 75–80). Aronson.

Liddle, H., & Saba, G. (1983). On context replication: The isomorphic relationship of training and therapy. *The Journal of Strategic and Systematic Therapies, 2*, 3–11.

Lowy, L. (1983). Social work supervision: From models toward theory. *Journal of Education for Social Work, 19*(2), 55–62.

Lusk, M., Terrazas, S., & Salcido, R. (2017). Critical cultural competence in social work supervision. *Human Service Organizations: Management, Leadership & Governance, 41*(5), 464–476. https://doi.org/10.1080/23303131.2017.1313801

Magnussen, J. (2018). Supervision in Denmark – An empirical account of experiences and practices. *European Journal of Social Work, 21*(3), 359–373. https://doi.org/10.1080/13691457.2018.1451827

McKibben, W. B., Cook, R. M., & Fickling, M. J. (2019). Feminist supervision and supervisee nondisclosure: The mediating role of the supervisory relationship. *The Clinical Supervisor, 38*(1), 38–57. https://doi.org/10.1080/07325223.2018.1509756

Mishna, F., Sanders, J. E., Sewell, K. M., & Milne, E. (2021). Teaching note-preparing social workers for the digital future of social work practice. *Journal of Social Work Education, 57*(sup1), 19–26.

Morrell, M. (2008). Supervision contracts revisited: Towards a negotiated agreement. *Aotearoa New Zealand Social Work Review, 1*, 22–31.

Morrison, T. (2005). *Staff supervision in social care: Making a real difference to staff and service users* (3rd ed.). Pavilion.

Munson, C. (2002). *Handbook of clinical social work supervision* (3rd ed.). Taylor & Francis Press.

Muskat, B. (2013). The use of IASWG standards for social work practice with groups in supervision of group work practitioners. *Social Work With Groups, 36*(2–3), 208–221. https://doi.org/1 0.1080/01609513.2012.753837

Nelson, M. L., Gizara, S., Hope, A. C., Phelps, R., Steward, R., & Weitzman, L. (2006). A feminist multicultural perspective on supervision. *Journal of Multicultural Counseling and Development, 34*, 105–115. https://doi.org/10.1002/j.2161-1912.2006.tb00031.x

Newgent, R. A., Davis, H., & Farley, R. C. (2004). Perceptions of individual, triadic, and group models of supervision: A pilot study. *The Clinical Supervisor, 23*(2), 65–79. https://doi.org/10.1300/J001v23n02_05

Noble, C., & Irwin, J. (2009). Social work supervision: An exploration of the current challenges in a rapidly changing social. *Economic and Political Environment. Journal of Social Work, 9*(3), 345–358. https://doi.org/10.1177/1468017309334848

O'Donoghue, K. (2010). *Towards the construction of social work supervision in aotearoa New Zealand: A study of the perspectives of social work practitioners and supervisors.* PhD thesis, Massey University, Palmerston North. http://hdl.handle.net/10179/1535; Accessed on 13 March 2022 from https://mro.massey.ac.nz/bitstream/handle/10179/1535/02_whole.pdf?sequence=4&isAllowed=y

O'Donoghue, K. (2015). Issues and challenges facing social work supervision in the twenty-first century. *China Journal of Social Work, 8*(2), 136–149. https://doi.org/10.1080/1752509 8.2015.1039172

O'Donoghue, K., Yuh, J., & P. W., & Tsui, M. S. (2018). Constructing an evidence-informed social work supervision model. *European Journal of Social Work, 21*(3), 348–358. https://doi.org/1 0.1080/13691457.2017.1341387

Olsen, D. C., & Stern, S. B. (1990). Issues in the development of a family supervision model. *The Clinical Supervisor, 8*(2), 49–65.

O'Neill, P., & Fariña, M. (2018). Constructing critical conversations in social work supervision: Creating change. *Clinical Social Work Journal, 46*(4), 298–309. https://doi.org/10.1007/ s10615-018-0681-6

Patridge, K. (2010). Systemic supervision in agency contexts: An evolving conversation with clinical psychologists in a mental health trust. In C. Burck & G. Daniel (Eds.), *Mirrors and reflections: Processes in systemic supervision* (pp. 309–335). Karnac.

Prouty, A. (2001). Experiencing feminist family therapy supervision. *Journal of Feminist Family Therapy, 12*, 171–203. https://doi.org/10.1300/J086v12n04_01

Rich, P. (1993). The form, function and content of clinical supervision: An integrated model. *The Clinical Supervisor, 11*, 137–178.

Sandu, A., & Unguru, E. (2013). Supervision of social work practice in North-Eastern Romanian rural areas. *Procedia – Social and Behavioral Sciences, 82*, 386–391. https://doi.org/10.1016/j. sbspro.2013.06.280

Schon, D. (1983). *The reflective practitioner.* Temple Smith.

Schreiber, P., & Frank, E. (1983). The use of a peer supervision group by social work clinicians. *The Clinical Supervisor, 1*(1), 29–36.

Sewell, K. M. (2018). Social work supervision of staff: A primer and scoping review (2013–2017). *Clinical Social Work Journal, 46*(4), 252–265. https://doi.org/10.1007/s10615-018-0679-0

Sherbersky, H., Ziminski, J., & Pote, H. (2021). The journey towards systemic competence: Thoughts on training, supervision and competence evaluation. *Journal of Family Therapy, 43*(2), 351–371.

Shulman, L. (1993). *Interactional supervision.* NASW Press.

Shulman, L. (2016). Addressing internalized biases and stereotypes of the group leader: A life-long professional task. *Social Work with Groups, 40*(1), 10–16.

Shulman, L. (2020a). *Supervision*. Oxford University Press. https://doi.org/10.1093/acrefore/9780199975839.013.385

Shulman, L. (2020b). *Interactional supervision* (4th ed.). NASW Press.

Stoltenberg, C. D., McNeill, B. W., & Crethar, H. C. (1994). Changes in supervision as counselors and therapists gain experience: A review. *Professional Psychology—Research and Practice, 25*(4), 416–449.

Storm, C. L., & Heath, A. W. (1985). Models of supervision: Using therapy theory as a guide. *The Clinical Supervisor, 3*(1), 87–96.

Suet Lin, H., Shui Lai, N., & Kwok Kin, F. (2010). Functions of social work supervision in Shenzhen: Insights from the cross-border supervision model. *International Social Work, 53*(3), 366–378. https://doi.org/10.1177/0020872809359864

Szymanski, D. M. (2003). The feminist supervision scale: A relational/theoretical approach. *Psychology of Women Quarterly, 27*, 221–232. https://doi.org/10.1111/1471-6402.00102

Szymanski, D. M. (2005). Feminist identity and theories as correlates of feminist supervision practices. *The Counseling Psychologist, 33*, 729–747. https://doi.org/10.1177/0011000005278408

Tosone, C. (1998). Countertransference and clinical social work supervision: Contributions and considerations. *Clinical Supervisor, 16*(2), 17–32.

Turner-Daly, B., & Jack, G. (2017). Rhetoric vs. reality in social work supervision: The experiences of a group of child care social workers in England. *Child & Family Social Work, 22*(1), 36–46.

Tsui, M. S. (2005). *Social work supervision: Contexts and concepts*. SAGE Publications.

Tsui, M. S., & Ho, W. S. (1998). In search of a comprehensive model of social work supervision. *The Clinical Supervisor, 16*(2), 181–205.

Van Kessel, L., & Haan, D. (1993). *The intended way of learning in supervision seen as a model* (Vol. 11, p. 29). Haworth Press.

White, M. B., & Russell, C. S. (1995). The essential elements of supervisory systems: A modified delphi study. *Journal of Marital and Family Therapy, 21*(1), 33–53.

Wilkins, D. (2016). How is supervision recorded in child and family social work? An analysis of 244 written records of formal supervision. *Child & Family Social Work, 2*(3), 1130–1140.

Wilkins, D., Forrester, D., & Grant, L. (2017). What happens in child and family social work supervision? *Child and Family Social Work, 22*, 942–951.

Williams, A. J. (1988). Action methods in supervision. *The Clinical Supervisor, 6*(2), 13–27.

Yan, M. C. (2008). Exploring cultural tensions in cross-cultural social work practice. *Social Work, 53*(4), 317–328.

Chapter 5
Critical Dilemmas and Challenges in Professional Supervision

Introduction

This chapter will discuss some critical dilemmas identified by supervisors in our interviews. As discussed in previous chapters, within the context of socioeconomic, political, and technological challenges (Chap. 2), social work is practiced in various organizational contexts and practice settings (Chap. 3). Although the purposes and goals of supervision – mainly administration/management, education, and support – and different paths to achieve those goals are well intended and sound (discussed in Chap. 4), social workers' experiences of achieving them appear problematic. Some supervisors and supervisees can do justice to all the purposes and goals, whereas others can attend to only one or two of the purposes and goals and some to none. For example, as discussed earlier, administrative/managerial supervision often occurs at the expense of education and support. It is also possible that education and support are sometimes provided at the expense of performance accountability. Are there any issues with how the roles of supervisors are structured in terms of combining surveillance and support? Are there any problems with structures dominated by the market and managerialism and resource allocation? What is the role of professional bodies? These questions are complex, as may be the responses to them. Is developing the unison between social work values and principles and power, hierarchy, and structure inherently problematic? Answers to some of these questions may be found in how supervisors and supervisees are responding to the context of professional supervision in social work.

After completing the planned questions in our survey, we asked supervisors to share additional thoughts on supervision. The analysis of their responses identified six dilemmas they have experienced in supervision. These are line-management supervision versus non-line-management (external) supervision, supervision in private practice, face-to-face supervision versus digital supervision, supervising social workers and non-social workers and new and experienced social workers, the role of the professional bodies in supervision, and the issue of developing qualities/character in supervisees. Their responses are presented below in their own words with brief comments. Finally, the chapter concludes by contemplating ways and means of resolving these and similar dilemmas.

Line-Management Supervision Versus Non-line-Management (External) Supervision

The issue of line-management supervision versus non-line-management (external) supervision is introduced and discussed in Chap. 3, including their respective strengths and limitations, and as models of supervision in Chap. 4. This issue is posed in the professional supervision literature (e.g., Egan et al., 2016; Davys & Beddoe, 2021), but without any planned solutions by the organization, though proper training is suggested (see Egan et al., 2016). This appears to be a critical dilemma for both supervisors and supervisees, perhaps due to the use of power and authority and hierarchy, and the lack of time and resources on the part of the supervisor and the fear of an abuse of power and a lack of trust on the part of the supervisee (Copeland et al., 2011). The role of balancing surveillance of performance and supporting professional development is a delicate one, but both are equally important. However, the narration of supervisors suggests that balance is often not achieved, and the dilemma continues.

While line managers seem to be more preoccupied with performance and accountability, supervisees seem to feel not so confident and safe. It may be that supervisees could engage and reflect better with a non-line manager without any hierarchy and power.

… but as a manager there's always a sense of accountability in the whole, in the setting. Whereas here for example, where we're doing peer supervision with each other, there's none of that and it seems to be a much better vehicle for reflection. People much more readily engage in the supervision in the reflective practice. And there's no one-up-down, thing.

No, and in some ways supervisees are not confident that they're safe enough to deal with it or to raise it in the organization. I think that's a big part of why they seek out external supervision.

A supervisor argued that even in non-line-management supervision, there is accountability one cannot relinquish.

There is. I think even in the professional supervision there is, because you are in the role of supervisor. So, ultimately we both know that. And the supervisee has come to supervision seeking support from someone who's got the technical knowledge or the practice wisdom or the clinical knowledge or whatever. So I don't think you can relinquish that role just because you're in partnership with, and that sounds a bit of a contradiction I suppose, but I think it is like that. It's a paradox isn't it really? [Laughing]

A supervisor in the public sector stated that hierarchy and ranking cannot be denied in lline-management supervision, but line managers can consciously come down to the level of workers. However, there is a dilemma that supervisors should be able to address.

> Because I think both happens at the same time. I think, yeah, I think you can have partnership but one party's always more, in a hierarchical sense, that's just, that's it. That's the way it is. You can't ignore it. It just is. So, what do you do with that? Well, I think, what I do with it is I try and maintain that partnership relationship but ultimately, I will, I don't want to use the word pull rank, I'm trying to think of something better than that, because I'm so institutionalized in the public sector hierarchy it's hard not to talk about rank. But in a supervisory relationship, I will take charge of the conversation or of the matter that we're talking about and particularly because if the person's grappling and they're struggling and they've come to you, well there's only so much of that that, it becomes circular for them. So, you've got to break, you're the one there who breaks that. So you have to kind of do, shift position. So now I'm in charge of this conversation and let's move it into this space. So, I think both is true.

Another supervisor stated that as line-management is often linked to performance management, there is an element of fear and stress. In peer supervision, through contractual arrangements, confidentiality can be maintained, with exceptions, to facilitate better discussion in supervision. As a non-line-manager, the supervisor said, they would not share supervision notes with the line-manager, and if there was a breakdown in the relationship with a supervisee, steps were planned before the start of the supervision. As performance management and workload are not on the agenda, they can reflect better.

> There is because of that issue around performance management so fear of being performance managed if you say something in supervision that you're not, and you're not performing for whatever reason. [Pause] And look the way I get around that is through the supervision agreement. I just say, I mean for every contract I have, private or within … Health, every contract I say "Supervision is confidential unless you're at risk of harming yourself or someone else". So, I just use that same rule. Or unless you know of criminal activity about to happen, that's always a bit of a curly one in the drug area I've got to tell you, but anyway. So, I name that and then I talk about, I've only ever had one line-manager ever ask me for the supervision notes and I refused. And what my contract with the supervisees is always I will, upon request from your line-manager I can give them, and this is the other, when they've got a different line-manager as opposed to me, but I can give them their, just the date, time and themes, full stop. Even if you're being performance managed, I won't give them the supervision notes. And they would have to subpoena me within the organization for them. I don't give them. If they've, but so that the safety net for someone who's being line-managed by me is the, if an issue arises within our supervisory relationship, what are we going to do. And so, then it becomes that "Well you look for another supervisor. We talk about it. I will help you find an alternative supervisor, or you find yourself a different supervisor, but we both know that that's happening because there's been a breakdown". So that's all nutted out before we start. It's pretty rare though that you've got to use that. I mean like I said once when a line-manager asked me. And what I find is rather than people say "I don't like how supervision's going", the biggest risk is they just drop off.
>
> Well, I think there's, you know, there's that tension between the performance management stuff and (pause) professional supervision. So I feel like I'm fortunate that I don't have to worry about the performance management and the workload stuff. The time that I spend supervising people, it is really reflective, and it is really time away from all the other stuff.

They can, you know, really have a reflective conversation with me. So, I like that model where the line-manager isn't part of the supervision, because they're having to think – they're having to worry about other things. So, this is really luxurious. I feel like it's really luxurious that we have that capacity to offer reflective supervision.

A supervisor stated that even in non-line-management supervision, it is important to probe difficult issues and it calls for courage. If the supervisee dislikes the supervisor, they are less likely to disclose issues, and in the case of external supervision, they might stop coming. Thus, it is important to model, in supervision, how to explore difficult issues.

They stop coming. So, they get, people don't like talking about an issue. Especially if they like you. If they like you, probably if they don't like you they don't like talking about it either, but if you've done something or said something in supervision that they don't like and they don't want to raise it, well then they're more likely just to disappear, and that's a shame. I think have the courage, have the courage to step up and talk about it. And I try and model that in supervision. Have the courage to go places that are difficult. But it doesn't work for everybody.

The following statement suggests that if there is a need, it is important to refer to external supervision. As a line manager in the public sector, the supervisor encourages external supervision if the supervisee is interested, but at their own cost.

Yeah, yeah. And so, I think, you know, I really – if that was the case here – I mean, in some of our teams the manager is a social worker, or was practicing as a social worker before they were manager, and they may have – may be very comfortable with supervision. And some people – I would support them seeking external supervision if they felt the need, rather than – you know, I think that's a valid reason to seek external supervision, because their manager is – yeah, it's a different relationship.

I think it depends on how comfortable the individual worker is. I would always encourage someone to get external supervision if they were interested, and I suppose they get money back on tax, a little bit, don't they?

A supervisor confirms that external professional supervision is quite different from line-management supervision.

Yes, I think so. But the space that I've created and I wonder whether it's true of other social workers in private practice that, to do that, it, I call it external professional supervision. And workers tell me constantly over and over that it is a different process than when they go to their manager or their go to their supervisor at work. Totally different.

Another supervisor stated that as line-management supervision can be caught up in organizational intricacies and issues, external supervision can offer insights without being constrained by unnecessary organizational intricacies and regimented structure. This helps to focus better on practice issues. Even the venue for the supervision can be informal.

I mean from my perspective as a supervisee, I've only ever received supervision from my direct line-manager within the department, but as someone who has supervised a person outside of the department, the biggest difference for me was around the organization and not having, I didn't need to understand the work environment within in which she worked to understand the hierarchy of where she fitted within the organization. All I need to know was, as a social work professional, what job she was doing and in order to be able to then understand what my role as her supervisor was going to be, around that administrative component of her supervision. I think it actually was a good thing to not know about her organization, I mean I know of her organization where she used to work but to not know all the intricacies around policy and government and, because it was a state government organization. To not know all the intricacies of that I actually think benefited me as her supervisor because we didn't get caught up in that. We didn't get caught up in the legislative requirements that came within the work that she was doing. We talked about the practice. We talked about what she doing as a social work practitioner and that was the bulk of our conversations every time we met and that was a monthly meet with her.

I think sometimes within the department we get very caught up on the structural side of our organization around the legislation and yes, that hierarchy of who is our immediate supervisor. You know, I do think sometimes it's quite debilitating, quite you know constrictive at times, but I don't have a lot of experience as I said earlier. I only supervised her externally for about four and a half months, so it wasn't a very long period of time but it was a most enjoyable period of supervision. It was often done at the coffee shop. It wasn't done in an interview room. It was a different environment. We never met at her workplace. It was always done outside of work hours and as much as that could be an impost at times, it was also, again, we set some very clear parameters around, you know it would be for an hour and a half. It wouldn't go for three hours and all of a sudden it's ten o'clock at night. It was very structured, but yeah, look I think sometimes the regimented nature of the supervision within the department can be quite restrictive, yeah, and that's not to say it's a bad thing. It's a different supervision. It does create a different element to the nature of supervision. Yeah, that's all.

One supervisor stated that often line-management supervision is preoccupied with unrealistic key performance indicators, whereas external supervision provides new perspectives and facilitates lateral thinking. Sometimes, line-management focuses on serving the organization, not the clients. So, the supervisor argues; external supervision fills this gap if supervisees can afford to pay for it.

I haven't got, I don't think I've had anyone in my team who's paid for external supervision, but I have at times in my career, and I've actually found it very helpful to get a different perspective and to get different theoretical inputs, which is outside of the restrictions and expectations of such a bureaucracy, which is very KPI, or Key-Performance-Indicator driven, because here we are judged on "did we go out on a visit in a certain time, did we substantiate or unsubstantiate the protective concerns, how long have we had a case open?" And to be honest, the key performance indicators around those timelines are completely unrealistic, because people sometimes are difficult to engage to begin with, and their issues are quite complex, so it takes a while to get an understanding of what's happening for them, so I think if I did have any of my workers having external supervision, it would enhance and enrich their work, because it would give them an opportunity to think laterally, and get different perspectives, and not be so confined to the standards that are imposed upon us, which are nothing to do with the clients and doing good work. The KPIs are about serving the organization, not serving the clients. So, I think it would enhance any worker who's prepared to pay for external supervision.

A supervisor stated that in line-management it is often difficult to find dedicated time for supervision. Often supervision was done informally, though the supervisor wished for more formal time. Organizations are risk averse and performance driven, whereas in external supervision dedicated time is allocated for supervision.

Sometimes, what happens is that we don't have enough staffing in the teams with the current model, to be able to provide the supervision that we would like, so sitting down and having that hour a fortnight for formal supervision is sometimes difficult to achieve, and a lot of it's done sort of on the run, on the hop. Most of the workers would bring their lunch in, or they'd go over the road to get their lunch and sometimes we find that we're having a conversation about cases over lunchtime, so you get a lot of informal stuff going on, which I think is a little bit, look, it's fine, it's just that I would like a bit more, sometimes I'd like a bit more formal time. I don't get any supervision myself, and I feel a bit like, now and again, like, if I'm worried about something I will go to my area manager and say, this is what's going on, and especially if there's a situation of organizational risk, I would let my manager know. Yeah, a lot of the work is really nurturing workers to be able to cope with the demands, and being aware, like looking at them when I come in, in the morning, and how are you going, and we have a morning catch-up every morning, what kind of day have you got planned, we've got this work coming in, I need this done and that done, and sometimes on the 40-degree days, I don't want to send anyone out, so I try to keep them in, so it's not ridiculous for them, running around the countryside. I've got one girl who's pregnant at the moment, so she does work at the desk. It's just trying to be mindful of getting the work moving through the unit, but also not flogging the workers to death [sigh], which some people do, they're so KPI-driven, they just, yeah.

You know that, you know I think too you know that, so there are also like social workers who are supervisors who, you know their issue is still about, quantity and they – you know they've got a lot of pressure and that's the way they'll go.

A supervisor stated that although there may be issues with line-management supervision that is what is practically available in some organizations and external supervision may not be practical.

I reckon there is an issue because clearly if someone is your boss, the likelihood of you being totally open with them about – I'm more surprised how people are about you know what their issues and insecurities and stuff are. And you know who you directly line manage. But I think the reality is any setting I've worked in the opportunity to have an independent person supervise you has never existed. It's not even remotely on the table. And so even though it would be the ideal it's so far, just in the settings I've worked in, it's not even a possibility, not in your wildest dreams.

Perhaps, in such situations, supervisees try to adjust to the supervisor and continue their practice.

Difference Between Line-Management and Non-line-Management Professional Supervision

In the field, professional supervision is offered by line-managers and external supervisors, whether in private, public, or non-government organizations. In some respects, as discussed in Chap. 3, both approaches appear to be problematic, though necessary in some organizations. The above narrations of supervisors show the dilemma experienced between line-management and non-line-management professional supervision. Drawing from those narrations, Table 5.1 summarizes the main differences between the two approaches, and those points are self-explanatory. In some organizations, the influence of managerialism has impacted the ability of line-managers to offer professional supervision, even if they want to, and in some organizations, there is no option except line-management supervision. However, critical

Table 5.1 Difference between line-management and non-line-management professional supervision

Line-management supervision	Non-line-management supervision
Use of hierarchy/rank/power/authority	No use of hierarchy/rank
Ensure administrative accountability	Ensure professional accountability
Constrained to engage and reflect	Better engagement and reflection
Performance management fear/stress	Contractual, confidentiality agreements
Personal disliking leads to non-disclosure of issues	Personal disliking leads to dropping out
Caught up in organizational intricacies	Not constrained by unnecessary organizational issues, focus on practice issues
Preoccupation with key performance indicators	Provides new perspectives and facilitates lateral thinking
Often difficult to find dedicated time	Dedicated time is allocated
Only option in some organizations	Not practical for some organizations

Source: Authors

issues experienced by supervisors and supervisees cannot be denied. This situation poses a serious threat to the professional development of supervisors and supervisees and in turn the quality of services provided to people and communities.

Although both approaches have their strengths and weaknesses, those who can achieve most purposes of supervision through line-management supervision are not prepared to give up on the ideal of line supervision. Contrary to the available evidence (Egan et al., 2016; Davys & Beddoe, 2021), in view of their experience of achieving administration, education, job management, professional impact, support, and service delivery functions through line-management supervision, they argue that there is no a priori reason why these cannot be achieved through line supervision. Indeed, there are reasons to think that exemplary line supervision has the capacity to achieve each of the purposes and goals of supervision far more adequately than any other form of supervision because of the intimate organizational knowledge and currency of the line supervisor. For example, in the areas of support, the line supervisor is also able to bring the organizational resources such as access to leave or employee assistance programs operated by the organization into the service of the supervisee. To achieve these outcomes, the supervisor and supervisee must reconceptualize power and authority, which is a core and delicate issue. Power and authority have become pejorative in their connotations; that need not be the case. Legitimate power and authority can be conceived in ways that are capacitating rather than coercive or threatening. Trust and relationship building and the recognition of legitimate knowledge and authority and structural acknowledgment are central to these considerations. By structural acknowledgment, we mean a clear separation of performance management issues and professional supervision. While there will be some overlap in practice, having separate and distinct processes minimizes any threatening capacity or aspect of the relationship. Authority and power in themselves are neutral concepts. They can be used for either good or ill – for illegitimate coercion or capacity building.

Hofmann et al. (2017, p. 1) write

The execution of coercive and legitimate power by an authority assures cooperation and prohibits free-riding. While coercive power can be comprised of severe punishment and strict monitoring, legitimate power covers expert, and informative procedures. The perception of these powers wielded by authorities stimulates specific cognitions: trust, relational climates, and motives. … coercive power increases an antagonistic climate and enforced compliance, whereas legitimate power increases reason-based trust, a service climate, and voluntary cooperation. Unexpectedly, legitimate power is additionally having a negative effect on an antagonistic climate and a positive effect on enforced compliance; these findings lead to a modification of theoretical assumptions. However, solely reason-based trust, but not climate perceptions and motives, mediates the relationship between power and intended cooperation.

Key considerations in line supervision must include an acknowledgment of legitimate power and authority and its positive aspects as well as limitations, considerations of the organizational climate, trust and relationship building, the prioritization of the supervisory relationship, and a strong commitment by both parties to developing the relationship.

In Table 5.1, the items listed under line-management supervision, except for the use of hierarchy/rank/power/authority, which requires a reconceptualization as indicated above, are operational constraints that can effectively be addressed by exemplary line-management supervision and organizational support for supervision, but these have largely evaporated under managerialism.

As an example, the co-author, A. W. (Bill) Anscombe, was a line supervisor in the probation parole service for an officer who was exemplary with all clients but was experiencing difficulties with a particular client and a particular class of clients. It was impacting his health severely. As we examined the reasons in supervision for his inability to work effectively with child sex offenders, it became clear that he had four young children and could not separate his emotions and act neutrally with clients who had offended against children. As the line supervisor and responsible for work/case allocation, it was within my legitimate authority and power to not allocate this officer clients who had offended against children for a substantial time while also having an understanding that he was prepared to take other clients with high needs and for whom he had a particular expertise. The legitimate use of power and authority in this way provided a temporary respite for the officer but also added to the unit's key performance indicators.

Supervision in Private Practice

On the one hand, managerialism has significantly compromised the ability of line-managers to offer professional supervision by increasing the demand for work outputs and reducing resources to do so. In some cases, line-managers have simply replaced professional managers. On the other, managerialism and privatization have also led to an increase in private practice. In the Australian context, social work private practice gradually increased, particularly after mental health support needs were recognized in Medicare. Qualified social work private practitioners also provide professional supervision to social workers. A supervisor who has been in private practice has faced some challenges over peoples' perceptions of private practice relating to competency and the charging of fees for services provided. Despite these challenges, the supervisor opines that supervision in private practice provides a crucial space for supervisees.

> … since I became an independent practicing social worker, one of the things that I had to deal with at the time was that I was being a failed social worker. Because I was working outside of organizations.
>
> That I was earning this pittance, and I had never earnt a very, it looks like you earn a lot per hour, but I can only do 3 or 4 contact hours per day, but I was doing 8 or 9 hours' work. So, I earn much less than I would earn in a social work job. And it irritates me that, I think that's become a lesser theme now anyway now the, as a matter of fact I think the AASW have done the opposite and they're over supporting independent social workers but anyway.
>
> But that you weren't quite living up to the ethics of social work practice because you were charging money for your work. I don't think that's the case now.
>
> And then over the years, I think that perception of private practitioners has changed. Although I would wonder whether that story is still there, I don't know. Probably not. But it doesn't really matter now. One of the things that I think that is of interest to me in this conversation is that I think that the space, people have said to me over and over, workers have said to me over and over that this space is really important to them. To come get away from organizations with another social worker and reflect on them and their practice in the supervision context.

If the market and managerialism have led to an increase in social work private practice, the questions posed by this supervisor are relevant. The ethics of the market and professional bodies are not necessarily the same, though professional bodies have provided clear guidelines for self-employed social workers and private practice. Organizational neglect of professional supervision and private practice eligibility requirements has created a demand for professional supervision. Many qualified private practitioners offer professional supervision on a fee-for-services basis to social work supervisees. Many social workers self-manage professional supervision, often paying the fee themselves and claim that such an arrangement is legitimate professional supervision (see King et al., 2017). Does this pose any ethical dilemmas? Is there any potential for cooption between the supervisor and supervisee as mandatory supervision hours must be completed to meet the minimum requirement for private practice? How does one deal with public perceptions about private practice, though such perceptions may have changed now? At the same time, it is important to acknowledge that it is meeting the demand for professional supervision, which many organizations are failing.

Face-to-Face Supervision Versus Digital Supervision

As stated earlier, supervision is not limited to a face-to-face mode. Many supervisors offer supervision through digital modes including phone, email, and online meeting platforms such as Skype, Zoom, and Google Meet. These platforms are recognized by professional bodies, and the same ethical standards apply as in face-to-face settings. Non-face-to-face supervision is perhaps becoming a norm following the COVID-19 pandemic.

> … as more and more supervision is not being done face-to-face, you know we've moving very much into a virtual environment of supervision being done off-site, supervision being done over web cams and the like or even just over the phone.

Digital supervision certainly provides access to supervisors and practitioners working in rural and remote areas. The following narrations by supervisors highlight a few advantages and disadvantages of digital supervision methods and the importance of observing non-verbal communication. Supervision by using only the phone and/or by using video mute functions blocks opportunities to observe non-verbal cues, which poses challenges to understanding the person and building a relationship. The following narration shows how one supervisor struggled with supervision only on the phone until a face-to-face meeting changed the whole perspective.

> And I think that was one of, just going back to the person, the one person who I've struggled with, the phone supervision, and phone supervision's very limited if you've never met the person. And I was very keen to do Skype and she just didn't want to. And it wasn't until I met her, I met her in-person and my whole world view of her changed. So, I went from talking to my supervisor about this one person that I just can't relate to, that I'm struggling with, that I wondered did I like her. Isn't that awful? I wondered did I like her. And when I met her, I really liked her. She was so different to on the phone. It was just bizarre. She was human. And I couldn't capture that at all with her on the telephone. I just couldn't capture it. But when I had all the non-verbal and we were standing talking to each other, the whole world changed. Interestingly though, we've never had phone supervision again after we met. So, she had something, there was something for her around that that …

A supervisor stated how she prefers using Skype, which allows her to observe the face of the supervisee, rather than just a phone call. She said it could take a long time to establish a rapport and understand the relevant issues when you had not met a supervisee.

> I prefer it (Skype), I should qualify that, I prefer it to phone if I've never met the person. But there are some exceptions to that, but on the whole if you've met the person face-to-face and then you have phone supervision it's fine because you've got a visual and you know something about them. But when you're just, you're meeting them for the very first time cold, going into supervision with zero knowledge of them, it takes much longer to build rapport in the relationship and it takes much longer, depending on the supervisor though, it takes much longer to get to the bottom of what the issues are or to build the trust so that they're willing to talk with you really openly about what's going on.

The same supervisor stated that as an exception, she had supervision on the phone with one supervisee and it was as good as a face-to-face session. It is inconsistent with what is stated above, but it also confirms that the phone can serve the purpose in some circumstances.

> And the exception I've got to that is a fabulous social worker but she's much older so I'm wondering if there's an age, the experience of social work across years makes a difference or just if it's her specifically, but we've only had phone supervision and she's, it's as good as face-to-face. So, it's as meaningful and genuine and connected as it is face-to-face.

Although initially hesitant to use Skype, one supervisor said she had started liking this mode of supervision. She acknowledged it was important to observe non-verbal cues and Skype helped to observe the face of the supervisee.

> I think they can. Because you've got all the, I mean you've got all the visual cues, you've got all the, you're looking at each other. [Pause] You can pick up little nuances that you can't on the phone. Yeah, the non-verbals are critical sometimes. I think for supervision and counseling I think you need the non-verbal communication. So that's why I'd put Skype and face-to-face on a par really.

> I think that you can see people's reactions and you see their faces and they can see yours. So, you have to actually monitor the conversation and in terms of just monitor the exchanges and allow for the delay. But people can see your face. And yeah, so I actually was really hesitant but as I said, I was actually approached for supervision by someone in Queensland and that's how I started. And she was really enthusiastic and said oh, you know, we could do Skype. And that actually worked really well. And I actually quite like it.

Although all these are important avenues of supervision, one supervisor preferred to balance online and face-to-face supervision. In this supervisor's opinion, online modes should not completely replace the face-to-face supervision method. Balancing modes of supervision is a critical issue. It is important to observe non-verbal communication in online supervision meetings, but face-to-face meetings are critical to know the person and build a relationship. The supervisor says:

> One of the things that I do is I try and visit with my staff twice a year, those staff who are in the country more than in metro Melbourne, but I do that because whilst I'll do supervision with them through other mediums, virtually, I like to still do the face-to-face if I can and even if that means a couple of nights away traveling or whatever, I do like to spend that time with them one-on-one. I often spend a lot more. It's not just the hour, hour and a half. It might be half a day and I find that it's quite rewarding for them, but when we do the virtual supervision either over the phone or through the webcams, because I've got the visual on the webcam and we've only introduced that in the last six months or so, where it's worked well, for me having sight of people gives me a much better impression of what they're getting out of supervision. So, if I think of where we're heading to in the future with virtual supervision, I think again, to have a relationship with your staff or a supervisee supervisor relationship, I think there's got to be an element of actually knowing your people and sometimes you get to know them by the gestures or the face, the way they might look at you if you ask a question or you know the hand gestures or the body language can tell you a lot about someone. When you only have that over the phone you don't get to see that. It can often make a big difference in the relationship with someone which is why, for me, having the webcam has been so critical to have it working well, but again I like to get out and actually meet with people as well and do face-to-face supervision. So, I'm happy to have a balance. I don't mind that and my staff in the country, they know, and even some of my staff in metro Melbourne, I don't get to see them face-to-face all the time so sometimes their supervision, as much as I might be in the northern suburbs and they're in the east, I might not physically be able to get to them but we'd use the phone and we use the webcams and that's great but I still try and do at least twice a year where I am face-to-face with them as well. That's me. That's the way that I try and supervise yeah, it's not to say everyone would do it that way or should do it that way, yeah.

The comments made by supervisors generally support the literature about geographically dispersed teams, where it is clear that optimal outcomes occur where people have occasions to meet face-to-face and the interim supervision can be done using telephonic systems. The co-author, A. W. (Bill) Anscombe's experience in supervising staff at a distance in a line supervision manner (eight direct supervisees on monthly line supervision with weekly administrative "catch-ups" spread over an area of 588,000 square kilometers) was that supervision could be undertaken by telephonic means provided it was supplemented by at least four face-to-face meetings per year. Thus, administrative matters were dealt with weekly by telephone. Professional supervision was undertaken with the supervisee monthly on the basis of a minimum of one session being face-to-face (with the supervisor traveling) and two being telephonic in the intervening months. At supervision sessions, there was no discussion about administrative matters and KPIs; rather, these sessions were dedicated to education, professional impact and development, personal and professional support, and career development (job management).

Supervisors' experiences of offering supervision through digital and face-to-face modes and the varying views about such options pose critical challenges and dilemmas in a technologically dominated world where social work is human-centered. Many organizations have established call or smart centers, and digital technology is used significantly to work with people and deliver services. Social workers must get acquainted with such technology, and thus using the same in supervision prepares supervisees to practice in a smart environment. Certainly, some social work practice can be done through digital means. However, these supervisors' narratives affirm the significance of human, face-to-face interactions not only in supervision but also in social work practice. When supervisors and supervisees use only digital technology without meeting people in-person and when organizations "over use" digital technology, there may be practice, moral, ethical, and human implications, notwithstanding the advantages.

Difference Between Social Workers and Non-social Workers and New and Experienced Supervisees

Although differences between these groups of supervisees are not in themselves an issue, these important variables need to be properly understood for the supervision to proceed smoothly. A supervisor stated that there is a clear difference between social work and non-social work supervisees, at least initially, and it needs to be properly understood as some supervisees may need some additional help in terms of better preparation and to ensure the focus in not solely on problems.

> The major difference is the social workers are ready for supervision, more than other people are. After some time, there's not a great deal of difference, I think, but the major things that, social workers are more prepared for it. They make better use of it, especially in the early stages.
> So, they (non-social workers) need to be educated about that. Encouraged.

> Social workers readily are looking at people in a social context more than other people do. Others are more inclined to be focused on the problem and on the individual. Social workers, while they might be focused on the problem, they can more readily start looking at others, the broader picture.

... So, they don't come really prepared, I guess the non-social workers, they're a bit more broad.

With the social workers, they're a little bit more, I feel they're a bit more self-aware. Like being aware of, taking on things to heart. I think they can also pinpoint models that they use. I actually tried to challenge my supervisees about, 'what model do you think you are using?' They're, from an educative point of view, saying, 'what were you thinking, what were you wanting to, what was your intervention?' I think social workers are better at that. Better at pinpointing whether they were using a problem-solving approach, or crisis intervention, or narrative, or (pause). They can label it more, I think.

Similarly, it is important to heed differences between new and experienced supervisees to facilitate better supervision.

I think there is a difference. And I think that's why it's really helpful to have a look at that model where someone is in their profession or where they are in terms of their experience or expertise.

The message from this is that supervisors cannot treat all supervisees the same way. They need to individualize each supervisee as there are significant differences between a professionally trained social worker and a worker without any training and between an experienced and inexperienced social worker.

The Role of Professional Bodies

Although the Australian Association of Social Workers, the peak professional social work body in Australia, focuses to some extent on professional supervision and has developed supervision standards, a code of ethics, and a dedicated website listing available supervisors, a supervisor was of the view that the social work professional body does not push for supervision like similar professional bodies do, but social work has much to offer, including its value base.

I'm surprised that there's not the same push with social workers as there is with psychologists to receive social work specific supervision. You know how with psychologists, if you were a clinical social worker where I worked we would supervise psychologists as well in terms of their supervisions. But there's very much a push from the APS that they must be, you know ...

And it's sort of interesting that – I'm not aware that social work has done the same and yet our values are so profession specific and unique. And you know – because I've supervised a lot of people who weren't social workers and you know they have all said, just the whole value thing of social work, brings something unique to the table for them.

Drawing from this comment, it is important to raise a question. What more can professional bodies proactively do? They are well aware of the significance of professional supervision, but many organizations are not providing adequate space for it, and when they do, supervision is often done perfunctorily by merely focusing on administrative aspects. The supervisor's remark that "there's not the same push with social workers as there is with psychologists to receive social work specific supervision" poses a challenge to social work professional bodies. There is also a dilemma for professional bodies; how much do they push and not push?

The Issue of Teaching/Developing Qualities/Character

A supervisor raised a fundamental question – how can you teach qualities/character? Is it feasible? Further comment questioned the relevance of developing qualities/character in supervisees as there may be some social workers without the required qualities. It is an important and relevant issue as people do come with certain qualities, but the challenge for the profession and education, supervision, and training is – how can they purposefully enhance the required qualities? We were trying to find out whether and how supervisors do it. A supervisor said:

> That's exactly right. And I think it's really hard to unpack, because is it an intrinsic quality or is it something that can be taught? You know, is it something that people have a sense of from their environment and who they are and their world view, and if it isn't entirely there, can it be taught? Because that's a really interesting concept for me. I've had a few students in our department that there's been a real tension and struggle with that. You know, you can give them tasks, you can do all that and they're quite capable, highly intelligent, very academic, their theoretical framework's great, writing's great, everything. Put them in a room with a client and it's just like seeing a different person, and it's like, "How can we teach that? How do we teach that?" You're right, and then what are we teaching people? Are we saying to people, "Well, what you're presenting to us is not right for a social worker?" Or is it that we need to present a picture of who social workers are and these qualities that help us grow in our profession and help us be effective. And then how can we teach that to people? And I'm teaching at uni now, and I can tell you even at uni, there's a few people I looked around the room and thought, "Oh no, please don't be social workers." [Laughter]

As a line-manager and supervisor, the co-author had a reason to address the question of dressing modesty with a staff member attending court. The staff member's immodest dress was raised in supervision and not well received by the supervisee. No change occurred until the person appeared in court to present a well-researched and comprehensive court report. The report was given no credibility, and the staff member concerned, in the next supervision session, believed that the report on the client had been dismissed clearly identifying the immodest clothing for court as the reason for the report's dismissal. The staff member considered that the client had been done a disservice because of that staff member's insistence on continuing with inappropriate clothing for the court appearance. In this supervision session, the cultural contexts (courts), which have their own particular subcultural norms (for better or worse) and our own response to those subcultural norms, were considered and discussed. The quality and character of the staff member relating to dressing modesty was developed.

Developing the qualities/character of social workers through supervision remains to be explored. If they cannot be taught through teaching in classrooms, can these be developed in the practice settings with the help of supervisors like the above example and what roles should supervisors play in this? The supervisor's remarks above suggest that there is a need to address this issue for better practice.

Conclusion and Summary

This chapter poses some of the dilemmas and challenges shared by supervisors. Despite some clear advantages, there seems to be convincing evidence (Egan et al., 2016; Davys & Beddoe, 2021) that line-management supervision as currently practiced is often unable to provide education and support to supervisees, though some line-managers are aware of what is expected of them (Wilkins et al., 2017). There are issues of hierarchy, power, trust, managerialism, being overburdened with administrative work and a lack of adequate time for supervision, and possible non-disclosure on the part of supervisees. On the other hand, most supervisees feel much more comfortable and supported and enjoy a better professional relationship with their supervisor under non-line-management supervision. Given the experiences of some supervisors and supervisees, it is important to revisit the question raised in the introduction. Is there any issue with how the roles of supervisors are structured in terms of combining surveillance and support, or is there any problem with structures dominated by the market and managerialism and resource allocation? The market and managerialism have placed a significant strain on supervisors and supervisees. Does it make sense to clearly re-delineate and clarify role expectations on the part of supervisors and supervisees? Since some prefer line-management supervision, and some seek non-line-management supervision elsewhere, it may be practical to leave administrative supervision to line-managers and educational and support-related supervision to other entities such as peer, private, or organized external supervision and allocate the resources necessary for this, rather than making employees pay for it. This needs to be arranged with the organization's support so that supervisees have the experiences of blended supervision for better practice and personal wellbeing. As some have already followed this path (e.g., some organizations contract supervision work, or employ consultants, social workers self-manage supervision), it appears worth standardizing it, and consequently, line-managers may feel less burdened. At the same time, the merits of line-management supervision, where they work, need to be pursued.

The market, managerialism, and government policies and programs have not only changed organizational contexts and service delivery mechanisms but have also given rise to the privatization of social work practice. As narrated by the supervisors, social work private practice raises perception and ethical issues, particularly when supervision is self-managed and self-paid. Perhaps, better regulation, monitoring, and auditing systems are needed to ensure that standards are maintained and likely compromises are prevented. What is the role of professional bodies in this? Can they do more than what they have been doing?

Supervisors have also pointed out the dilemmas and differences between supervising social workers and non-social workers and experienced and inexperienced social workers. As each supervisee's needs are different, the supervision needs to be tailored accordingly. In a digitally dominated world, there is a choice between face-to-face supervision and digital supervision. Following initial resistance, some social workers have significantly engaged in online social work practice. The supervisors' suggestions for developing the balance between the two have some merit, given that social work is a human-centered profession. Finally, the question of how to develop and build the qualities and character of social workers is an important challenge. Almost all social workers join the profession with certain desirable qualities and character traits. However, can they be taught, can they learn, and can they be shown are the critical questions and challenges both supervisors and supervisees need to consider. The next chapter will discuss the processes followed and contents discussed in supervision.

References

Copeland, P., Dean, R. G., & Wladkowski, S. P. (2011). The power dynamics of supervision: Ethical dilemmas. *Smith College Studies in Social Work, 81*(1), 26–40. https://doi.org/10.108 0/00377317.2011.543041

Davys, A., & Beddoe, L. (2021). *Best practice in professional supervision: A guide for the helping professions* (2nd ed.). Jessica Kingsley Publishers.

Egan, R., Maidment, J., & Connolly, M. (2016). Who is watching whom? Surveillance in Australian social work supervision. *The British Journal of Social Work, 46*(6), 1617–1635. https://doi.org/10.1093/bjsw/bcv098

Hofmann, E., Hartl, B., Gangl, K., Hartner-Tiefenthaler, M., & Kirchler, E. (2017). Authorities' coercive and legitimate power: The impact on cognitions underlying cooperation. *Frontiers in Psychology, 8*(January), 1–15. https://doi.org/10.3389/fpsyg.2017.00005

King, S., Carson, E., & Papatraianou, L. H. (2017). Self-managed supervision. *Australian Social Work, 70*(1), 4–16.

Wilkins, D., Forrester, D., & Grant, L. (2017). What happens in child and family social work supervision? *Child and Family Social Work, 22*, 942–951.

Chapter 6
The Process, Essentials, and Content of Professional Supervision

Introduction

This chapter will discuss the processes followed by supervisors, the essentials of supervision, and the broad content of professional supervision. As discussed in Chap. 4, Davys and Beddoe's (2021) reflective model of supervision includes the beginning process under step one, which refers to preparation for the supervision in terms of building a relationship and an agenda. It would be interesting and useful to explore the general process followed by supervisors in this study. The first section of the chapter discusses supervisors' narratives of the general process they follow. Their supervision process ranged from open, flexible, and informal to structured and contractual. The second section looks at what should be the essentials of supervision as narrated by supervisors. Our analysis categorized 17 broad essentials, such as focusing on practice/work, reflection, relationship, trust and empathy and strengths, and balancing work and private issues. The third section shares the main themes or content of supervision identified by supervisors. These included 10 broad content areas, such as self-care and safety, personal issues, difficulties with the organization, practice issues, and developing competencies. Overall, this chapter gives a broad overview of what supervisors do in professional supervision in terms of the general process followed, the essentials that should be used, and the contents covered.

The General Process of Supervision Sessions

The general process of supervision refers to how supervisors approach supervision sessions and what they do. A semi-structured interview question we posed to them was: "What is the general process of your supervision sessions?" The analysis of supervisors' responses suggested that there was no specific prescribed process to follow in the supervision sessions. It differed from one supervisor to another. However, a few processes may be identified based on the analysis of their responses. Their supervision sessions appear to involve a combination of informal and formal processes. Each process has its strengths, depending upon the context. We have categorized these processes into open, flexible, informal and conversational, clarification of expectations, recapitulating, structured/contracted, supervisee-led, two-way, task/issue/goal-focused, and reflective. These processes are discussed further.

Supervisee-Focused Open, Flexible, Informal, and Conversational

In their model, under step 1, Davys and Beddoe (2021) state that it is important to demonstrate respect, regard, trust, and warmth according to the cultural context. Similarly, in Cojocaru's (2010) appreciative supervision model, the first step involves recollecting past successful cases. A few supervisors in this study seem to follow an open, flexible, and conversational process that involves beginning where things are for the supervisees. They said supervision is a space for supervisees.

> So, when we first meet, I say, I talk to them about what is useful for them in our working together and we have a look at what has worked well for them in the past. ... I always say, "It's your time, it's your space. So, let's talk about it."
> And let's look at a format that's flexible in what's going to work for you in how we're going to set up this space for you.
> So, I don't have a general process that I impose on it, it's more a conversation where, but I say to people what would they like to be looking at today. And then we would begin to work around that. That's it, not very involved ...
> I'm open to flexibility around being able to have them say, I've got to deal with this crisis first.
> I generally start with how are they, how are they feeling, get an overview of what's happening.
> It tends to be that there's a bit of an informal catch-up at the beginning.
> ... but it can be a pretty informal, I'm finding that. Or it can be more structured.

These responses suggest that the supervision process is generally open, flexible, informal, and conversational to make space for supervisees. In their narration, the choices of phrases such as "what is useful for them," "it is your time," "what is going to work for you," "I do not...impose," "have them say," and "how are they" suggest that the purpose of remaining open and flexible is to focus on supervisees and provide space for them. Supervisee-focused supervision is not only the desired process but also a good supervisor virtue.

Clarification of Expectations

Often issues arise or are not addressed due to a lack or misunderstanding of and or mismatch of expectations between the supervisor and the supervisee. Thus, to some supervisors, it was important to clarify mutual expectations as part of the supervision process.

> At the point that they engage, I meet with them, which isn't a supervision session; it's a meeting for us to work out whether it's going to work and I'm keen to hear from them about what they expect from supervision, what they want it to be, what their past experience of supervision has been and I talk with them about what I expect in supervision. And so, it's kind of an opportunity for us each to work out whether it's going to be a good fit or not.

Clarifying whether the supervisor-supervisee relationship will be a "good fit," what each party expects from each other, and sharing their past experiences appears to be a good process to follow before accepting the respective roles.

Recapitulating

Recapitulating or briefly recounting what happened in the previous supervision session is an important aspect of the supervision process. It not only has an element of reflection but also provides link and continuity/follow-up to the supervision from one session to another. A supervisor stated that their supervision process begins with recapitulating points discussed in the previous session.

> We do a little bit of the reviewing of what we last discussed … but we talk about, is there anything they wanted to discuss.
> … I also keep notes myself to remind myself of what we've talked about.
> So, I will draw in things from previous sessions …

Note keeping both by supervisors and supervisees is an important practice and aids the recapitulating process. Succinctly recapitulating is a skill that needs to be developed by practicing so that supervision time is used efficiently.

Structured/Contracted

As discussed in Chap. 4, supervision may be organized by developing a mutually agreeable contract between the supervisor and supervisee and sometimes the employing agency. The contractual process makes clear for both parties their roles, tasks, and expectations. It makes the supervision process systematic, certain, accountable, and assessable. So, the following responses suggest that some supervisors prefer to follow a structured approach for their supervision sessions. Sometimes, it may involve a written format.

And so that just simply is "Let's develop the contract around how we're going to work together, what do you want to get out of it"?

... in the initial phase we develop some rules and an agreement about the type of super-, or the responsibilities of the supervisee and the supervisor. And expectations are established.

... it focuses on, what are the challenges, what have been the highlights of the month, things that have gone well, things that have not gone well.

I make it a point of them keeping a running journal of topics to talk about, or clients to discuss,

... that the person would come prepared with issues that need to be addressed that they would have a significant impact into the development of the agenda for the supervision session, that they would take notes, that we would agree on the tasks to be followed up and that we would agree on any other issues that actually need to be taken up.

The supervisor's choice of the phrase, "what do you want to get out of it?" suggests that even in the contractual process the focus is on the supervisee. Further, the contract includes mutually agreed rules, roles, and responsibilities with an emphasis on the supervisee coming prepared, developing the agenda, and keeping a running journal.

Supervisee-Led

In many of the above processes, particularly, under the supervisee-focused open, flexible, informal, and conversational process, it was clear that most supervisors preferred the supervision to be led by supervisees. That approach is reinforced in the following narrations. A few supervisors stated that they leave the supervision sessions to be led mainly by supervisees.

But it's always, I suppose, my biggest thing about my own supervision, it's always got to be driven by the supervisee. I want them to come, not to sit down and start thinking when they get here. They've thought about what the issues for them are before they come.

And as I was saying, I like the space to be there for them. Not for me.

But I always let them be in charge of what they wish to talk about.

I expect the supervisee to bring what it is that they want to talk about so I'm clear with them that it's their responsibility to fill the hour.

... but I largely leave it up to the supervisee to determine how they want to use the time.

... but basically, my view is the supervisee brings the agenda. It's their responsibility and their business and my job is to respond to that as best I can.

So, I allow them to dictate the scenario a little bit as well along the way, but I don't like supervision to be just about me delivering to them.

The above narrations reinforce that the supervisee is the center of the supervision process and the supervision is not about the supervisor. External supervisors may be more comfortable with this approach. However, where the professional supervision is done within a line management structure, employing organizations use professional supervision as a way of ensuring accountability to clients and that client and worker safety is being met. Thus, line-managers who are also professional supervisors may want to have a say in the agenda, lead parts of the supervision, and raise issues that the supervisee may not want to hear. In such contexts, the following two-way process may be more effective.

Two-Way Process

Although supervision is supervisee-led and focused, one supervisor viewed supervision as a two-way process, suggesting that supervisees and supervisors must play their roles.

It's a bit of a two-way conversation with the staff.

I think it's important that for our professional development that we understand that there's a commitment to undertaking supervision and that that commitment has to be a two-way thing. It's not just about me pushing it. It's not just about them coming to me and saying, "I need supervision." It's got to be a two-way street. If you haven't got that, I don't think either party can then commit to supervision fully, so that's probably the most important element for me.

The above narration suggests that the supervision process needs to take cognizance of the supervisee's and supervisor's professional development, which requires a commitment to undertaking supervision. That is why supervision must be a two-way process. This does not contradict the supervisee-led focus but highlights that the supervisor also has a critical role in making the supervision a two-way process.

Task/Issue/Goal-Focused

Many supervisors stated that their supervision process focuses on tasks, issues, and goals of the supervisee.

… that it might be a particular case, or it might be a theme around a number of things they're seeing in cases, or it might be around their own sense of performance or efficacy within the workplace, or it might be a particular strategy or technique that they want to develop further.

… if I'm concerned about people at risk and, you know, I don't have a sense that it's being adequately managed then I do have a responsibility to do something about that and that might involve speaking to a person's line-manager at work or somebody in management.

I try to work to people's goals. So, it depends where they're at. So, if they're coming to prepare for accredited mental health social worker status, I'm really quite structured in terms of making sure that they know CBT.

I really closely talk about ethics and try and, I actually try to draw problems, mental health problems back to the wider social world.

… helping people build their own resiliency and capacity because of the nature of the work.

I have developed a contract with the person identifying what the goals of the supervision will be generally and those include what the policy of the organization is, which is the case issues, as well as wellbeing of the worker and in some instance, of course, the administrative stuff that is a requirement of the role that I would hold in that position.

The above response captures so many aspects of the supervision process in terms of administration, education, and support (Kadushin & Harkness, 2014) and simultaneously focuses on the supervisee's needs. The task/issue/goal-focused process confirms that supervisors provide professional inputs according to the requirements of each supervisee.

Reflective

Reflective practice or reflection on practice is a method and strategy as well as a process in many professions, including social work. As discussed in Chap. 4, it is also a model of professional supervision (Davys & Beddoe, 2021). Thus, it is hardly surprising that a few supervisors indicated that they would like to follow a reflective process in their supervision.

> … it's more about getting them to think …
> Then we ask them to think about what learning and development that they would like.
> I like to just offer reflective supervision.
> I actually do use the critical, the Fook and Gardner's critical. So, what's going on for you, let's draw out the assumptions, let's link those assumptions to theory. So, I will be doing that as an overarching thing.

The reflective process is critical in supervision as it helps supervisees and supervisors think about their learning and development and improve their practice.

Overall, by synthesizing these responses, it may be argued that supervisors' general process of professional supervision in social work may include any combination of supervisee-focused and supervisee-led open, flexible, informal, and conversational discussion, clarifying each other's expectations, recapitulating the main points discussed in the previous session, developing and following an agreed contract/structure, maintaining a two-way commitment to supervision, focusing on tasks/issues/goals, and following reflective supervision. Their narrations certainly captured the process at the beginning of and during supervision, but the ending process was conspicuous by its absence.

Essentials of Professional Supervision

Supervisors were asked to share their views about elements/essentials of professional supervision. The actual question posed to them was: What do you think should be the elements of professional supervision? The analysis of their responses shows 17 essentials of professional supervision. We did not find specific essentials that were common across the responses. However, the essentials of supervision identified make a useful guide for any supervision, depending upon the supervisee's circumstances.

Being Clear at the Beginning

As discussed under the process, to one supervisor, being clear at the beginning about expectations is an important element of supervision.

> So, again, as part of the contracting stage, I'm clear with people that they're coming for supervision and not for counseling.

Establishing clear expectations at the beginning helps both supervisees and supervisors to focus on mutually agreed specific tasks/areas and maintain boundaries to distinguish between professional supervision and counseling relating to personal issues, though in some situations there may be a connection between the two. It may call for careful balancing, as discussed below.

Focus on Practice/Work

Some supervisors stated that focusing on work/practice is an important element of supervision.

> I think it's looking at best practice.
> … it's got to be some focus about practice.
> I work with, for me it would be about how the person's work, how they do their work, the factors that influence their work in negative and positive ways.
> I think there's always got to be a focus on the work performance as part of supervision and that can be good or bad at the end of the day. It can be responding to feedback; it can be responding to customer criticism or customer congratulatory messages that I receive. It can be about how they're managing their workload; you know so, very much there needs to be an element there.
> I think there needs to be a discussion about the actual work and what is the actual work that is actually developed.

It makes sense that the core element of supervision is practice/work-related, whether it is performance, customer feedback, or improving practice. This element is further discussed in Chap. 8.

Balancing Between Work Issues and Private Issues

While discussing work issues, supervisees' private issues may naturally emerge during some supervision sessions. It calls for supervisors' judgment to address or not address them, depending upon the supervisor's remit. Delicate balancing may be needed to distinguish between the two, though they may be connected, as pointed out above. Some supervisors believe they are not counselors and do not deal with private issues and refer them appropriately. In contrast, others thought that supervisors should be able to balance the two in supervision sessions.

> So, I have, I go to supervision meetings here and people say, "You don't talk about private stuff." And I always say "I don't think you can totally separate work issues to private issues" I don't think it should solely be a counseling session, however if we're looking at transference and countertransference, I think we need to look at ensuring that when we're reflecting on issues that those personal issues don't get in the way of their work. And so that's really important.

We don't discuss much about their personal life really, it's all pretty much clinical. But if it does come up, we then find commonalities, or links to ways that may impact on their decision-making or the way they process things.

Yeah, and I do think that that's probably, you know, in my head I think there are things that lie clearly with the supervisee so, I think, I think it lies with them to bring something along to talk about but that's something that I think probably lies more with the supervisor; not exclusively but I think that it is a supervisor's responsibility to kind of monitor that grayness and be supportive of hearing the information but also being clear about when it might need to be dealt with elsewhere.

Part of the conversation that I had in that first session is about the continuum between the personal and the professional and where do we want to put that line. And what I say to people is, "As far as I'm concerned, that's your call." I as an individual think it's all of a piece, but while obviously there is a difference between the personal and the professional, it's all of us that does the job." So, if you're coming for supervision I don't have a difficulty with you saying, what I really need to talk about today is some particular that might have arisen in their personal life because inevitably, that will be impacting on their professional functioning, but I guess I think that's a call for the supervisee to make because some people will say, home is home, work is work, I just want to come here and talk about work and that's okay. Other's will say thank goodness because I'm putting my mother into aged care at the minute and every client I see has a mother who is driving them nuts or whatever, so they're really relieved to find a place where that totality is acceptable and I think that's the call for the supervisee to make, but I think it is an important call and it's also one that can change over time, but I think it always needs to be renegotiated.

It appears that there are three views on this issue. The first is that professional and personal issues are different, they cannot be mixed, and the supervisor may refer them to appropriate services. Secondly, as they are interconnected, supervisors must balance the two carefully. The third is that it is up to the supervisee; implicit in this is that supervisors can provide such support if the supervisee asks. On this issue, further research may be needed.

Focus on Workplace Context

A few supervisors stated that it was important to focus on the supervisee's workplace context as it may impact the worker and the work.

I think it's really important if a service is being, has lost funding and is winding down. Workplace context can get really rugged. Because everyone's afraid. And so, I'm just recalling a case like that, a supervisee who was in that position and we had more frequent supervisions and it was a lot more about how am I feeling and how can I make this process the best? So, I think that there needs to be a lot of linkage to context.

That needs to be part of it. I think there needs to be an aspect of how is the worker traveling in that work and how is the worker traveling in the agency?

How is the worker traveling as part of ... a member of the team? What is currently happening for the worker in the workplace?

The organizational context is critical as it can directly impact the worker, services, and people. In extreme situations, supervisees' wellbeing may be a prime concern.

Focus on Reflection

Many supervisors stated that they facilitate supervisees to reflect on what they have done well, what they have not, and how they can improve.

> I think you need the one-on-one for people to reflect well.
>> ... and a real structure about reflective practice.
>> ... together some discussion as to be self-reflective.
>> It's a bit about self-reflection in a way.
>
> ... a place for reflection.
>
> ... we never get a chance to actually sit down and be reflective.
>> So, from a social worker there should be that reflection on key theoretical practices and what that person is experiencing as a practitioner ...
>> I see it as my responsibility as a supervisor to assist the worker to reflect and to gain some insight into some of the strengths as well as some of the struggles and assist the worker in developing a way forward to either pursue further strengths and/or address any of the struggles.

As discussed in the previous section, reflection is fundamental to any supervision, and supervisors have identified it as basic to supervision to focus on strengths, work toward improvements, and move forward.

Focus on Positives/Strengths

For a few supervisors, identifying the positives and strengths of the supervisee and consciously using them are essential aspects of supervision.

> So, there's a lot of the problems stuff, positive stuff ...

> To have an approach you know where we can be strengths-based wherever possible.

> There should also be an element of what are some of the strengths that the worker has and how those strengths can be further enhanced and what are some of the issues that are making the worker struggle at any level and what are some of the strategies that could lead to that worker addressing those issues?

This essential of supervision is closely connected to reflection, as discussed above, as it helps look at strengths and strengths-based practice.

Professional Development

To some, professional development was an important element of supervision as supervisees need to learn and grow.

> ... to grow and to develop, personally and professionally.

There has to be some elements on what learnings would be good.

… a place for development.

… for me … I think it's about helping that person grow. So, you want to help them actually be able to blossom and feel safe.

I think there also needs to be an element around professional development, areas of expertise that they need to enhance, so looking at options or opportunities for where they can develop and grow.

… I'd like to think that it's not only the individual cases that you consider, but I'd like to think that it is the total development of the worker.

Professional development of the supervisee as an essential of supervision includes so many aspects of the profession, practice, and the supervisee. So, it is a loaded and comprehensive element of supervision.

Identifying Themes/Issues

Some supervisors thought that identifying themes and issues in supervision is an important element.

Or ethical situations where you have to make a clinical decision. That's where I like to sort of try to tease out when we're talking about clinical caseload. Look at what might have been challenging. What did they learn from it? What did they find? What did they find easy? What did they find difficult?

So, for me anyway, I think it's about putting that stuff on the table. Not shying away from it, because otherwise, it reduces the benefit I think, that can come from supervision.

So, for me the, maybe I could say I'm trying to work it out as I go, that the elements are often frequently the kinds of factors that impact upon the work that this person's doing, that's often organizational factors, political factors, funding factors and knowledge limits. And the kinds of knowledges they are drawing on, those kinds of factors. So, we're looking at those elements. What this person, what this worker does. How they turn those, what do they, how these factors impact upon the worker. So, the effects on the worker. And then definitely the kinds of work that a worker is able to do given all of that. And how they story that.

Although at times challenging, "putting that stuff on the table" is critical, and further linking it to possible organizational, political, and economic factors and vis-à-vis the knowledge and ability of the supervisee is equally important.

Focus on Values and Ethics/Links to Professional Ethics

Professional values, principles, and codes of ethics are the foundations of any profession. Some supervisors rightly stated that drawing on professional values and ethics should be an important element of supervision.

I think being upfront and being honest. Ethics, values, morals. Being non-judgmental.

I think that there should be clear links to professional ethics.

… to incorporate the values of social work as often as we can.

… while maintaining our professional values is really important, which is why supervision is so important because you can start on a slippery slope and unless you've got a good supervisor to bring you back to all that – and I've seen it quite a few times Manohar … where people haven't had good social work supervision and you can see values-based issues slip.

Without values, principles, and ethics, "a slippery slope" may occur, as expressed above. Thus, a good social work supervision must include the foundations of the profession. Further details are discussed in Chap. 8.

Accountability/Responsibility

While discussing the elements of supervision, a few supervisors referred to accountability and responsibility as follows.

… being accountability.

But for me there's a responsibility I have in this seat that is to the people that this person's working with. So, this worker has their clients, and I always imagine their clients in a room with me. 'Cause the work that I do with this worker will have an impact, I believe, on the work that they do with those people.

Professional supervision in social work must have accountability and responsibility from the perspective of self, the profession, the organization, and people and communities. The above statement captures many of these perspectives.

Offering Support

For a few supervisors, as stated below, offering support should be an important element of supervision.

… and a place for support.

I think that's important to be able to think about that and hear that and provide some support around that within the supervision relationship but in terms of working to resolve whatever that might be creating that should be happening somewhere else.

But also, there needs to be workload and self-care, and any performance issues also should be, and some case notes auditing, that type of stuff, or some auditing of their work should be also covered in supervision, which I don't tend to do.

As articulated by several scholars (see Chap. 4), providing support to supervisees is one of the main purposes of supervision. To a few supervisors, relationship-based support and self-care focus constitute the support element of professional supervision. Supervision is essentially "a place of support."

Being Present/Listening

A few supervisors stated that being present and listening with a presence of mind should be a crucial element of supervision.

> So, I think it's about, for me it's also about being very present, and having that space. You can de-brief anytime.
>
> But supervision is especially for that person, and it's about listening and really being present. And so often for our work we never get a chance to actually sit down and be reflective, and to really think about what we're doing. So, I think that's a very important.
>
> Yeah, look I think [pause] I think you've got to have really good listening skills, and I think you have to be genuine, really be there with the person. People can sense when you're, it's just a process you're going through.
>
> But I think being human. I know that sounds funny but it's like don't let the administrative paperwork side take over the supervision. It becomes too false and bureaucratic, I think.

Being present and active listening are fundamentals of social work practice. As narrated by supervisors, being present and listening requires "good listening skills, being genuine, really there with the supervisee," and this is less likely to occur in the current managerialist, bureaucratic context, unless dedicated arrangements are made for it.

Sharing Own Experience

For one supervisor, sharing one's own relevant experience should be an important element of supervision.

> … and sometimes I'll relate a bit to my own experience. And I try not to do that too much because it's not about me. It's not my supervision session. But I might draw on a similar story from my own life or my own practice, that kind of signifies that I understand. It's different but I understand some of that fear or some of that anxiety around that particular issue. So, I use that a little bit as a connection but yeah, you got to be very careful not to do that too much otherwise it becomes all about you.

Appropriately sharing relevant experiences of supervisors may guide and support supervisees and can enhance the authenticity of the supervision experience. However, as suggested, it needs to be done carefully so that it does not dominate the supervision.

Empathy

Depending upon the context, supervisors sharing some experiences may facilitate empathy. As such, supervisors may also need to appropriately empathize with supervisees. A supervisor stated:

> I try and get them to feel that I'm with them, so I use the word "we" a lot. "Look we need to think through what this might look like so that," and "We're going to share this problem, and we are going to share this responsibility", because I think when you do that it's not, it takes the weight off them and supervision is supposed to be supportive, so I just think that's been quite a nice strategy to use in supervision.

The "we" approach has a solidaristic spirit. Supervisors supporting with empathy are quite different from just supporting. Empathy is broader than the "we" approach but can include an element of it.

Relationship and Trust

A few supervisors were of the view that forming respectful relationships and building trust should be an essential part of supervision. They said:

> So, it becomes a mutually respectful relationship, that helps build the trust in the supervisory relationship.
> I think that there should be a space where clinicians can talk about, or social workers can talk about what's going on for them in the context of their work.

> Well, I think there's always got to be an element of the personal. It is about having a relationship with your staff, so I think there's always a need to talk with people about how they are and how their family are and how, you know if they've had illness, or if they'd had a break from work. How was their holiday or are they well now after they're back from a few weeks personal leave? So, I think there's always got to be that personal.

> … to have a respectful attitude.

Building relationships, trust, and having a respectful attitude are critical requirements in any profession, including social work practice with people. It is hardly surprising that supervisors view that it should be one of the essentials of professional supervision. The way of achieving it may differ from one supervisor to another. Here the supervisor suggests taking a personal interest in the supervisee beyond work. There may be other ways as well. Its significance is apparent when we experience no progress because of a lack of trustful relationship and respect between the supervisor and supervisee.

Asking Curious Questions

One supervisor believed that asking curious questions should be an element of supervision.

> And I think asking curious questions is really important so that very non-judgmental, being open to hearing anything and everything, and being able to hold your own stuff. So that maintaining the boundary, maintaining the composure, and not showing that behind that face you're kind of thinking "Oh my gosh, this is really big". So, there's that. And I think that's, but being able to do that and still connecting with the person, and that connection happens through the curious questions and the listening ...

This supervisor has explained it well and offered additional insights. Asking curious questions helps to remain "non-judgmental" and "open to hearing anything." It is a useful suggestion that supervisors can "connect" with supervisees by raising curious questions and listening.

Using Theory, Sharing Resources

In addition to discussion between the supervisor and supervisee, the purposeful use of theories, evidence, and sharing resources should be an element of supervision. A supervisor said:

> And I try as well to contribute to the supervision in a way that's using evidence, so sometimes I'll draw upon a particular theory, or I'll ask the person about a theory that they might prefer or that they've used or talked about, to help understand what's happened with the client for example, or I might say "I've read a really good article on mental health recovery recently. I'll send it to you". So, I do that after the session. So, I try and give them resources. And what that does is that some of them, not all of them, some of them start sending me articles then on topics. It's quite nice.

> So, I think that I am really good at drilling down to the different theories people are using.

This suggests that supervisors have an important to role to discuss relevant theories and their application to the supervisee's practice. In a particular practice context, sharing an article and asking the supervisee to read it helps the supervisee to think about its application in work. The educative role of the supervisor is well reflected here, and it is one of the main purposes of the supervision as discussed in Chap. 4.

Overall, the respondent supervisors think that these 17 essentials should be used in supervision. As each supervision context differs, the 17 essentials are not exhaustive, and some supervisors and supervisees may find some other essentials that work for them. However, these essentials are closely linked to the purposes and goals of the supervision – administration, education, and support – discussed in Chap. 4. It is interesting to note that, of the 17 essentials, only two are related to the administration – focusing on the workplace context and accountability and responsibility. Four essentials are related to education. These were focused on practice/work, professional development, values and ethics, using theory, and sharing resources. Only two are related to offering support, which included balancing work and private issues. Of the 17, over half (9) were "dos" for supervisors. Supervisors should focus on being clear at the beginning, reflection, positives/strengths, being present and listening, sharing experiences, empathy, building relationship and trust, and identifying themes and issues and asking curious questions. Another interesting and insightful aspect of five essentials – the use of reflection, positives/strengths, being present and listening, empathy, and relationship and trust – is that they all flow from casework practice in social work. (See section "Casework, Clinical Practice, and Therapy-Oriented Supervision Models" in Chap. 4.) As raised elsewhere, professional supervision in social work tends to draw knowledge and skills from work with clients, but the relationship between the supervisor and supervisee is not like the relationship between the social worker and the client/people. Although there is nothing wrong with using the same knowledge and skills in professional supervision, if it works, it is important to be aware of the differences between the two types of relationships to guard against the potential of messing-up the supervision. On the whole, we believe these 17 essentials of supervision will be of some help to supervisors and supervisees.

The Main Theme or Core Content of Professional Supervision

Having explored the essentials of professional supervision, we asked supervisors to share the main theme or core content of their professional supervision sessions. A guiding question was: What is the main theme or core content of your professional supervision? The analysis of the narrations of supervisors helped to identify 10 main themes/core contents of their supervision, though some of them may be merged under other related themes. A couple of supervisors did not mention any themes or content but stated that it all depends on what the supervisee brings to the agenda, it is self-directed by the supervisee, and what they as supervisors do is active listening and guiding. However, this does not mean the themes/content presented here are not driven by supervisees. What it suggests is that supervisors often focus on the following 10 themes/core contents in their supervision sessions.

Self-Care/Safety for the Worker and the Client

As already discussed, one of the main purposes of professional supervision in social work is to provide support to supervisees, and the ultimate purpose of supervision is to deliver better quality services to people and communities. Thus, for some supervisors, self-care/safety of the worker and client was an important component of their supervision sessions. They said:

Safety for the worker and for the people that they're seeing, that's coming from mental health, that's really important. And that's around boundaries. That's around the safety of the worker and for the person in terms of those values and morals and rights, ethics, are those all being thought about and abided by. Supervisor, am I doing the right thing? So, I'm always thinking about those things, when, for example I've actually worked with people, supervisees, and I've needed to do mental health checks on my supervisees. They've been unwell in terms of mental health issues ...

So, and I've had to talk to them that I needed to talk to their team leader. "Look, I noticed that things aren't quite okay here, what's happening?" "Oh, I haven't been sleeping well. I've been really stressed." So even as a supervisor, it's our responsibility, still, to look at safety. ... And they need to have time off. And that's for their reputation, for the safety of themselves and of the safety of the people that they're working with. And it's being upfront and honest. I would like someone to be honest with me.

Self-care. Not getting too involved, from a, not getting personally, like kind of trying to distance yourself from, they may have a case where it might trigger an emotion, or a past experience that they've been through personally. Where they feel like it's challenged them more. Knowing that they're doing a good job and they need to find balance. And not to take work home. Not to give, they need to be able to find that distance and being able to switch off when they get home and look after themselves.

... and I would also have to say how are they, as individual workers, managing the stressors that are presented to them? What kind of assistance would be of value to them, and supporting the workers to think outside the square, not only for their clients, but also for themselves? One of the other things which is demanding and challenging for me, is managing performance when it's under particularly, and the department has a very clear process that you have to go through, which is totally exhausting for everyone, and how you manage the team culture when you do have someone on a management plan, is also tricky.

In the context of mental health issues of supervisees and their clients, supervisors have focused on self-care and safety of the supervisee and their clients. When they refer to "being upfront and honest," supervisors expect supervisees to honestly disclose what is happening to them, even in sensitive situations where the supervisor may need to confer with the supervisees' managers to adhere to ethical guidelines. This would be a highly sensitive and complex supervision. Asking the supervisee to be upfront and honest when there is the possibility of having to discuss the same matters with their supervisor or line-manager is not easy.

Self-care also calls for controlled emotional involvement on the part of the worker. Transference and countertransference occur not only between the worker and client but also between the supervisee and supervisor. Preparing to disconnect between work and family is easier said than done, but one needs to learn it consciously. Stress can quickly compound if it emanates from both client-related work and managing performance; consequently, some workers may struggle. Perhaps, being upfront and honest helps so that supervisors may gain an understanding of the situation, and both supervisors and supervisees together can explore "outside the square" solutions. Depending upon the issue and context, these may include a change of clients/work/team/department or further training and capacity development or a short break to rest, or a combination of these. There are also clear ethical and practice guidelines to take steps to ensure the safety of the client and related individuals and families.

Maintaining Boundaries

Supervisors helping supervisees understand and maintain personal and professional boundaries with the client and organization is critical (Pugh, 2007; O'Leary et al., 2013). A couple of supervisors stated that one of the main themes of their supervision was maintaining boundaries.

> Gosh, that's a really interesting question. Probably one of the things that comes up nearly always – probably not always but nearly always – is thinking about boundaries with clients, you know, or boundaries within the work setting. And I think that's a really great thing to be talking about in supervision because it differs from workplace to workplace and from individual to individual. So, that I think would certainly be a theme. What else? I think the rest is kind of really mixed.

> And it's linked with the boundary stuff as well, isn't it, you know, like an emotional boundary in the sense of being able to say, "That situation could all go to hell in a hand basket tonight or before I get back to the office next week but if it does, that doesn't sit with me, that's not my fault". Yeah

Boundary maintenance in social work is both a professional practice and ethical requirement as dual relationships are prohibited between the practitioner and client. It is also important to disconnect between work and family to maintain emotional boundaries. This theme is revisited in Chap. 8 as one of the main issues discussed in professional supervision.

Personal Issues

In the previous section, balancing work and private issues was discussed as one of the essentials of supervision. Apparently, in the supervision sessions, supervisees' personal issues emerged as a major theme. One supervisor stated: *Sometimes it will be the personal things.*

Personal and work issues of supervisees may be perceived as separate by some supervisors, but it is also important to note that they may be interconnected. Work issues influence personal issues and personal issues affect work issues. Each supervisee's situation will differ and supervisors may need to employ professional discretion to work with supervisees dealing with difficult personal issues. This issue is further discussed in Chap. 8.

Difficulties with and Conflicts Around the Organization

Since the 1980s, due to the influence of neoliberal ideology, the free market, privatization, and managerialism, the work culture of the organization has significantly changed. This has been reflected in "doing more with less resources," which has generally had a significant impact on organizations, their values and principles, and on employees' morale. The following narratives of supervisors show that one of the important themes of their supervision was supervisees having difficulties with and conflicts around working in organizations.

> Whatever that might be, whether it's their committee of management, whether it's their teammate, whether it's their line-manager, whether it's their whatever. That tends to be the stuff that is generally more challenging …

> But once upon a time workers would come in and talk a lot about the work they did with their clients, or within the communities that they were working. And that was probably the more dominant set of themes in the talking that we did.

> And then I reckon, I don't know, somewhere over the last 10, 12 years, that changed. And the more dominant theme now is, I don't know how to name it, but something like workers surviving their organizations. Something like that. Surviving the impact of policies, procedures, funding, restrictions. Management practices. Workers talk a lot about that, the impact of that on them and on the ability to do their work.

The organizational issues appear to be more challenging for supervisees. Client/practice issues are no longer a dominant theme in the supervision, but "workers surviving in their organizations" due to the impact of changes and management practices of "more with less." This is further discussed in Chap. 8.

Client/Practice Issues

As a supervisor has narrated above, client/practice issues were once the dominant theme of supervision. Even if they are no longer so, they remain a critical theme as supervisees regularly discuss practice issues with supervisors.

> So, someone's got a client, for example, that's got a personality disorder. I might provide some education about personality disorder. And then talk about some strategies that the clinician might use in that context. Yeah. Or whatever. You know. So, if a clinician's feeling stuck with a client, often it's a matter of working out, without going into their full past life, you know, what's the psychological element of that stuckedness? What assumptions have I made and can I link them to my social work theory? And okay, so this is where you're sitting with this, but here's some skills, some specific skills as well, that you can use. And you know this, but you do need some skills as well.

> Because, I actually firmly believe in mental health, that you need to use skills, purely because it's such a litigious area and you actually need to be able to write your case notes up and you know, I have actually recall spending one whole session on a client just about writing case notes.

> I'd have to say it would be the case management …
> One of it is, trying to work through and understand the issues that, be facing our family. You know the families that we work with and the kids that we work with.
> The practice, the actual practice, what is the worker doing with the clients that she's actually working with or he's actually working with and where is that practice coming from and how is that practice being representative of the policies and the legislation and what is it that they're meant to be doing in that particular role. With that comes the level of skills that they have in order to provide that service.

First, along with the supervisee, supervisors need to understand "where the supervisee is at" and what knowledge and skills need to be provided to move to the next level. As shared by supervisors, the discussion of a client/practice issue may include education about the issue, understanding where the supervisee is feeling stuck, clarifying theories, focusing on specific skills, learning to properly document case notes, case management, relating practice-work to policies and legislation, and developing the required knowledge and skills to deliver the service. This content is further discussed in Chap. 8 as one of the core issues posed by supervisees.

Feeling of Inadequacy in Work Performance

How supervisees have performed in their work and how they can perform better are important areas of discussion in supervision. A supervisor stated that one of the main themes in their supervision was some supervisees feeling inadequate in their work performance.

> Probably the other common theme that comes out is people feeling inadequate in their work performance …

Supervisors helping supervisees to perform better according to key performance indicators is possible when both supervisors and supervisees focus on understanding and identifying knowledge and skills deficiencies and accordingly developing the competencies of supervisees. This issue is further discussed in Chap. 8.

Critical Reflection

As discussed earlier, reflection is used as a process and is one of the essentials in supervision. It is also identified as one of the main themes or contents in supervision. A couple of supervisors narrated as follows:

> So, but yeah, so I suppose the overarching theme is I am a social worker and I supervise social workers. The theme is critical reflection, but I will drill down to various areas if I need to.

> But as I said earlier, I think the other thing that really motivates, my supervision of other people is, the concentration on not just our families but the person who's delivering the service, as trying to help and support them to deliver the best possible service that they can. And you know to help them build resiliency and, you know through – especially through critical reflection, to be able to grow and feel – you know I just believe that old paradigm about if you can help people feel competent, they'll be confident and then deliver a far better service.

Whatever model of reflection is followed, critical reflection helps to "drill down various areas." What supervisees did; what they did well and not so well; how they can do better. "Concentrating" on and supporting workers help to deliver better services to people and communities. As narrated above, critical reflection can be used for the professional development of supervisees, to develop resilience and to make them feel competent so that they feel adequate and confident to work with people and deliver the best possible services.

Modeling Values

One supervisor stated that modeling values and behavior was an important theme/focus of supervision. Certainly, deeds are more powerful than words.

> … as someone who's in a management role or whatever you like to call it, that I have to model the values that I want from other people. So, I'm very careful at supervision to, you know talk about how we are working on these issues not just – not just some hierarchical top-down approach.

In addition to the supervisory discussion, supervisors need to model values and behavior so that supervisees learn by observing them. Putting aside the hierarchy and managerial/administrative power, supervisors need to model practice with people, translating values and principles and knowledge and skills. It appears that modeling is an effective method of supervising.

Professional Identity

The subject/issue and experience of professional identity comprise a relevant theme in professional supervision, particularly for those supervisees who have just begun their career in social work. Even for experienced supervisees, the social work professional identity may become an issue if they are working in multidisciplinary teams in which the social worker's role/contribution is sidelined or ignored. A supervisor said:

> The core content is actually that I am supervised as a social worker. And I think that in social work there can be a loss of professional identity, especially if you're working in a multidisciplinary team.

> And I think that professional identity is probably one of the values in the AASW values and the code of ethics, that's not fully explored.

As discussed earlier in Chap. 2, the social work profession faces de-professionalization challenges due to managerialism and competing professions where social work has a secondary role and, perhaps, due to the decolonization process. As professional identity and a lack of it raises serious questions for practitioners, professional supervision provides necessary space for constructively discussing it from several perspectives, including values, ethics, and professional character.

Learning/Training and the Future

As discussed in Chap. 4, education is one of the core purposes and functions of supervision, and learning/training is embedded into it. One supervisor stated that learning/training and the future of supervisees should be the content of supervision, but often it is not.

> There's not enough, but there should be more of a theme about learning, training, where we want to go to from here. That should be there, often missing, I think.

It is normally expected that learning/training and future directions for the supervisee should be an important aspect of professional supervision. If this is often missing, it raises the need to reconsider, rearrange, and challenge the professional supervision practice.

The analysis of supervisors' responses shows 10 important themes/content in their supervision as presented above, though they may not focus on all of them. Self-care and the safety of the worker is an important issue as many social workers work in demanding, stressful, and sometimes risky situations. Maintaining boundaries and addressing personal issues are in a way related to self-care and safety. Working with client/practice issues is an important area of supervision, and it may involve a particular focus such as mental health and recovery focus, strengthening workers' competency, and reflection. It appears that supervisors do not find it difficult to work with the practice issues, with one supervisor describing it as a "breeze." However, what they find difficult and challenging are the organizational/systemic issues presented by supervisees, such as issues involving value conflicts. A shift from client/practice issues to organizational issues being dominant is concerning. This finding has implications for further research and training social workers and other professionals. For one supervisor, developing a professional identity was an important theme. Another supervisor stated that the learning/training and development of the worker should be the main theme of supervision but was missing. Overall, their responses did not make an explicit reference to focusing on the virtues/qualities of social workers in supervision. However, there may be implicit elements of this in the supervision theme of self-care and the safety of the worker. One supervisor stated, "I have to model the values that I want from other people." Such a supervision theme is likely to impact the virtues/qualities of supervisees, but it may be the desired response as our project was researching this area.

Conclusion and Summary

This chapter presents an overview of what supervisors think about professional supervision in social work. In particular, it has discussed the supervisors' views about the general process, essentials, and themes/content of professional supervision. Although the supervisors' description of the supervision process was varied and flexible, informal, and formal, it was mostly determined and led by the supervisee under the supervisor's guidance. The process must be a two-way commitment focusing on clear goals and tasks/issues. As the narrated process mostly focused on the beginning and main discussion parts of supervision sessions, it is important to look at the ending process of supervision, which appears to be neglected in the professional supervision practice. The 17 essentials of supervision narrated by the supervisors captured well the administrative, educational, and support functions of supervision, but more than a half of them focused on what supervisors should do. It is important to heed these dos. It is critical that both supervisors and supervisees should try to be clear at the beginning and facilitate reflection, positives/strengths, presence of mind, listening, sharing experiences, empathy, building relationship and trust, identifying themes and issues, and posing curious questions. Although using knowledge and skills of clinical practice in supervision may be useful, some caution may be needed to prevent the parallel of worker-client relationship. The 10 themes/content of supervision – self-care/safety, sustaining boundaries, personal, organizational and client/practice issues, recovery, enhancing competencies and confidence, critical reflection, modeling, professional identity and learning/training, and career development – confirm not only the content of supervision but also provide additional insights. The shift from client/practice-focused supervision to a focus on organizational issues discussion, at least in some contexts, should be noted and addressed in the interests of people and communities, workers, organizations, and the profession. Reflective supervision should be underscored as it cuts across the process, essentials and theme/content of professional supervision. In the supervisors' narratives, we did not find the theme of professionally ending the supervision, which needs to be explored in future research. The next chapter discusses the expectations of supervisors.

References

Cojocaru, S. (2010). Appreciative supervision in social work. New opportunities for changing the social work practice. *Revista de cercetare [i interven]ie social, 29*(1), 72–91.

Davys, A., & Beddoe, L. (2021). *Best practice in professional supervision: A guide for the helping professions* (2nd ed.). Jessica Kingsley Publishers.

Kadushin, A., & Harkness, D. (2014). *Supervision in social work* (5th ed.). Columbia University Press.

O'Leary, P., Tsui, M.-S., & Ruch, G. (2013). The boundaries of the social work relationship revisited: Towards a connected, inclusive and dynamic conceptualization. *British Journal of Social Work, 43*(1), 135–153. https://doi.org/10.1093/bjsw/bcr181

Pugh, R. (2007). Dual relationships: Personal and professional boundaries in rural social work. *British Journal of Social Work, 37*(8), 1405–1423. https://doi.org/10.1093/bjsw/bcl088

Chapter 7
Supervisors' Expectations

Introduction

In the previous chapter, clarifying expectations as a process and being clear about expectations at the beginning as an essential of supervision were discussed. Due to its importance, this chapter further considers the expectations of supervisees and supervisors. Munson (2002, p. 137) argues that "Failure to work through varying perceptions of supervisor and practitioner can lead to conflict and frustration." A mismatch between supervisees' and supervisors' expectations may result in confusion, misunderstanding, and not meeting the needs of the supervisee and thus not achieving the purpose and goals of supervision. On the other hand, understanding and aligning the expectations of supervisees and supervisors are likely to result in better professional supervision (Peters et al., 2020).

Drawing on the analysis of narratives of supervisors, the first section of this chapter discusses supervisors' perceptions of supervisees' expectations. Supervisors think that supervisees expect supervisors to make themselves available, support, respect, provide space for ventilating, have a plan/direction/advice, help solve problems, enhance learning, facilitate reflection, share alternative perspectives, offer honest feedback, be accountable and maintain continuity, and provide therapy and counseling. In the second section, supervisors' 13 expectations from supervisees are presented. Supervisors expect supervisees to come prepared; take follow-up action; analyze issues from different perspectives; discuss ethical dilemmas; be critical, honest, and responsible; and have a proper focus. These expectations help reflect on the purpose and goals of supervision discussed in Chap. 4. In the final section, under the conclusion and summary, similarities and differences in supervisees' and supervisors' expectations are indicated to enhance professional supervision in social work.

M. Pawar, A. W. (Bill) Anscombe, *Enlightening Professional Supervision in Social Work*, https://doi.org/10.1007/978-3-031-18541-0_7

Supervisors' Perceptions of Supervisees' Expectations from Supervision

We tried to explore what supervisors think supervisees expect from their supervision. The guiding question posed was "What do social workers/supervisees expect from your supervision?" As stated in the introduction, the questions produced a range of responses from supervisors. However, one supervisor stated that they did not know what to expect. The analysis of their responses has been organized into the following 10 supervisees' expectations.

Availability, Support, and Respect

We do not think professional supervision is possible without committing specific time for supervision, respectful relationship, and offering support. Some supervisors stated that supervisees expect support, respect, and availability from supervisors, particularly when there are crises, difficult cases, or critical decisions to be made.

> I mean they expect me to be able to support them, to be non-judgmental, they expect me to be available and respectful.

> What I hope is that they would expect me to be respectful and to prioritize that time and be available at that time and to have no distractions and to really make that time as a special time, discreet time, for them so that they feel that they can completely talk about what they want. ... So, they'd expect a degree of confidentiality and respect.

> To feel that they are supported, to feel that they're part of something more than just coming in and plodding through the tasks associated with case management.
>   I think they would, and I would want to offer them some forum where they feel someone is thinking of them, holds them in mind, and has their back, because when you work for a department such as this, and when you work in such a stressful, challenging environment as child protection, which is risk-laden, there are cases that maybe change very quickly, and you might have a child death on your hands, or you might have a complaint to the minister about you, and I would want my workers to know I had their back, and I would support them ...

> They sometimes see supervision as surrogate parenting, as parenting and they want you to meet the needs of a caring parent. So, it's sort of balancing knowing – trying to meet people's needs that are reasonable while focusing on professional issues.

> They're also looking for support. ... my worker that I'm supervising at the moment is looking for support in terms of managing quite a demanding workload. ... She's also looking for me to support them should there be a crisis or an issue of concern or should there be questions about their decision-making ...

These are reasonable expectations of supervisees as perceived by supervisors. As pointed out earlier, due to administrative workloads and managerialism, some line managers were not able to allocate adequate time for supervision, though they were aware that they are meant to. Meeting supervisees during tea or lunch breaks and having a quick catch-up is not uncommon. However, such practices cannot substitute for a specific dedicated time for supervision. Supervisors need to make themselves available for supervision; if they cannot do so, organizations should look at alternative ways of arranging professional supervision for supervisees. Committing time to supervision shows the importance attached to it and demonstrates respect and support. In addition to day-to-day work-related matters, supervisees expect supervisors' support, to "have their backs," especially in stressful settings such as child protection and the court system. Sometimes, support may involve more than simply professional matters. Some supervisees will have significant personal and professional issues and supervisors will need to balance their support.

Space for Ventilation/Debriefing

As discussed earlier, professional supervision is a space for supervisees. Many supervisors thought that supervisees expected supervision sessions to provide a space for ventilation and debriefing.

> … they would probably say, "maybe just to vent." As a colleague. They might side-along with me as another social worker colleague and feel a bit more comfortable that we're on the same page, that we understand each other.

> Generally, people say "Oh, just somewhere to talk about cases and my work generally" – you know, it tends to be these sort of very broad statements.

> They'll often talk about getting some more clarity or getting some more … just being able to talk about different issues that might have come up.

> I hope that they would go out feeling like they're … like a bit of a weight is off them.

> But I think as well the thing that comes up is they're looking for the experience, they're looking for someone to share a problem with, and to be able to walk out of supervision feeling uplifted, feeling buoyant.

> They expect to feel better at the end.

> They're looking for an opportunity to debrief …

Space for ventilation/debriefing suggests the significance of an individual supervision meeting, though some ventilation/debriefing can occur in group supervision. Implicit also is the supervisee's pent up feelings, emotions, and issues and the need to share the same with the supervisor in a safe and nonthreatening environment. Along with this, there is also an expectation of an outcome that, following the ventilation/debrief, supervisees should "feel better/uplifted."

Have a Plan, Direction, or Advice

Professional supervision is a planned and purposeful activity. Some supervisors said that supervisees expect to have a plan, direction, or piece of advice.

> They expect to have a plan at the end, which is, I think is fair enough.

> I think they expect direction. I think they like sometimes to be told what to do and where to go to find different things and how to explore or access an avenue of support for something.

> I think they expect to have some direction.

> … they're generally looking for guidance and advice.

> And she's looking for advice on how to manage some of the difficulties that the role presents for her.

These expectations suggest supervision is not an ad hoc, casual conversation between the supervisee and supervisor. Supervisees expect a clear plan, direction, guidance, and advice. The supervisor may need to ensure that practical plans are developed and future directions are provided.

Have Answers and Problem-Solving

A couple of supervisors believed that supervisees expect answers or problem-solving for specific problems or issues.

> They expect me to have the answers, a lot of the time.

> And I think when you've got a good supervisor who you can strategize with or problem solve with, then you can achieve that.

Social work practice in some settings, such as child protection, mental health, and domestic violence, can be challenging and complex, and, despite much consideration and contemplation, decisions can be doubtful. Supervisees often wish to discuss such problems with supervisors to seek answers or solve problems or develop some strategies.

Learn Something More than What They Know

This expectation directly fits with one of the purposes of supervision – education. A few supervisors stated that supervisees expect to learn something more or know more than what they already know.

> They want to come away knowing that they've learnt something.
> … they want to come away knowing that they've learnt something more than what they've come to the supervision with.

That they're going to learn more about, or in a deeper level, about probably with their therapies or theories or practice theories that they already know about. They probably want to
know that they're coming to see someone that has an understanding about social work theory, and practice.

But a lot of them also want some teaching from me.

Undoubtedly, supervisors are a source of practice experience and knowledge for
supervisees. Supervisees expect to learn from supervision or "know more than what
they already know." It may include particular theories or therapies, depending upon
the case problem they discuss with supervisors. It also suggests that, to meet such
an expectation, supervisors need to plan and prepare well for each supervision
meeting.

Facilitate Reflection

As discussed earlier, supervisors have identified reflection as a process, an essential
and part of the content of supervision. The following responses are consistent –
supervisees expect a time of reflection on their practice/work/cases during the
supervision.

That they have been able to reflect on the difficulties of the problems that they've come to
supervision.

They expect me to help them think through things.
    … someone to talk to, to do some skill development or someone to bring some difficult
cases to or someone to reflect on, you know …

Supervisees often come to supervision to discuss difficult cases or problems. As
discussed above, instead of readily providing answers or solving problems, supervisors have an important role in facilitating supervisees' reflection on the practice
issues they have tabled in the supervision. Supervisors need to engage supervisees
in the reflective problem-solving process. What supervisees' have encountered,
attempted, assessed, and thought of options to work with need to be constructively
and critically discussed by supervisors.

Looking for Affirmation

Looking for affirmation can also be a part of the reflective process. One supervisor
stated that supervisees look for affirmation, which we think is a good practice in
supervision when it is appropriate and done appropriately.

… I think they're looking for affirmation, to say that they've done a good job. But if they
were, that's more than anything, I think that's the common, that's more of the most of it. To
kind of, find out that they were on the same page, I think that's the reassurance they're looking for. Yeah. That's probably the highest, the common theme. Then the next would be,
"How might I have done that different?" Or "I'm stuck, I don't know which way to go."

In supervision, as part of the reflective process, supervisors can facilitate supervisees' thinking, confidence, and alternative options by affirming, reassuring, and confirming that they are progressing toward the desired direction. When appropriate and necessary, supervisors may also share what they would have done differently or the same.

Providing a Different Perspective

When supervisors share how they address the same issue or need differently, it may help provide a different perspective. A supervisor stated that supervisees expect to have varied perspectives on the problems they face in their practice.

> But because I'm a narrative practitioner, people come and want questions that invite them to look at things from a different angle, from a different perspective. So, they like the questioning, I think. And they like the political questioning that's going to invite the politics of their work world and their workspace into the conversation.

As discussed in Chap. 6, asking curious questions was one of the essentials of supervision. Supervisors posing questions help supervisees to think about different perspectives and consider options. Such questioning may also help gain insights beyond practice cases as organizational politics and workspaces may be connected to practice issues, at least in some situations.

Honest Feedback and Understanding

Honesty and understanding between the supervisor and supervisee are needed. A supervisor stated that supervisees expect a good understanding and honest feedback from supervisors.

> I think honesty is really critical that they get some honest feedback, that they get some insight into how I feel that their performance is occurring, and I think they expect me to know them personally and I think over the years that I've developed that understanding with people.

To develop a good understanding, honest feedback needs to be given to supervisees. The feedback needs to be based on evidence. Some supervisees expect a realistic assessment of their performance and areas for improvement. Such honest discussion and feedback generally occur where supervisors and supervisees have a good understanding.

Accountability and Continuity

Earlier, accountability was discussed as one of the essentials of supervision and so is follow-up or continuity as a supervision process. A supervisor stated that supervisees expect accountability and continuity during supervision sessions.

> … I think there's an accountability around some note taking and some reflection back on that a month later or six weeks later to be able to say, "Look we talked about this at that stage, where have things moved on from?" So, it's about that continuity of knowing your staff member and being able to actually keep abreast of where they're at and know where they're at so that they don't feel like you didn't listen to them last time. You know that you didn't hear what they were saying so you know I think, again, they're probably some of the elements that I think my staff expect of me …

Both the supervisor and supervisee need to be accountable in the supervision. Supervisees expect supervisors to take and keep notes from supervision sessions, refer and reflect on them, and in the subsequent session maintain continuity by asking supervisees how they have progressed and what stage they are at. Although accountability is more than this, it shows as an example supervisees' expectations from supervisors.

Therapy and Counseling

References to therapy and counseling may naturally take us to supervisees' work with people and clients, which is an important subject of supervision. However, here it refers to therapy and counseling for supervisees. A supervisor stated that sometimes supervisees also expect supervisors to address their personal issues during supervision.

> But to be honest what I also get at supervision quite a bit and even quite senior workers, is people want – come to supervision sometimes with – they want you to be their therapist (laughs) …

> … I'm actually coming to supervision to have a whole range of other needs met. And that's always really tricky to help people build capacity, if their issues are actually not ground in professional issues.

In Chap. 6, supervisees' personal issues were discussed as part of the process and content of supervision. Some supervisees expect supervisors to offer therapy and counseling to deal with their personal issues, but it is delicate and "tricky." Some supervisors were clear that they do not entertain this as part the supervision and refer them to appropriate services, whereas others try to balance the work and personal issues. To meet this expectation, whatever approach they take, supervisors need to ensure that ethical standards are adhered to and boundaries are maintained.

Do Not Know What to Expect

Those who are new to social work practice, new supervisees, may not know what to expect from professional supervision, though this may not be the case with all new supervisees, and it may be a wrong assumption on the part of supervisors. However, a supervisor stated that some supervisees do not know what to expect, particularly if they are new.

> … but frighteningly, a lot of people don't know what to expect from supervision if they're fairly early on in their career I think and I don't think I would have either.

> … But I don't know that people will have clear ideas about what they want it (supervision) to be.

> … more often than not, I have a sense that people aren't sure what to expect. Yeah, which is alarming at some level.

First, this assumption needs to be checked, and, if it is confirmed, supervisors are responsible for educating supervisees about what to expect from supervisors and the supervision process. One way of achieving this is to openly discuss the expectations at the beginning and or clearly articulate them in the contract setting stage of supervision. If a formal contract is used, these expectations should be reviewed periodically (3 or 6 months).

The above analysis of supervisors' perceptions of supervisees' expectations suggests that many supervisees expect supervisors' support, availability, and respect. Supervision sessions should provide a space for ventilation and debriefing so that supervisees feel better at the end of the session. Supervision should also help them have a plan, direction, or advice. A couple of supervisors thought that supervisees expect answers or problem-solving and to learn something more than what they already know. Other expectations included facilitating reflection, gaining a different perspective, receiving honest feedback and affirmation, developing a good understanding, maintaining accountability and continuity, and addressing personal issues. Most of these expectations are relevant, reasonable, and valid. None of their responses directly referred to the development of qualities/character or virtues as supervisees' expectations. However, indirectly or implicitly, some qualities/virtues such as honesty, accountability and continuity, learning, support, and respect may be deciphered from their responses. A limitation of this analysis may also be noted that these expectations are not directly elicited from supervisees, but, as earlier qualified, they are supervisors' perceptions. It is not clear if supervisors' perceptions of supervisees' expectations in any way influence what issues supervisees bring to supervision. If there is a clearly developed supervision contract that excludes some of these expectations, some relevant issues may not appear on the supervision table because either the supervisor or supervisee may perceive them to be outside the relationship. However, we believe that the analysis offers some insights and guidance to both supervisors and supervisees about how and what to prepare and how they can mutually benefit from supervision.

Expectations of Supervisors from Supervisees

We also explored what supervisors expect from supervisees. An interview guiding question was "What do you expect from social workers who come for the supervision?" The analysis of their responses suggested 13 expectations, as presented below. These are discussed according to their own narratives.

Come Prepared and Bring Agenda Items for the Meeting

About one-third of the supervisors expect the supervisee to come prepared for supervision sessions, bring agenda items, and have something to raise, which may be about their work/case, organization, or themselves.

> My expectations are that they'll come prepared, firstly. And that they will have thought about the whatever issues they're going to raise, in some detail. They will also, they'll know what's going to be talked about, so they should have thought about most of it before they come through the door.

> I expect them to be prepared … a little bit of preparation, at least a little bit of forethought into what they're going to be talking about. Rather than just coming and rattling on about, you know.

> My expectation, if someone's coming to prepare for accredited mental health social work status, that they would do the homework and the additional learning I set.

> … I expect them to come with suggestions and ideas and ways to move forward …

> … but I do say it would be helpful if they come to the session with something to talk about. … Pull anything out of a hat … I say it really is helpful if you can bring to the session or the appointment something to talk about, whether it's clients or participants, whatever term they use, to the session. Something that has been troubling you, something that grabbed your attention, that was difficult or great. Something that was really sparkling or rewarding during the week. Something that was difficult with a colleague.

> I expect the supervisee to bring what it is that they want to talk about so I'm clear with them that it's their responsibility to fill the hour, if you like – it might be a particular case or it might be a theme around a number of things they're seeing in cases or it might be around their own sense of performance or efficacy within the workplace or it might be a particular strategy or technique that they want to develop further.

> … I do say to people "Come in with something that you want to pull apart." I say that can be something problematic in a bit of work you're doing with someone, or it could be a practice direction that you don't like that's happening in your career or it could be a set of ethics that it's hard to hold onto in particular spheres of work. Or it might be something you've done that you're really proud of. That we can pull apart and learn from.

> I expect that people coming to supervision come with an ethical or clinical question, that we can work on.

> … I expect them to bring things to supervision whether they be the opportunity to debrief, the opportunity to vent.

The message from the above narratives is that supervisees should come prepared and bring the agenda to the supervision meeting. Supervision is not just about coming and "rattling." Supervisors expect supervisees to think through the issues to be raised, complete any homework or exercises if given in the previous supervision, and come with ideas to move forward. Supervisors have indicated they cover wide-ranging issues from practice with clients to organizational issues and achievements to performance issues. Supervision can also include debriefing and ventilation. It appears that the responsibility of preparing for the supervision rests with supervisees, but supervisors also need to be well prepared.

Follow-Up from the Previous Meeting

Follow-up from previous supervision sessions or continuity in supervision or recapitulation has been discussed earlier. Similarly, a supervisor expects supervisees to follow-up on previous meetings based on the notes taken.

> … I might say to someone – and sometimes I will do this at the beginning if it's something that's kind of pressing – I might say, "You know, last time we mentioned this, and you wanted to go away and think about that or you wanted to try this. I'm interested in how that's gone."

This suggests that supervisors are keen to see the progress made since the previous meeting and expect supervisees to update them on how they have employed some of the suggestions, advice, or discussion from the previous supervision session. This is a useful practice, where it is relevant, and it would be beneficial if both supervisees and supervisors reinforce it.

Talk About Issues from Various Angles

Social workers often work with complex cases and complex solutions, and there are many perspectives to issues and solutions. Two supervisors stated that they expect supervisees to discuss issues from various perspectives.

> I expect them to be about to talk about various, talk about an issue from various angles. If having difficulty with that, it'll be my job to help them think about that, from another point of view.

> "Let me put up on your board a really difficult case and let's work through how we could approach this." So – or "This is a case I've had for months, I'm getting nowhere. Can we talk it through and pick out what I could do differently, or I might have not have – I might have missed?"

Supervision discussion should help the supervisee see and think about the issues from various angles. There is not "only one way" of doing things in social work. Discussing cases from various angles and supervisees leading this process with the aid of the supervisor is likely to enhance supervisees' learning and professional practice.

Discuss Ethical Dilemmas

While each issue has several perspectives and approaches, certain approaches or decisions in social work practice may pose ethical dilemmas. Such dilemmas, for example, may emanate from organizational practices, using discretion in socio-legal settings, and discharge planning and opting between home and an institution. A supervisor shared the following example to demonstrate how the discussion of ethical dilemmas helped supervisees clarify their views about certain practices. Thus, supervisees are expected to bring ethical dilemmas for discussion. Needless to say, supervision is an appropriate platform to discuss ethical dilemmas if supervisees have experienced or observed them in their practice. The supervisor said:

> I like people to come to me with those ideas of talking about ethical dilemmas and identifying ethical dilemmas to think about. Yeah. I think that's something that gets ignored in everyday practice. Yeah. So, I think supervision's a good place to talk about those things.

For example:

> I think what happened was there was a person who worked at the school who had a very close relationship to the family, she was like an SSO at the school, and the family – the parents had disabilities, but they didn't like to identify having disabilities, they didn't want any support from a disability agency. But they had a child and they needed some respite from – they needed to have a break. They didn't like the idea of respite in the disability sense of the term, but they liked the idea of having a babysitter. And because that's what other people use, you know, like regular families use babysitters not respite providers. So, what happened was the school spoke to the disability agency and they decided to tell the family that this woman who knew the child well could provide some babysitting for their child; and the family were happy to accept that. And they were aware that the disability organization was happy to pay her on their behalf, and they accepted that. They knew her and trusted her; they saw it as a babysitting thing. And the child had a break from the family. It was a bit of a hard family. Anyway, this social worker took exception to that, she felt that it was a (pause) the – she felt the service wasn't being honest with the family because they called it babysitting not respite. And she thought that we should – yeah, it was a wrong thing to do. And she thought that the agency was colluding with the school and tricking the family, and she had an ethical problem with that. She aligned to, like, the Stolen Generation. And so, she felt it to be ethically wrong and that we – that the disability agency was at fault in not coming clean and saying it's being funded through the respite program or something. You know. And yeah, so we talked it through. It was an ethical dilemma for her. But in the end, I think she could see that the outcome – the outcome for the child and the family was beneficial, and so she was willing to, sort of, put her issue aside. Yeah.

This example shows how the use of the term babysitting in place of respite caused ethical concerns for the practitioner and how the supervisor clarified it by focusing on the best outcome for the child and family. Other ethical dilemmas in practice may not be as simple as this, and thus supervisees discussing them with supervisors may help clarify and support appropriate decisions or follow practice approaches that do not compromise ethical standards or the interests of the people and communities they work with.

Aware of Issues, Disclose Concerns, Defend Practice, and Disagree

Practitioners need to be thoroughly aware of the presenting issue and systematic ways of addressing it. A supervisor expects supervisees to be aware of issues surrounding a case, disclose concerns and defend their practice, and be able to disagree so as to facilitate rich discussion and better learning.

> I expect them to be aware of some of the issues … some of the dilemmas that they have in decision-making. I expect them to feel … well, I hope that they will feel able to disclose concerns, issues, shortcomings. I also expect them to be able to … well, to defend their practice.

> And I also expect them to … I hope that they would be able to disagree with me. The environment that I try to establish is one of trust, transparency, safety in terms of, "It's okay to disagree with me, please do. Let's do this because I'm learning."

This is an important expectation of supervisors, and it is critical for social work practice. Supervisees should be aware of their practice issues and be able to present all the necessary details in terms of assessment and a problem-solving plan or approach. They should also be able to disclose their concerns, doubts, and shortcomings to the supervisor. At the same time, supervisees should also be able to defend their practice by presenting systematic evidence and disagreeing with the supervisor where appropriate. Supervisors need to create a trustful, transparent, and safe supervision climate to facilitate such contentious discussions and mutual learning from them.

To Be Reflective

As discussed earlier, a reflective approach has a dominant presence in social work practice and professional supervision. Supervisors and supervisees need to be reflective both in practice and supervision. A few supervisors stated that they expect supervisees to be reflective.

> … to be more reflective in that space. So, it's not just a chat …

> … I think I need and want them to be very reflective and very insightful … because I'm like, "Oh it's a core thing of social work to be reflective and insightful [laughing] and if you haven't got that how have you been in social work and how are you with your clients?"

> If someone comes here to spend an hour, an hour and a half reflecting on their work I suppose I expect them to prepare to sit and reflect a bit, which they do in varying degrees.

As reflective practice is core in social work, both supervisors and supervisees need to be reflective in their practice and insightful in the supervision sessions. The above narrative asserts that, without reflective practice, one cannot be in social work and cannot work with clients. "They do in varying degrees" suggests that all supervisees do not engage in reflection to the extent that they should. Dedicated time to reflect on what has been done and how, what is the outcome, and how can it be done better in the future will contribute to both personal and professional development and better service delivery to people and communities.

Vision and Responsibility

While working with individuals, families, groups, and communities, supervisees necessarily focus on the here and now and current problems, though this may require looking into the past in some cases. However, beyond that, a supervisor expects supervisees to have vision for the people they work with and a sense of responsibility.

> … so, I want workers who've got a vision for their cases, and workers who have that sense of their role is critical to the welfare of those kids, and to the families as well, so they have their own sense of responsibility.

These two expectations supervisors have of supervisees of developing vision for their cases and having a sense of responsibility are both meaningful and profound. Beyond solving the presenting problem or crisis, which often challenges and dominates the world of the worker, supervisees' visioning for children and families, perhaps, provides new directions and perspectives. Likewise, developing one's own sense of responsibility helps supervisees to be self-motivated and self-directed. These are excellent attributes for any practitioner.

Take Risks and Have Passion

"A complex interplay between human behavior, emotion, evidence of fact, professional values and organizational systems" (Whittaker & Taylor, 2017, p. 375), in many respects, makes social work practice risk oriented, not risk averse. A supervisor stated that supervisees should be able to take risks and have passion.

> I don't want workers who come and say, shall I put my left foot in front of my right, and don't hold any risk, like you've got, it's a question of human dilemma, and you have to weigh up the information and work out, well, okay, there's risk in this case, but there's enough strengths to enable this family to go on with their life in the community with maybe some supports, we don't have to be going down the legal route, because the legal route always brings with it its own difficulties. So, I want people to have a bit of oomph and passion about them.

How do you develop risk-taking ability and passion in supervisees? Are passion and risk-taking ability positively connected? Supervisees need to develop the skills of "weighing up the information," evidence, facts, and socio-cultural and emotional situations and "work out" the likely harm and gains of impending practice decisions. While weighing the risks, the supervisor suggests looking at the strengths of the family and using them to enable the family to move on with their lives. "Legal routes," perhaps, have more risks than rewards. The supervisor expects supervisees to bring energy and passion to their analysis and action. Supervisors can play a role in this as well.

Punctual

Being punctual is an important and good quality in any professional practice. Supervisees need to be punctual – a supervisor said:

> I expect them to prioritize that time and not make excuses. I expect punctuality and to value that time …

Being unpunctual may send many unintended messages to the supervisor. These may include that the supervisee is uninterested, unprofessional, not serious, irresponsible, does not value the time, and disrespects others' time. Maintaining punctuality is a basic expectation that supervisees should be able to meet by dedicating and prioritizing specific time to supervision sessions. Beyond supervision, it is important to be punctual in all aspects of professional practice.

Take Supervision Seriously and Value It

To value supervision and take it seriously, professional supervision in social work should not be an externally imposed activity; it should be voluntary and come from within. A few supervisors stated that they expect supervisees to value supervision, take it seriously, and be committed to it.

> I think I expect that they're going to take the supervision as seriously as I do. So, I have a high expectation in that regard. If you're going to come to me for supervision let's do it properly or otherwise don't waste my time.

> I expect them to actually, oh well, yeah, I wouldn't work with someone if I didn't think they were valuing the supervision, if they were just doing it because they felt compelled to do it.

> I hope they see the value of supervision, and that it doesn't become the first casualty of a really difficult workload. Because I say to people, you can always put supervision off, but eventually it's one of those things, it's like, you know there's always something else to do than re-paint your house. But eventually the gutters are going to you know rot if you don't. And – so it's the expectation that people are committed to supervision. That they will honor the times that are put in there …

The above narration suggests that supervisors highly value supervision and take it seriously, and they expect the same from supervisees. Supervisors' remarks, such as "let's do it properly or otherwise don't waste my time" and "I wouldn't work with someone if I didn't think they were valuing the supervision, if they were compelled to do it," suggest that supervisors are not interested in perfunctory supervision. A high workload and limited organizational resources should not be an excuse for not arranging professional supervision. Both individual practitioners and organizations should value professional supervision and translate that value into practice. Professional bodies have prescribed mandatory supervision in certain settings, but such requirements become meaningful if individual practitioners and organizations value and commit to supervision. The supervisor's analogy – "eventually the gutters are going to you know rot if you don't" – is a compelling reminder to value professional supervision and take it seriously.

Tell Truth/Be Honest

Under line-management supervision, honest disclosure may often be an issue, though it is much needed for healthy discussion and supervisees' professional development. Whether the same phenomenon exists under non-line-management supervision is not clear. A couple of supervisors said they expect supervisees to tell the truth and be honest.

> I want them to tell me the whole truth, the complete truth, and nothing but the truth, if they've stuffed up, and we all stuff up. I want them, as soon as they realize it, when they have that [intake of breath] minute, to come to me and say, oh, (participant name), I'm a bit worried about this, and I think I might have done the wrong thing.

> Well, I expect them to be open and honest and I expect them if supervision is not working or we're not addressing the issues that they need that they feel that they can be honest about that.

"We all stuff up" is a way of empathizing with supervisees. Supervisors expect supervisees to honestly disclose how they practice, their decisions, concerns, and mistakes. Sharing openly and honestly in supervision and reflecting on it helps to address the issue and improve practice. If sometimes supervision does not provide answers or does not work, supervisees should respectfully communicate this to the supervisors.

Focus on Supervision, Do Not Bring Other Agendas

As discussed in Chap. 4, professional supervision has clear purposes and goals – administration, education, and support – it should be focused accordingly. A supervisor expects supervisees to focus on the supervision and not to mix it up with other agendas.

... and that you know hopefully, that, there aren't other agendas to be worked out at supervision. You know stuff that, you could do at a different time, then don't do it then. Don't bring a whole sheaf of paperwork and say can you sign all this off, and I spend the next half an hour signing stuff off. So, it's that – you've got to focus on what supervision is supposed to be about.

... some people like very focused supervision where they have a number of goals that they want to reach professionally you know and they want, almost coaching with that at supervision.

Supervisees may have a lot of matters on their table, but they should be able to distinguish and prioritize tasks based on the purpose of supervision. They should be able to present an appropriate agenda in the supervision to effectively use the limited supervision time. The supervisors' message is clear; supervisees should not mix up the agenda and should squarely "focus on what supervision is supposed to be about."

Link Supervision to Performance Appraisal

Although professional supervision is and should be beyond key performance indicators (KPIs) and appraisal, they are inextricably linked. A supervisor expects supervisees to connect supervision to their performance appraisal from the perspective of learning, where it is necessary and relevant.

And yeah (pause) also, formally I suppose, we want to get their supervision linked into the performance appraisal format. I see it important to link performance appraisal with the supervision sessions, so that the performance appraisal isn't a tick the boxes form, put it away, like it can be in many organizations. It's about developing a learning plan.

From the perspective of learning and improving practice, a performance appraisal may be discussed as part of professional supervision. The observation above that "the performance appraisal isn't a tick the boxes form" but is treated this way in many organizations needs to be taken seriously. Have line managers created "a tick box" culture due to managerialism and work pressures? Line managers as professional supervisors should ensure that the performance appraisal is a constructive learning and improvement tool. In the case of non-line-management supervision, supervisees may openly discuss any concerns about their performance as per the KPIs and develop strategies with supervisors to help meet the KPIs. The scope of professional supervision is more than the KPIs, but supervisors and supervisees should address the KPIs, if that is the concern, to realize the potential of the broader scope of the professional supervision.

Another view to note is that if the line manager is the professional supervisor, it is important to separate performance management from professional supervision as they involve distinct processes. Mixing the two may pose challenges for creating a climate of trust and openness in supervision if there remains a threat to employment or career development. However, such a separation may result in trust and openness. In the case of organization-supported external supervision, where the supervision is to inform performance management, those links need to be clear to both the supervisee and supervisor, and they need to be written and endorsed by the organization.

Overall, the above-presented analysis of supervisors' expectations from supervisees suggests that these expectations are reasonable and fair. They expect supervisees to come prepared with a clear agenda. Following-up on previous supervision sessions, looking at issues from various perspectives, and being reflective are useful in any professional practice. Further, supervisors expect supervisees to be fully aware of the issues surrounding their cases, raise ethical dilemmas, defend their practice, and constructively disagree with the supervisor to facilitate critical discussion and learning. Supervisors' expectations relating to supervisees developing a vision and their own sense of responsibility; taking risks and having passion; being punctual; valuing supervision and taking it seriously; being truthful, honest, and focused; and meeting performance requirements suggest the implicit presence of qualities and character in professional supervision in social work.

Conclusion and Summary

Analyzing the narratives of supervisors, this chapter has discussed the supervisors' perceptions of supervisees' expectations from the supervisor and supervisors' expectations from supervisees. Discussing and clarifying mutual expectations is critical as it helps identify similarities and differences in expectations, mismatches and contradictions, and additional complementarities in supervision practice. Such an understanding and insight may be employed to consciously reduce differences, match expectations, and add complementarities to enhance the quality of professional supervision for the benefit of supervisees, supervisors, and ultimately of people and communities. It also helps us link to and think about the purpose of supervision discussed in Chap. 4. A comparison of supervisors' expectations from supervisees and supervisors' perceptions of what supervisees expect from the supervision suggests that only four expectations matched. These were being reflective, looking at issues/cases from different perspectives, keeping continuity or follow-up, and being honest. Although the remaining expectations did not match, they were complementary and added further needed perspectives to the supervision. Supervisees' expectations of support, space for ventilation, receiving direction/advice, problem-solving, learning more, and counseling from the supervision are apt. Similarly, supervisors' expectations of preparing well, being punctual and serious, raising ethical dilemmas, awareness of issues and defending practice, having a vision, sense of own responsibility, passion, risk orientation, and a clear focus on the part of supervisees should help both supervisors and supervisees to prepare well for the supervision. The analysis found these complementarities, but not contradictions. Although without directly referring to virtue/quality development of supervisees, supervisors' responses suggest several virtue elements such as reflective practice, having vision and responsibility, taking risks and having passion, valuing time and supervision, committing to supervision, learning, and being truthful and honest. It would be interesting and useful to further explore whether and how supervisors develop these and similar qualities in supervisees.

As pointed out earlier, supervisor and supervisee expectations vis-à-vis the supervision contract need some consideration. Often, a supervision contract, depending upon how it is written, may not cover all expectations unless there is a proviso to amend it as needed. As already qualified, another important limitation is that supervisees' expectations are supervisors' perceptions of what supervisees expect. Further research may be needed to directly interview supervisees to understand their expectations, which may match our analyzed expectations and add additional expectations. Future research may also look into expectations of line and non-line-management supervisors and employed and self-employed supervisees, including in private practice. Overall, we hope that the discussion of these mutual expectations may lead to better professional supervision practice. The next chapter will discuss the issues posed in the supervision.

References

Munson, C. E. (2002). Practitioners' reactions to supervisor styles. In C. E. Munson (Ed.), *Handbook of clinical social work supervision* (pp. 135–148). Taylor and Francis.

Peters, S., Clarebout, G., Aertgeerts, B., Michels, N., Pype, P., Stammen, L., & Roex, A. (2020). Provoking a conversation around students' and supervisors' expectations regarding workplace learning. *Teaching and Learning in Medicine, 32*(3), 282–293. https://doi.org/10.108 0/10401334.2019.1704764

Whittaker, A., & Taylor, B. (2017). Editorial: Understanding risk in social work. *Journal of Social Work Practice, 31*(4), 375–378. https://doi.org/10.1080/02650533.2017.1397612

Chapter 8
Issues Posed in Professional Supervision

Introduction

The chapter discusses some of the supervisees' issues and needs presented in the supervision as narrated by supervisors. In Chap. 1, our conceptualization of professional supervision in social work included people and communities, agency supervisee and supervisor, professional attributes, and organizations and institutions. The issues discussed in this chapter revolve around these areas. The guiding question posed to supervisors was "What issues and problems do supervisees often present in supervision?" Their responses have been categorized into nine broad areas. According to supervisors, supervisees often present issues relating to the organizational context and clients and practice. The other related topics of discussion include reflection, maintaining boundaries, competency and skill development, social work theories, personal issues, and the recognition of good work. These categories appear similar to an earlier section on the main theme or core content of professional supervision discussed in Chap. 6. However, in this chapter, these issues not only confirm the consistency in responses but also elaborate some of those themes. The nine issues discussed in the chapter point out that supervision is not just about issues; it can and should include good practices and achievements.

Issues Supervisees Present in the Supervision

Issues Relating to the Organizational Context

In Chap. 3, we discussed a range of organizations, from GOs to NGOs, and observed that organizations play a critical role in social work practice. If social workers have issues with the organization, those issues need to be understood and addressed. As

M. Pawar, A. W. (Bill) Anscombe, *Enlightening Professional Supervision in Social Work*, https://doi.org/10.1007/978-3-031-18541-0_8

discussed in Chap. 6, working with organizational issues appears to be a dominant theme in supervision. Many supervisors stated that supervisees often bring organizational issues to the supervision, whether it is working with structures, teams, or staff members or value conflicts. The issues relating to the organizations are presented under four themes: change management and structural issues, value conflicts, shortage of staff and work-related stress, and staff-related issues.

Change Management and Structural Issues

Often workers find themselves in a helpless situation as it is difficult to change organizational systems and structures on the one hand and operating hierarchy on the other. It is challenging for supervisors to help supervisees navigate within such systems and yet bring change to clients' lives. Supervisors said:

> … the first thing I'd say is it's never the clients that are the problem, or rarely. That's not true. Sometimes people will come with really complex clients they want to talk about, but that tends to be easier for people. The tricky conversations are the ones that are usually giving people more angst, are the things that relate to their organization.

> So, sometimes it's the relationships in teams, sometimes it's the hierarchy and the management structure that's creating problems, and then sometimes it's the work context or the environment. So, when there's massive change going on in the organization and some people struggling very much to cope with the changes.

> … so, in a lot of the time it's dealing with the frustrations and the limitations imposed by organizational factors.

> But the theme does appear to be more a structural type of dilemma, in terms of systems. In terms of referring people on and not being able to do much with the client.

> … certainly, bring up issues around departmental policy and government legislation and the impact that that's having upon the client. I think about issues that they raise, probably the majority of them would be around the departmental issues which we don't have a lot of control over. We don't make the legislation. We enforce it, but we don't make it, but we can influence it and I think that's where I often talk with them in supervision about how do we as social workers influence change and the best way to do that is through case studies. The best way to do that is to empower our customers to talk with their local MPs and the like…

Supervisors' observations of supervisees' "angst," "frustrations," and "limitations" suggest that many supervisees often find themselves helpless against imposing organizational structures, unable to cope with change management due to policy and legislative changes. A sense of professional guilt may also be apparent when workers refer people or clients rather than work with them. Supervisees at the grassroots level often have no control over the massive organizational structures. Under this seemingly cloudy situation, discussion with the supervisor may help. Social workers can still have an influence by documenting cases and empowering and encouraging customers to approach lawmakers and policy decision-makers.

Value Conflicts

Value conflicts and ethical dilemmas are not uncommon in social work practice. There are personal, professional, organizational, and people/community/cultural values, and they may not be congruent all the time. Value conflicts in silence can cause stress and inner suffering for some supervisees and practitioners in general. The following responses show how workers experience value conflicts emanating from the organization, community and the cultural context, and their own self and how supervisors discuss them.

> … the one person who I was talking about comes from the public service. And that has conflicted with her values around social work. So, one of the things that has really helped us is going back to the AASW website around ethics and values. And that has really helped her to see oh, this is why I'm having this conflict. How can I work with this in a way without knowing that I cannot change what I'm working with? So, how can I use my skills, my values, my morals in working with the people that I'm working with and know that I can't be the change agent for this organization. But I can maybe be the change agent for the people that I'm, and the supporter for the people that I'm working with. And maybe even, that might have a flow-on effect for the people above me. And that had a significant impact on her stress levels.

> How do you hold your own values when there are questions of judgment that you may or may not agree with? So, there are some of these dilemmas. I mean, I had a situation. A worker was very distressed at one stage when I was a team leader because she had found out that one of the children in her caseload … an Aboriginal child had actually been taken into a community and had been circumcised and she was just absolutely … she couldn't accept that we weren't doing anything about that issue, that we weren't actually taking the parents to court for whatever, that we weren't actually raising all up in arms.

> So, it was a difficult conversation to have at one level, but it was a wonderful opportunity to talk to the worker about values, ethics, cultural issues, self-determination, the importance of community, the importance of walking between two cultures, ethnic issues as well as their own values and how you need to manage professional and personal values. How do you manage information? How do you record information? And this was an interesting case because she had to make a file note in relation to what she had found and we reviewed the file note in terms of how did her biases, her personal biases, how were they reflected in the way in which she wrote and what would the meaning of the language that she was using have for the different players that would actually be impacted by that documentation.

> … our people deserve as much professionalism as anyone. Why should we lower our standards, or our bar, or why shouldn't we have very good transparent practices, and follow our code of ethics, and that sort of thing, no matter where we're going in terms of administration, and a whole range of different things. So, I think that's one of the things that we, as social workers, can bring in.

A good deal of learning may occur from the above narrations. When we experience or sense value conflicts, it is good to revisit professional codes of ethics and identify the source of conflict as a first step. Where relevant, reframing from the change agent of organizations to the change agent of people and communities and its likely flow-on effect on organizations is a good guidance. When experiencing value dilemmas, holding onto professional values and looking at all stakeholders' value perspectives, keeping in mind people's and the community's interests, may provide further insights. It is also important to examine how value biases are reflected in one's own writing and the impact such writing is likely to have on stakeholders. Supervisors recommend sticking to professionalism, standards, and transparency.

Shortage of Staff and Work Stress

Due to managerialism, rationalization, and outsourcing, many organizations have reduced staff members, and, as a consequence, other staff members have to pick up the extra work, which often creates work pressure and stress. In such organizational contexts, supervisees often bring issues relating to staff shortages, stress, and burnout to supervision sessions.

> I guess it's still in the establishing phase of working out what's best practice. But under that, but in that same phase there's actually a lot of stress amongst other co-workers that aren't handling the clientele referral, there's not enough on the ground to do the amount of work that's presented. So, it's a lot of burnout happening, at a very early phase.

> … this guy was experiencing, battling, or working through his caseload, but also how does he deal with waiting lists. And if there's a need, immediate need, then if they've been told that they've gotta wait two weeks, then, it's working out a solution as to how might they prioritize clients. So, then there isn't such a long wait. So that's a constant organizational challenge that, that comes up a lot.

> Change happens slowly, but in the meantime the co-workers are going on stress leave. If one's away, then the rest of them have to pick up the load. They're already …

Even under normal circumstances, in some settings such as hospitals, child protection, and domestic violence, staff members experience more than usual stress due to crises they often deal with. When organizations implement rationalization strategies, staff members are pressured to do more with fewer resources, often under demoralizing conditions. The above examples of staffing shortages, dilemmas of attending to urgent needs against long waiting lists, and picking up the work of staff members who suddenly go on leave show the kind of issues and stress supervisees are dealing with in organizations and the kind of support they need from supervisors. These issues are also closely connected to the self-care and safety of workers discussed in Chap. 6 as one of the core areas of professional supervision.

Staff and Team Interpersonal Issues

As an employee, a social work practitioner, or supervisor or manager, how one maintains interpersonal and collegial relationships with coworkers, teams, and interprofessional groups is important for a conducive working climate within an organization. Many supervisors stated that supervisees present issues relating to working with colleagues and teams and sometimes supervisors and managers.

There's been staff issues between how different members of staff have got on with different members of staff that I've had to ... that's always interesting.

But if we're talking about issues, sometimes I've had issues where people have brought in, I'm struggling with that other staff member, or ... does that make sense.

The core content and common theme is around staff-to-staff problems.

So, peers, yeah. Working in teams, working in organizations. The organizational stuff dominates, and people will say, most supervisees would say "Oh the client work's a breeze. It's dealing with my colleagues that are the problem"

But sometimes it's about team dynamics. Sometimes it's about managing another staff member and some disharmony that's happening in their team.

They often talk to me about issues with their supervisor, so if I'm talking to an entry level social worker who might be having difficulties with their own supervisor, so again this might be a more informal supervision session. They might talk with issues around their peers.

Supervisors' descriptions of supervisees "struggling with a staff member," having "staff-to-staff-problems," and "difficulties with supervisor" suggest the experience of interpersonal relationship issues with workplace colleagues due to whatever reasons. This can significantly impact the health of supervisees, employees, and the quality of work performed. Honestly discussing these issues in professional supervision meetings may help supervisors and supervisees work together to deal with such issues.

The above narrations relating to organizational structural issues, value conflicts, staff shortages and stress, and interpersonal issues have a lot of loaded content, and each issue has much to discuss. It is a real struggle for supervisees and workers in general to put up with an organization that they cannot change or feel they cannot change. Living with value conflicts and contradictions can cause and build stress in workers in the long run. Change management, restructuring, line manager, colleagues, team members, budget cuts, and work stress have become the dominant discussion topics in supervision. The view that "working with clients is a breeze, but the organization is a problem" suggests the need for practitioners to develop skills and strategies to work in organizations. This area certainly calls for innovative approaches so that workers can work effectively rather than resentfully.

Issues Relating to Clients/Practice

As discussed in Chap. 6, working with people and clients and, generally, social work practice issues are one of the core areas of professional supervision, though their dominance has waned as earlier indicated. Supervisors stated that supervisees bring to the supervision issues relating to clients and practice, which include personal caring issues of clients, complex cases, community practice, making decisions, recovery, and work stress. Some of these are illustrated below by supervisors.

Personal Care Issues Relating to Clients

Personal care issues, though they may appear simple tasks, can be very challenging in some settings such as mental health, nursing homes, aged care facilities, disability, and home-based care as they relate to real life, day-to-day needs and issues. The following example shows how personal hygiene can be a critical issue for certain people or clients.

> For example, when we're dealing with people who've got a severe mental illness, personal hygiene always suffers. Caring for themselves and caring for their accommodation. So, we often come thinking about, 'How do I get him to have a shower? How do I get him to tidy up his room? How do I do that, making it something that he wants to do rather than something I'm trying to persuade him to do.' So, it's strategies about getting people to be motivated and that type of thing. The issue about motivation, but not being directive.

Arranging personal hygiene care for those who cannot take care of themselves is one challenge for supervisees if there are no resources to do it (e.g., organizations may not employ adequate staff members to organize care and support). Another challenge is people not able to care for themselves for various reasons (e.g., mental health, drugs and alcohol, people under supervision such as probation and parole). For both types of challenges, different strategies may need to be discussed in the supervision meetings. The former may require working with organizations, invoking compliance with set standards, and, as stated by the supervisor, the latter may involve "strategies to motivate people without being directive." It is also important to consider the impact of work health and safety regulations on the practice of social work. For example, some organizations require a home risk assessment before a worker visits to undertake tasks. This is particularly relevant for service providers in the disability and aged care sectors. The issue is often that the homes are unsafe as a workplace; therefore, services can either be denied or ameliorated so as to not have any impact. These are serious practice issues, and there may not be readymade solutions. This highlights the importance of supervisees and supervisors discussing such issues during supervision meetings to try to find strategies to solve the issues.

Complex Case Issues

The following example shows supervisees presenting complex cases for discussion in the supervision. A supervisor narrated:

> … a young child who had an intellectual disability and he lived with his father – I think he was removed from his mother's care when he was maybe five and placed with his father when he was about seven. And he was about nine at the time of this session. And his father – the social worker was really struggling with ways to engage with the father and felt that he was having to do everything for the father, and include – you know, any intervention that he had with the father there would be no follow-up on the father's side. So he was really struggling to get the father on board with Centrelink, and you know, healthy food for the child, and he understood that there was a lot of external factors that were impacting on the father. And he had – he was an alcoholic himself and so he had some impairment himself, and the child's mother was also financially abusing him – and his older son was also financially

abusing him. And so it was a complex group of difficulties. Yeah. So I guess he – we talked about some strategies to maybe harness the father's energy, and yeah.

But I think there's also – a lot of the time the issues that arise are about the intractability of some of the problems. They're intergenerational, they're entrenched, there's very little that can be done, systemically to help. So there's – often people feel hopeless and helpless.

Sometimes it's just, well, this is the situation, that the family are resistant, or the family present as aggressive, that's a big concern, and how you work through aggression, how you work through an attitude of the parents being dismissive of child protection's involvement. I often find that workers will come when they're stuck, as well, but I like them, even within that stuckness to think of, well, what could happen, and sometimes workers will come to me if they are in that dilemma, and it's six of one, half-a-dozen of the other, which way should they go?

We'll often talk about particular case studies, so particular individual customers and their circumstances and how could I, in understanding their circumstances better, how could I then offer a suggestion as to what they might be able to go away and do with that particular customer because again, keeping the customer as the center of our work and everything that we do, it's about how can we better improve their circumstance?

How do you engage with clients or people who do not want to engage? Supervisees often work with "intractable, intergenerational, and entrenched issues in which people feel hopeless and helpless." Sometimes clients, people, or families resist, turn aggressive, and dismiss the agency's involvement, and supervisees feel "stuck." Understanding a range of factors and circumstances impacting the client or person is a beginning step in the helping process. The supervisor emphasizes customer-centered work and improving their circumstances. The discussion of such cases in the supervision shows the significance and necessity of professional supervision for supervisees.

Community Practice

As observed elsewhere, professional supervision in social work is often dominated by clinical practice, working with individuals and families. It is less common for social workers in community practice to seek professional supervision. However, the following example shows a social worker engaged in community practice activities posing questions to the supervisor.

I'm working with a woman who's working, who's just begun a community development work, community development role at the moment and she came in after a month and she said, "I don't know what I'm doing." And I was able to say, "Well that's what most people say when they're doing a community development-type role. You've got to sit in it for a while. Make relationships, build networks." And so, we talked about the kinds of relationship that, the kind of networks that she's building, the kind of relationships forming that she's doing in the organization and in the community and by the time we had the conversation, she realized that she's doing quite a lot. It's just hard to put a tick in boxes.

In community development work, the feeling of "I don't know what I'm doing" appears familiar, particularly when one is new to the community or at the beginning stage of the community development work. The supervisor's empathetic response, advice to "sit in it for a while," and discussion on building relationships and networks made the supervisee feel better about the work. It appears that more work needs to be done to offer professional supervision to community practitioners.

Making Decisions

Making decisions in practice-related work is one of the important issues supervisees bring to supervision. Despite legal and procedural guidelines, codes of conduct, and ethical guidelines, making decisions in certain practice circumstances or settings is challenging, particularly where ethical dilemmas are present. As discussed in Chap. 7, supervisors expect the supervisee to bring ethical dilemmas and decision-making issues to the supervision. A supervisor said:

> Some of the dilemmas that staff come through is how can they make decisions in the best interest of the child when they may have limited information to do that. The issue … the self-determination issue is a really difficult one for some staff to deal with. The issue of authority, the skillful use of authority as to … you know, once you knock on the door and you say that you're from the department that people already create a view as to who you are, what you are there to do and they respond to you in a certain way.

Decision-making and determining the child's best interest are difficult when limited information is available. In a setting such as child protection, there are many challenges to self-determination. The agency social workers represent has an impact on the views of parents and families, and that also influences the disclosure of information and decision and how people and communities perceive that decision. As it is difficult to make decisions in some practice contexts, professional supervision is a good platform to discuss and reflect on decision-making.

Recovery Focus

Depending upon the organizational context, often the issue of supervision changes. Due to the nature of a particular agency, for one supervisor, the main issue posed in their supervision was the recovery focus. The supervisor said:

> … (pause) The recurrent theme is always the issues and the problems that I'm having at the moment. There's always a theme about that. Currently what I see is (pause) the theme of, what we call, the recovery focus. That's related specifically to this agency, which we drive them pretty hard, that philosophy, so that theme comes up pretty often.

In organizations that are engaged in working with mental health issues, the recovery focus is emphasized at the policy level, but often workers find it challenging to translate it into practice—perhaps due to a lack of resource commitment and support from the organization or ignorance of it at the top management level. Perhaps this is why the supervisor stated, "we drive them pretty hard," and the recovery philosophy is a frequent subject of discussion. This also shows that supervisors can help the agency address the committed agenda. Similarly, the nature of the organization, whether it is child welfare or protection, a women's refuge, or school social work, determines and influences the issue posed in the supervision.

Client and Practice-Related Stress

In the organizational context, work-related stress due to staff shortages, work pressure, and staff relations issues has already been discussed. Client or practice-related stress is about working with challenging cases and risky situations, deadlines, vicarious trauma, burnout, and related issues. Some supervisees raise these issues in supervision. A supervisor said:

> … So, usually leading up to that at no matter what level there are great – there are a lot of issues of stress that you'll be talking about, and how they manage that and, you know as I was saying before the building of personal resiliency and stuff like that.

This practice-related stress cannot be avoided. It is the nature and part of social work practice in some settings. Most social work practitioners experience stress to different degrees. Professional supervision provides a critical platform to ventilate experiences of stress, and as such providing support to practitioners is one of its main purposes. As stated by the supervisor, two approaches are important and useful: on the one hand, it is important to develop strategies to manage stress and, on the other, to build personal resilience to cope with the stress.

Overall, issues relating to clients and practice are varied and many, and it is not practical to cover them all. For example, we have discussed challenges of personal care issues relating to clients, intergenerational and entrenched complex cases, supervision support for workers engaged in community practice, the recovery focus, and stress emanating from practice with people. All these and more are critical issues for professional supervision.

Reflection on Practice

Supervisees seeking reflection on their practice in supervision is normal and expected; not doing so is an issue. As discussed in Chap. 6, supervisees and supervisors have identified reflective practice as a process, an essential element, and the core content in professional supervision. That spirit is well reflected here. Reflective practice is a framework that supervisors and supervisees can use for any aspect of social work practice. Some supervisors stated that their supervision focuses on reflective practice, which helps supervisees improve practice, gain clarity, and find answers on their own.

> I guess that's my hidden agenda, is looking at best practice. When you think about it. Is looking at, 'What is it that we could have done differently? Or were you happy with the way that, how that unfolded? Or was there anything else you could have done that would have changed the outcome?' I always like to try and stimulate their brain, try, and look from a different perspective.

...they don't work out as we had hoped and how great it is to reflect it on "Could I have done something better" but also being able to have that ability to say, "I did the best that I could in that situation and the outcome isn't dependent on me."

And that's not to say that we don't talk about clients. I didn't mean to minimize that, but those conversations tend to be much easier and they're more reflective about, you know, "This is what I did. I'm not sure. Could I have done it differently?" A bit of unpacking of that sort of stuff.

And sometimes it's - I mean, sometimes it's just the need to talk about a difficult case and just to feel that they're – a difficulty that they're having is shared almost. I mean, sometimes they come to an answer themselves just in talking through, it helps them to formulate a strategy of where they're heading, it helps them to gain some clarity in where they're heading by talking about it. And often that's the case; it's the tricky clients.

To employ a reflective practice framework, supervisees and supervisors should understand what reflective practice is. A supervisor said that reflective practice "stimulates the brain" and helps look at practice from different perspectives. It also helps to focus on doing better and best practice. Simply talking about the case, actions and inactions, and consequences sometimes helps develop clarity and new strategies. Repeated mention of reflective practice in supervision by supervisors suggests that it is used as a common framework in supervision.

Maintaining Boundaries/Rural Context

In Chap. 6, maintaining boundaries was stated as one of the main themes of supervision. Many supervisees bring issues relating to maintaining boundaries about their clients' work and not getting impacted by their trauma. In the rural and remote context, maintaining boundaries becomes more complex and delicate.

And how the hell do, "I'm going to put some boundaries around this so that it doesn't swallow me up."
... in rural practice and regional practice there's a very complex interdependency between community and the practitioner. So, a lot of the questions in rural practice, from rural and remote social workers, are about how do I manage these really complex networks? How do I manage secrets? It might be an agency secret, or you know, change in practice. You can't talk about other people.
How do I manage going to a community event and seeing, you know, the person I've just been counseling? How do I put boundaries around that? So, there's a lot of boundary work.

As supervisor of someone in a remote or regional area, you have to understand their need to be able to put quite rigid boxes around different parts of their life because of the nuanced interdependencies and the fact that you, you know, you might be seeing someone, and she might be the mother of your daughter's schoolteacher. Or something like that.

And I think that that actually requires a different skill set, much more focus in supervision on those interdependencies in the rural environment, much more about context. Much more.
It becomes a hindrance in rural practice ... was the really difficult situations social workers can get in to through no fault of their own, because of family connections, children's connections.

> And also, you know, if there's not many people in your town and you're single, it can be hard because there's not going to be much separation about meeting people.

> And then we followed up with a conversation of the kinds of boundaries, how she was going to protect herself from some of the enormity of the trauma and its impact upon her …

Social work, as a relationship-based profession, must maintain boundaries. Social work codes of ethics clearly outline how these relationship boundaries should be maintained and not crossed (e.g., AASW, 2020; NASW, 2021). On the one hand, social workers strive to form honest, trustful professional relationships with clients and families, and, in response to that, clients and families place their trust, form relationships, and disclose sensitive or personal information. However, this occurs only one way, from client to social worker, and thus already the boundary and the relationship logic have an imbalance. Due to the dynamic nature of the work and contexts (e.g., interprofessional links, rural areas, Pugh, 2007), there are possibilities of compromising these boundaries, and some contexts may be confusing for workers as there are negotiable (greeting in other contexts, appropriate and controlled disclosure of a worker's personal details, sharing food and drink, taking calls, or meeting out of office hours) and non-negotiable boundaries (money, discrimination, substantial gift, preferential treatment, public disclosure, irrelevant questions, and sexual relations; see O'Leary et al., 2013, p. 144; Reamer, 2021), and mix up between the two is possible and must be avoided. What is also noteworthy in the above narration is maintaining an emotional boundary.

Work Performance Issues

As identified in Chap. 6, some supervisees may feel that they cannot work according to the expected standards or are keen to improve their work performance levels to meet key performance indicators of their organizations. One supervisor stated that supervisees bring up the issue of improving their work performance.

> … you know, that at some level they feel like, "I'm not doing a good enough job" or "I've not done this particularly challenging case and it didn't work out as well as I had hoped and, you know, I wish I had done better." And so, wrapping our heads around the fact that in the kind of work that social workers do, there's always going to be situations where things don't work out well.

How social workers and supervisees feel about their work performance is a relative and individualized phenomenon. A worker or supervisor may do a very good job but still feel inadequate in their performance. Another worker may do an average job but feel great about their performance. Supervisors have a critical role in identifying which one is the case. In the case of the former, reassuring the good work done and building confidence may be needed. In the latter case, carefully examining and discussing strengths and areas for improvement may be needed. In both cases, it is also important to reinforce doing their best in the given situation and carefully detaching from the outcome. Feelings of inadequacy in work performance are closely linked to knowledge and skills deficiencies or a mismatch between tasks and skill sets. As discussed below, enhancing the required competencies and skills may help address the issue.

Skill Development

Acquiring knowledge, developing skills, and gaining experience are all connected to developing competencies. A supervisor stated one of the issues supervisees often discuss during supervision is their skill development.

> … I think the issues that come up a lot of the time are, people being concerned that they – that there is some skill they need to have to be able to resolve an issue. So, it's about, you know the acquisition of skills, skills development. You know some sort of critical feedback, how they learn to – they want you to listen to what they're saying and help them you know say unpick a really tricky problem.

Depending upon the specific or specialized task, some organizations provide or arrange training programs for employees to orient them to the necessary knowledge and skills to do their jobs. Based on the discussion and their own assessment, supervisors may also recommend knowledge and skill development in specific areas. In both these cases, the suggestion to acquire knowledge and skills comes externally to the supervisee. However, when supervisees identify their need to develop knowledge and skills in required areas and seek guidance and support from supervisors to pursue it, they are internally driven and motivated to improve their competencies and practice. Thus, supervisors can play a critical role in stimulating the internal drive of supervisees to acquire skills and improve practice.

Theoretical Frameworks

Generally, significant theoretical inputs are provided to students during their graduate and postgraduate studies in the tertiary sector. Post-qualifying, once they become fully-fledged professional practitioners, most practitioners are busily engaged in practice issues and find very little time to read and gain further theoretical understanding unless they are asked to undergo relevant training programs. Professional supervision provides an important opportunity to fill this gap. A few supervisors stated that some supervisees were keen to discuss theories during supervision.

> They'll often want to talk to me about perhaps some philosophical ... sorry, some frameworks. So, with (supervisee) he might want to talk about different frameworks, or different parts of social work practice, what might unpack different things, so might unpack a gender analysis as opposed to a human rights analysis, or how do we blend the two. So, we'll often do ... have conversations about theory.

> … Sometimes people are wanting to maybe reflect a little bit more deeply about theoretical underpinnings or even what they're bringing to their practice.

Professional practice bereft of theories or theoretical frameworks can be problematic, though it should not bind the practice. There is a seamless connection between theory and practice and practice and theory. Therefore, it is important to guard against the tendency to focus on practice by ignoring theory. There are often new and complex practice situations that defy old theories, but there are also certain practice issues that require examining from different theoretical perspectives and frameworks to gain further insights and identify causes and effects so as to think about appropriate solutions. Supervisees and supervisors discussing theoretical frameworks vis-à-vis practice issues—whether it is gender analysis, human rights, needs analysis, race, systems theories, patriarchy, therapies, or cultural dimensions—may open up new insights and perspectives.

Personal Issues

In Chap. 6, balancing work and private issues as one of the supervision essentials was discussed. It is further confirmed by supervisors that supervisees often raise personal issues during supervision.

> Oh, as I said personal issues, how that's impacting on the ... how personal issues are impacting on the practice.

> It might be personal health things that are occurring – how to manage that, career decisions, which again, is potentially – if this is external supervision and is working well – it's a good place to at least test out some of that before you go to your boss and say, "I want to look at six months' leave without pay" or whatever. So, there will certainly be those sorts of decisions, conversations. There will be professional conversations that, "I'm not sure that I'm cut out for social work. What the hell am I doing?"

Supervisors discussing personal issues as shared or raised by supervisees may offer needed support to supervisees. As narrated above, these may range from personal health issues to professional career decisions. "Am I cut out for social work?" and "What the hell am I doing?" are serious career questions, and supervisors have a critical role in helping supervisees to make appropriate decisions. Work impacting health or health or family situations impacting work are critical issues at one level, but the question of "am I suitable for social work?" takes the issue to another level. Supervisors suggest that supervisees may test ideas with external supervisors, so they can feel confident to discuss the same with line managers, if and when appropriate. Since supervisees' personal situations are posed as important issues in supervision, as discussed earlier, supervisors may need to carefully consider and balance work and personal issues during supervision.

Recognizing Good Work

Professional supervision in social work need not and should not always be issue or problem focused. A lot of learning and improvement can occur by reviewing and reflecting on good work and achievements and replicating good practices. A supervisor stated that supervision does not focus only on issues; supervisees discuss good work done and achievements.

> It's not always issues, because I really do encourage people to bring something into supervision that we can celebrate, so it's things that we can celebrate. And that's lovely work. To grow people's sense of proficient competence through what they're doing well.

> I mean it's not all bad, don't get me wrong. They often bring a lot of very positive things to supervision as well ... we do bring a lot of positive things to supervision as well.

Just as we often learn from mistakes, we can also learn from recognizing and reflecting on good practices. Appreciation, positive reinforcement, hope building, and encouragement can play an important role in coping with stress, building confidence, and approaching issues with optimism. Supervisors encouraging supervisees to celebrate achievements and explicitly recognizing good work done may help supervisees in many ways. Supervisees may feel emotionally better, emboldened, and enthusiastic and may eagerly approach subsequent practice issues with confidence and proficiency.

Conclusion and Summary

The analysis of supervisors' responses regarding issues supervisees present during supervision shows that supervisees and practitioners experience difficulties and dilemmas while working in organizational contexts, both people in organizations and organizational structures. The organizational policies and procedures, conflicting values, a shortage of staff members, and interpersonal issues can affect the organizational climate and increase the stress levels of supervisees, particularly in the context of organizations following the approaches of managerialism. The organizational issues appear to be more challenging to them than the issues they experience while working with people or clients or in their practice. Practice issues included personal caring for people and clients, complex cases, making critical decisions, and work-related stress. Other notable issues relate to developing competency, in terms of skills and knowledge, and maintaining boundaries. Sometimes, supervisees bring personal issues to supervision, and it is important to attend to them in a balanced way. As in previous chapters, the use of a reflective practice framework is common. Supervisees discussing different theoretical frameworks relevant to their practice issues help them have different insights and perspectives. It is emphasized that supervision is not just issue or problem oriented; good things, good aspects of the work, and achievements are also discussed. The nine issues discussed in this chapter are consistent with and confirm most of the core themes and content of supervision presented in Chap. 6. They are also consistent with the purposes and goals of supervision discussed in Chap. 4. Three content areas—modeling values, professional identity and learning/training, and the future—discussed in Chap. 6 were not reflected in the supervision issues discussed in this chapter. Three additional issues added in this chapter—skill development, theoretical framework, and recognizing good work—were not identified as core content of supervision in Chap. 6. However, together they provide further insights for supervisors and supervisees to reflect on supervision practice. The supervisors' responses did not make any explicit reference to the development of qualities or character of supervisees, though these may be implicit in their narrations. For example, one supervisor stated, "working with client issues is a breeze," which suggests a virtue/quality that they enjoy working with clients or are passionate about it. Similarly, referring to "best practice, making relationships, keeping the customer at the center of work, focus on understanding, harnessing energy, transparent practices, holding on to values and change agent for the people, empowering customers, and recognizing good work" suggests the presence of supervisors' virtues and qualities in their work. The next chapter will discuss the use of concepts and theories by supervisors.

References

AASW. (2020). *Australian Association of Social Workers Code of Ethics 2020*. AASW.
NASW. (2021). *Code of Ethics of the National Association of Social Workers*. Accessed on 2 Feb 2022 from https://www.socialworkers.org/About/Ethics/Code-of-Ethics/Code-of-Ethics-English
O'Leary, P., Tsui, M.-S., & Ruch, G. (2013). The boundaries of the social work relationship revisited: Towards a connected, inclusive and dynamic conceptualization. *British Journal of Social Work, 43*(1), 135–153. https://doi.org/10.1093/bjsw/bcr181
Pugh, R. (2007). Dual relationships: Personal and professional boundaries in rural social work. *British Journal of Social Work, 37*(8), 1405–1423. https://doi.org/10.1093/bjsw/bcl088
Reamer, F. G. (2021). *Boundary issues and dual relationships in the human services*. Columbia University Press.

Chapter 9
Concepts and Theories Employed in Supervision

Introduction

The main purpose of this chapter is to explore concepts or theories used by supervisors in professional supervision. Although the meaning of concepts, models, and theories are different, some use them interchangeably. They can be or are interconnected as, generally, concepts (ideas, viewpoints) are considered at the beginning stage of model or theory building, and models (tentative patterns of relationships) are built on confirmed concepts, and theories (logically interrelated and verifiable propositions to explain a phenomenon) are developed based on confirmed concepts and models (Scott, 1988; Homberg et al., 2019). However, the terms, concepts, models, or theories were used loosely in this research to give flexibility to supervisors to respond, and we use them interchangeably in this chapter. The concepts and theories discussed here are similar to the models of supervision discussed in Chap. 4, and the analysis presented in this chapter confirms that some supervisors use those models to offer supervision, while some use other concepts and theories.

To understand what concepts and theories supervisors use, we asked them the following question: What conceptual or theoretical approaches do you use in your supervision? The analysis of their responses showed the use of 24 concepts or theoretical approaches in supervision. These included reflective practice, adult learning, task focused, systems theory, postmodern, strengths-based, anti-oppressive, social constructionist, feminist, narrative therapy, family therapy, sensorimotor psychotherapy, psychodynamic, cognitive behavior therapy, and an eclectic approach. They also referred to authors and trainers like Kadushin, Middleman and Goldberg, Margaret Morrell and Kolb, and their frameworks. Accordingly, the supervisors' responses are presented below with brief comments. It may be noted that our purpose is not to elaborate on these concepts and theories but to develop an understanding of what theories supervisors use to supervise supervisees. The analysis shows that supervisors use a range of supervision models presented in Chap. 4 and beyond,

M. Pawar, A. W. (Bill) Anscombe, *Enlightening Professional Supervision in Social Work*, https://doi.org/10.1007/978-3-031-18541-0_9

and those frameworks are closely connected to social work practice. Some of these concepts and theories are drawn from social casework or clinic practice models, whereas some are from broad educational and adult learning models. Most of the supervisors seem to use these models in combination or by mixing other ideas. Finally, the chapter ends with a conclusion and summary, emphasizing the significance and usefulness of these concepts, models, and theories in supervision.

Conceptual and/or Theoretical Approaches Used in Supervision

Reflective Practice/Critical Reflection Framework

As discussed several times in previous chapters, reflective practice or critical reflection is a common theme and basic principle, tool, or framework in professional supervision. It is frequently referred to in social work education, field education, and practice. The following narrations show that some supervisors use a critical reflection framework, including raising questions and probing in-depth in their supervision.

> So, they're talking about their clients or their participants, and they're reflecting on what has come up for them, what has been difficult. And they're reflecting on that. And using whatever has come up for them and it's just a natural process. So, it's not like you're stopping and saying, "Okay, let's roleplay that. What, let's have a look at a case scenario. What, so what do you think would happen here?" Rather we're just saying, "Okay, so do you feel comfortable talking about what's happening here. I noticed your leg is jiggling a little bit there. What's that about? Do you feel comfortable telling me about that?" And they just go with it. They don't feel uncomfortable, 'cause we have that relationship, that rapport.
>
> The structure, it's a more pragmatic kind of thing, I like this sort of, (pause) people to be able to talk about the whole situation, under those various headings. What's been good? What's not been good? And particularly issues. What might be other strategies and do a bit of reflection stuff.
>
> You can just about present the whole thing, and then come back and start saying, well, (pause) "What about? And how did you feel about that? And I noticed that you were very agitated when you were talking about this thing? And how do you feel about that? And what do you think that's coming from?"
>
> Offering supervision is the critical reflection framework.
>
> So, I'm interested in what's happening, what triggers have you got? Has anything major happened since I talked to you? Then I would be really interested in unpacking that in-depth, linking that to what's happening in the supervisee's wider social life. And professional life. Linking that to theories and the coming up with a plan about how we can do things differently.
>
> As part of that plan about how we can do things differently I will talk, we will do specific skill training, perhaps in an area of mental health.
>
> So, I would use a critical reflection framework and a psychodynamic framework to flesh that out. And then there's this other part, which is the goals, what are my professional goals? So, they're all hung over by this is all just, this postmodernist is all discourse, and then the critical reflection framework and then there's these columns underneath which I actually keep quite separate in my head. Does that sort of make sense?

I use a range of tools, so I use a lot of reflection. I use different elements of appreciative inquiry.

Critical reflection in supervision calls for a good and comfortable relationship between the supervisor and supervisee. The supervisee must honestly share what is happening, both good and not so good, and what are the difficulties and the gaps or shortcomings. Based on the listening to that recounting, the supervisor raises a series of questions to the supervisee to reflect and share those reflections. Such reflective discussion may lead to planning and doing things differently or similarly, depending upon the context. As the reflective framework is just a tool, it is always in relation to something that may be professional goals, a practice situation, or a particular theory or skill. Morrell (2003, p. 30) has suggested supervisors consider the following series of reflective questions after their supervision session.

What was the range of interventions/suggestions I used in this session?
  Is this range similar to what I usually use with this supervisee? If not, why not?
  How does the range compare with what I use with other supervisees?
  If different, why was this? How did I choose my interventions/suggestions?
  Was it a conscious choice based on the supervisee's stage of development, our contract, the session's agenda, and my understanding of how the supervisee best uses supervision? Or was it an unconscious choice based on my personal style, my stage of development, my experience of other supervisors, my counter transference to this supervisee (how I am "triggered" by him/her), or
    even just how I feel today?
  Would a different choice of interventions/suggestions have led elsewhere in the session?
  Could a different choice of interventions/suggestions be useful in the future?

Following the supervision session, supervisees may also consider the following or similar questions for their reflection. How or what am I feeling after supervision? What was my agenda today for the supervision and did we achieve the agenda? What did I discuss and share with the supervisor? What suggestions/advice did I receive and what is my thinking about such advice? How will it help me to change/improve my practice or myself? What change/improvement am I going to try? Reflective supervision practice should occur both from supervisor and supervisee perspectives.

Adult Learning

Adult learning approaches are mostly influenced by andragogy, in which learner-centered learning-teaching occurs. With so much firsthand experience and observation of the world, the way adult practitioners learn differs from how pupils learn in classrooms. Adult learners are self-directed and self-motivated, can connect learning to life experiences, are keen to solve real-world problems, and want to realize change through learning (Knowles, 1989). Thus, adult learning approaches are relevant in professional supervision. One supervisor spoke of adult learning as follows.

… how do adults learn best? And it's not … you're helping them to actually think about … you're not telling them, you're helping them elicit it for themselves, helping them to think about it.

From the adult learning perspective, this supervisor believes that supervisees need to seek information and learn themselves, and supervisors have only a facilitative role without providing any direct help beyond helping them to think. For supervisors, it is important and useful to apply adult learning principles in supervision so that supervisees learn effectively and meaningfully.

Kolb's Learning Cycle

The use of Kolb's learning theory/cycle in supervision is a good example of an adult learning approach as well as a reflective process. Kolb's (2015) experiential learning cycle includes a mutually integrative and supportive process of four stages: first, begin focusing on concrete experiences; second, reflect on the experience; third, learn and conceptualize from the experience; and fourth, apply the learning by experimenting and testing. It also includes four styles of learning: accommodating (feel and do), diverging (feel and watch), assimilating (think and watch), and converging (think and do). A supervisor referred to the use of Kolb's learning cycle during supervision.

> … So the Kolb cycle, I've used that. I mean that Kolb cycle of exploring and then – like, defining the issue and exploring it and making a bit of a plan, and then I guess sometimes that cycle is useful in supervision as well. You know, trying out a plan with the supervisee and then coming back to it, seeing how it went. I guess that can help too in thinking about, you know, session after session, if you're seeing someone that regularly. I think my sessions are spread a bit too far away for that to be too effective. I mean that whole Kolb cycle, that's useful for me to think about clinical work as well.

According to this supervisor, Kolb's learning cycle is a useful tool in supervision as developing practice plans, reflecting on them, learning from them, and implementing or testing the plans, and discussing this process in supervision sessions enhances a supervisee's learning and practice knowledge or "clinical work." In our view, professional supervision provides a critical platform for supervisees and supervisors to practice deliberate experiential learning to sustain lifelong learning (see Kolb, 2015) to constantly refine and improve practice.

Task-Focused Instructional Theory

Task-centered instruction theory or learning is essentially rooted in real-world problems and based on the assumption that people learn by solving real problems. According to Merrill (2006, pp. 1–2), "This task centered approach puts the emphasis on real world examples (show me) instead of on the abstract concepts (tell me).

The abstract concepts are still taught but in the context of real tasks." Further, Merrill states that "when learners acquire new skills in the context of real world tasks that they are more motivated to learn, the information they learn is more easily retrieved and the new skills they acquire are more easily applied when they later attempt to use their skills." The instructional theory is based on five principles: task/problem centered, activation, demonstration, application, and integration (Merrill, 2012). A supervisor preferred to use a task-focused instructional theory that helps to work on specific tasks and do a systematic follow-up.

> I suppose, again, being very task focused I always like to have the supervisor, either myself or the supervisee have specific tasks that we set out to achieve after supervision, and so each supervision session then we relate back to those when we come into the beginning of the next session. I like to be very structured, but again, I also like to be free flowing, so it's about having a balance of the two. I think being organized and having a framework is really important, so I think that's where that task focused instructional theory comes into play.

This instructional theory is useful to those supervisors and supervisees who prefer to work on specific tasks or problems and learn by addressing them. It also has an element of reflection. The theory helps to organize learning according to the five principles. However, it is important to have a balance between structured and flexible learning.

Systems Theory

While the task-focused instructional theory helps to look at a specific problem and its solution, the systems theory goes beyond the specific problem or individual to understand how the problem is caused by and connected to various subsystems, suggesting that solving the problem may require understanding and addressing a cause that may be hidden or located elsewhere in other subsystems. Systems theory is one of the major theories taught and used in social work education and practice. Originating in biology, systems theory suggests the interdependence and interrelatedness of various systems and subsystems in both objective and subjective worlds. A change in one system or subsystem affects other systems or subsystems. The structure of the systems continues as they adapt to changes, maintain or extend their boundary, and try to maintain equilibrium dynamically to adjust to environmental changes and survive. These basic concepts are extensively used in social work to analyze and work with individuals, groups, families, communities, cultures, social networks, and organizations, which form the systems of change agent, client, target, action, and professional (see Scott, 1988; Pierson & Thomas, 2010; Holloway, 2016; Payne, 2021). Two supervisors stated that they use systems theory in their supervision.

> I also work within a system, work within a structure, work within a bigger structure. So, I definitely have those ... that structural framework too.

I also use an element of systems theory because I think that once you understand how the different elements of what you do actually are interchangeable and interlock and relate to each other, so I use some elements of that.

Viewing all parties connected to supervision as sub/system (supervisor, supervisee, organization, people/communities) and analyzing and discussing issues presented by supervisees from the systems theory perspective offer insights to see the interconnectedness of issues and accordingly develop plans and strategies to work with people and communities (Holloway, 2016).

Kadushin Model/PASE Model

As briefly discussed in Chap. 4, Kadushin's (1985) model of social work supervision includes administrative, educational, and support functions. Later, better service to clients was added to it (Kadushin & Harkness, 2014, p. 9). The PASE (Practice, Administration, Support, and Education) model has a similar focus, though it is evidence-informed with clarified roles for the supervisor (Harris, 2018, 2020; Harris & Slattery, 2021). A few supervisors clearly stated that they use Kadushin's model, and one referred to the use of the PASE model.

That's probably the one that I talk about with people because I think it's a good way of describing what goes on in external supervision.

So, part of, if we think about the Kadushin framework, part of that is the teaching/learning bit, so I would talk to people about what I can and can't provide there.

I will sometimes talk about the whole basic Kadushin framework about the person at work is interested in whether you're seeing enough clients and whether your letter writing is appropriate for the agent. I'm not interested in that, and I have no authority in any of that. The bits that we can do here, teaching, learning and the personal professional and for those bits it's particularly, the relationship I think is particularly important, so I'll talk about, this needs to be a place where it's okay for you to walk in and say, "Gee I think I stuffed up today," without thinking I'm going to jump down their throat, but it also needs to be a place where I would suggest that, you know, if I think what you're doing is not okay we're going to have a conversation about that, then, "Are you okay with that?"

I know it's the oldest one in the world, but I always remember you know like Kadushin's model, who know the information advocacy, and support or whatever. And I think that's really important ...

And I've mentioned the PASE model, which is really Kadushin's model of supervision, so I quite like that as well.

This narrative demonstrates how supervisors cover educational, administrative, and support functions of supervision. It also shows how they supportively seek supervisees' consent to discuss practice issues, "what you're doing is not okay," to build the capacity of the supervisee.

Four Domains Approach to Supervision

One supervisor followed an approach consisting of four domains: accountability, reflection, development, and support.

> I kind of have always thought about it in terms of the four elements that we tend to talk about, being accountability, a place for reflection, a place for development and a place for support. And the weight that falls on each of those differs depending on whether it's somebody that I'm supervising within the organization, so a line-management kind of supervision or an external supervision.

Like Kadushin's supervision model, the accountability domain may be related to administrative aspects of supervision. It may include accountability to self, the organization, people or clients, and the profession. The reflective domain may be related to the practice issues. The development domain may be related to educational activities. Finally, the support domain is self-explanatory. It is important to note the supervisor's observation that the emphasis on each domain differs and depends upon whether the supervision is a line-management or external supervision.

Middleman and Goldberg's Model/Holistic Model

One of the early models of working with clients along with related structures and systems was conceptualized by Middleman and Goldberg (1974; Goldberg-Wood & Tully, 2006). The four quadrants of the model are (1) direct practice with a client concerning the client's particular situation, (2) direct practice with a client out of concern for the situation of others like the client, (3) direct practice with others concerning the particular situation of a category of clients, and (4) direct practice with others concerning a particular client's situation. A supervisor referred to using Middleman and Goldberg's framework during supervision.

> Middleman and I cannot believe how much I've referred to that across time in explaining social work identity, or the quadrants that we could be working in and probably shouldn't need to be working in to be, if we're working holistically and if we are holistic in our practice, then this is the model that just has stayed with me forever, and I use that in supervision. I kind of go, "Well what are you doing in this space, and what are you doing in this space?" Or even mentally I might be thinking, "Gee, they're heavily weighted in this individual client position. What are they doing with the families and what are they doing with the policies, and what are they doing?" So that really influences how I do supervision, I think.

The supervisor considers Middleman and Goldberg's conceptualization as a holistic model as it helps supervisors and supervisees consider the client's or people's issue from both individual and structural perspectives and plan, practice, and action at the individual level; at the group level to mobilize similarly affected clients, with other workers and professionals directly or indirectly engaged in working with similar clients and issues; and at the policy and program level, including resources mobilization to initiate larger change to benefit many individuals, families, and communities experiencing similar needs and problems. The model may also be linked to a systems approach and practice at the micro, meso, and macro levels. Middleman and Goldberg's conceptualization highlights the importance of the concept the person in the environment. It seems to us that many problems in professional supervision occur when the concept of the person in the environment has not been adequately addressed, and the concentration is specifically on the person rather than the environmental context. Environment means the physical, economic, social, and political environment. Increasingly, it also means understanding climate change, environmental social work, adequate food security, housing, and so on. The remarks in the narrative are profound as "social work identity" is created from what they do. "The quadrants we could be working" suggests that social workers often do not work in all four quadrants and are mostly engaged in quadrant one. It is an insightful observation that if social workers holistically engage in all four quadrants in a balanced way, a need for the worker to engage in all four quadrants may not arise. "The model that has just stayed with me forever" suggests the supervisor's commitment and passion for a holistic—individual to structural—social work practice.

Margaret Morrell's Framework

Margaret Morrell's (2005, pp. 41–42) framework for supervision is based on two fundamental beliefs: forming an effective partnership or working alliance between the supervisor and supervisee; and the outcome of the supervision should be effective and productive, benefiting the supervisee; employer, if any; and client or community. Drawing on the relevant literature (e.g., Kadushin's supervision model and Kolb's learning cycle), the framework includes the concept of a good supervision, supervisees' awareness of their needs and wants, the supervisor-supervisee relationship with contractual clarity, the scope of the issues to be considered in the supervision, the principles of reflective practice, and the preparation for and evaluation of supervision. This framework was employed by a supervisor who stated:

> Well as I said before, I love Margaret Morrell's framework for supervision … which is really about the supervisee taking – having control really, or having a lot of input for what they're wanting. So, they come with an understanding of what they're wanting to achieve from the supervision session. And they come with a question. So, they – this is the model – not everyone is able to do that, but I like them to, sort of, have an idea, and I show them this model in the hope that they will come – 'cause it makes it very – it makes it a very useful supervision. If they have a think about it first and then they come with a predetermined idea of what they're struggling with and how they would like the session to help them. So, whether it's about, you know, I think Margaret talks about five different reasons, purposes, of supervision. And so that – if the supervisee's aware of the purpose, and then they can think of a situation and devise a question around that. So, I like them to come with quite a clear idea of what they're hoping to achieve from supervision. Yeah.

This framework is used and appreciated by the supervisors, perhaps because the supervision is led and directed by the supervisee under the supervisor's guidance. It makes supervisees be aware of their needs, roles, and responsibilities and prepare well to achieve the best from the supervision. Supervisors appreciate supervisees coming with a clear idea of what they hope to achieve from the supervision.

Postmodernism

Along with modernism-based social work practice—values, principles, positivist assumptions, rationality, evidence, observation, experiment, and explanation— postmodernism-based social work practice helps supervisors and supervisees to explore alternative, unconventional, and multiple ways of looking at problems and solutions by critically examining, critiquing, and deconstructing language, culture, social relations, and identities. Payne (2021, p. 301) states that:

> The idea of discourse allows social workers to rise above any particular interaction and ask about the social constructions and power relations represented within it. By helping people to deconstruct discourses in their lives, social workers can give people greater power in their relationships with others.

A supervisor stated that their supervision includes discourses from a postmodernist perspective.

> Well, I use postmodernism in the critical reflective approach. But I'm also very strongly, as a postmodernist, they're all just discourses.

The application of postmodern thoughts in supervision and discourses, whether it is a client, organization, or community context, provides opportunities for supervisors and supervisees to critique and question modernist-based social work practice and seek additional and alternative insights to work with people, organizations, and communities to change their world and/or perceptions and beliefs of their world. However, there is a constant struggle between the current roots and nature of social work in modernism and postmodern thoughts.

A Strengths-Based Perspective

The strengths-based perspective was referred to in Chap. 4 as part of Cojocaru's (2010) appreciative supervision model and casework, clinical practice, and therapy-oriented supervision models. In social work practice, the use of a strengths-based perspective has revolutionized the way practitioners approach clients with a problem and pathology focus. A shift in strengths not only creates hope but also enables social workers to tackle issues confidently. Some social work practitioners seem to use the knowledge and skills of the strengths-based perspective in the professional supervision context. A few supervisors clearly stated that they use a strengths-based perspective in their supervision.

And so, I try and use a strengths-based perspective with them. So when we first meet, I say, I talk to them about what is useful for them in our working together and we have a look at what has worked well for them in the past. This is how I work, and I tell them that. Is that okay. So that's the first place that we start, where we meet. 'Cause there's no point continuing on if this isn't going to work for them.

I definitely come from a strengths-based perspective.

... the strengths-based, you know, the old chestnuts that social workers have been using forever and a day, but what I want them to do is take some core theories, and amalgamate them with their own style, and that becomes their way of negotiating through the interviews in a way that's almost that they're not even aware of consciously, so you go in with a nucleus of ideas from your theories, that match your personality. It doesn't really matter what the theory is, to be honest, you can use Freud if you like, as long as it works for you.

... I use elements of certainly strengths-based approach. I do start from an inquiring strengths-based sort of situation. I guess it's mostly the strengths-based narrative which is all sort of part of that sort of approach.

In this narrative, the repeated use of the phrase "strengths-based" suggests the supervisor's strong belief in the approach. The approach has clear merits as it looks at "what has worked well in the past and what is useful" for the supervisee in working together with the supervisor so that they can offer improved services to people. The supervisor translated the strengths-based approach in terms of supervisees choosing suitable knowledge, skills, and theories, which dovetail with their styles and personalities to work best for them. As pointed out earlier, it is important to remember that supervisees are not clients but practitioners.

Anti-oppressive Framework

The anti-oppressive framework involves identifying, analyzing, and fighting the sources of oppression, which include the unequal distribution of power, poverty and socio-economic disadvantage, and all forms of discrimination based on race, ethnic origin, gender, disability, class, age, sexual orientation, gender reassignment, religion, or belief. Sometimes, anti-oppressive practice is interchangeably used with anti-discriminatory practice, though these can be distinguished as the former involves, among other things, power analysis, whereas the latter focuses on the sources of discrimination, which also cause oppression (Pierson & Thomas, 2010). A supervisor referred to the use of the anti-oppressive framework in the supervision.

I have an anti-oppressive framework I guess that I understand ...

To Clifford (1995, p. 65), anti-oppressive practice,

looks at the use and abuse of power not only in relation to individual or organizational behaviour, which may be overtly, covertly or indirectly racist, classist, sexist and so on, but also in relation to broader social structures for example, the health, educational, political and economic, media and cultural systems and their routine provision of services and rewards for powerful groups at local as well as national and international levels. These factors impinge on people's life stories in unique ways that have to be understood in their socio-historical complexity.

Where relevant, supervisors may help supervisees understand work with people and communities using an anti-oppressive lens. An anti-oppressive practice requires enabling people and communities to critically understand their current conditions and causes, link individual circumstances to oppressive institutional factors, and fight those factors to overcome the oppression (Pierson & Thomas, 2010; Thompson, 2016; Okitikpi & Aymer, 2010). Supervisors and supervisees may potentially have an empowering discussion and translate the same to people and communities to initiate change.

Social Constructionist Approach

The social constructionist approach is a part of postmodernism. A social constructionist approach suggests that "through social interactions with each other, using language and shared ideas expressed in language, people develop shared pictures of the world in the social and historical context over time. Through such interactions, people develop common understanding of their socio-cultural world that they share" (Payne, 2021, p. 295). Further, the social constructionist approach calls for analyzing human interactions to identify the formation of identity and behavior in human relations and using that understanding to create similar purposeful interactions to change people's perceptions and social constructions to change individual/group behavior and social relationships (Payne, 2021, p. 297). One supervisor used a social constructionist approach within narratives and storytelling.

> I approach the conversations that I have from a narrative point of view but also from a social constructionist point of view, so I imagine that here's the work that this person's doing, whether it's in community or overseas with a community or wherever it is that they're doing the work. And then also here's this person reflecting on that work and telling stories about that work. And my belief is that the stories that this worker has about their work, those stories will shape how they do that work tomorrow. And so, my responsibility is to help, not just to listen, but to help re-author those stories, to help shape the stories that this person has spent their work in ways that will assist her or him to do the work, but also in ways that will assist this client, or this group or this community in their lives. So, a shorthand of that, I suppose, is that I'm wanting to assist workers to actually step into their preferred idea of themselves as a worker.

According to the supervisor, the social constructionist approach essentially involves not only listening to stories told by supervisees but also reshaping those stories in such a way that they will help both the worker and lives of clients, people, and communities. Reshaping requires relooking at human interactions in stories in terms of identity, human behavior, and social relations and changing people's perceptions and social construction to change behavior and social relationships. Most importantly, it helps supervisees realize their preferred ideas and approaches to social construction.

Feminist Framework/Gender Perspective

In Chap. 4, we briefly introduced feminist supervision models, which provide alternative ways of analyzing and addressing power, hierarchy, and authority in supervision and practice. As discussed, Szymanski's (2003) four steps involving collaboration, power analysis, diversity, and modeling empowerment provide a useful framework to practice feminist ideas. A supervisor referred to the choice of a feminist framework or gender perspective in supervision.

> I do have a gendered analysis, I guess I come from a feminist framework, so again that's about having a lens on power and what that means.
> I think that the understanding of the power lens is very, very important … definitely feminist theory.
> … but my own is often to bring – try and bring a feminist lens and to try and look at – at the phenomenological lens.

Patriarchy and power are critical aspects of feminist analysis and action. The supervisor's reference to "lens of power" and "what that means" suggests that it is critical to uncover power dynamics and how power is unfairly distributed and used to oppress not only women but also several weaker sections of society, children, the disabled, the elderly, and similarly marginalized groups. While the feminist framework may not have answers to all issues, it does provide new and alternative perspectives to challenge the status quo on sound grounds and change it.

Narrative Therapy

Unlike expert-centered therapies such as psychoanalysis and psychotherapy, narrative therapy is mostly client and people centered. A narrative is "a series of events that are linked together in a particular sequence, through time, according to a specific plot" ("the dominant construct of how one understands oneself") (Bruner, 1991; White, 1991; White & Epston, 1990, as cited in Hall, 2016). With the hope of changing the dominant negative construct affecting the self and well-being of the client, the practitioner and the client collaboratively expose and externalize the problem; trace the effects and personify the problem; deconstruct and reconstruct the life story, event, or narrative; and experience the change and celebrate it. In the newly reconstructed stories, the client or people will identify resilience and strength and positive self (see Hall, 2016). Like other therapies, narrative therapy has limitations as it has a flexible structure, is non-expert based, and makes it difficult to build hard evidence (Hall, 2016). A supervisor specializing in a narrative approach explains how it is used in supervision.

> I mean I like narrative therapy. I think it's very human, it's connecting, it's nonhierarchical, but you know that you're there in the supervisor role, so that's that the supposed experts in the room, whatever that means.

But I try and foster that narrative approach of we're problem-solving together. I've got that on my, that's my little mantra for (name of organization), you see, my private practice, it's "Problem-solving together." So, I like that connection. So, I think I draw on narrative a lot for that.

… my work has informed my thinking and who I am is informed by that narrative perspective, but also by a belief that as professionals, I think the dominant culture of professionalism in the Western world is that you have to look after yourself. And you have to do lots of self-care and drink lots of water and go and get supervision, and if you don't look after yourself well enough, you'll end up burnt out. That's not being very respectful of it, but that's, whereas I think we have a responsibility to support each other. To walk with each other, to encourage each other, to acknowledge each other. And in my case, to help people story their work in ways that are really helpful and useful. So, I, not only do I do the work from a narrative perspective, I believe I'm working with narratives, but I also have a belief as a worker that I want to lend myself as a social worker, I want to walk with other social workers to help them do their work. 'Cause I think it's in that kind of relational being in supporting each other, that we can be powerful. So, I don't want to be sending somebody off feeling alone in their work. So they've come, got charged up, can go back to their work and do better on their own.

Clearly, the supervisor likes narrative therapy as it is collaborative, nonhierarchical, and egalitarian, and it helps the supervisor and supervisee solve problems together. Distinct from the ethos of "looking after yourself," the philosophy of narrative therapy helps to walk together and support and encourage each other. So, supervisees' practice stories can be deconstructed and reconstructed in ways that are helpful to both. The supervisor states that, with this approach, the supervisee does not feel alone in the practice; the supervision helps to "charge them up" so that they can practice and "do better on their own." Although the narrative therapy concepts seem to be well applied in supervision, as raised earlier, it is unclear how the worker-client situation is prevented during supervision sessions between the supervisor and the supervisee.

Family Therapy

Family therapy is not one model or one theory; it is a range of models and theories; for example, cognitive behaviour therapy (CBT), narrative, and solution-focused therapies may be used (see Franklin & Hopson, 2013) depending upon their relevance and the practitioner. In a way, family therapy is the first step to moving further from focusing only on the individual to other related systems. Thus, the ideas of systems theory, Ecomap Genogram, etc., are applicable. The systems theory or approach helps understand circular relations among family members and "how each member behaves affects the way everyone else behaves, and so on" (Pierson & Thomas, 2010, p. 226). Generally, the focus is on understanding and addressing problematic family interactions and relationship patterns. By remaining neutral, the practitioner "explores with the whole family how to achieve a different overall pattern and how to view behaviours more positively with a hope to enable the family to change attitudes, viewpoints and behaviour" (Pierson &Thomas, 2010, p. 226).

Besides the family, the practitioner may also work with other systems such as schools, hospitals, and other relevant agencies to enhance the family's functioning (Franklin & Hopson, 2013). A supervisor with a family therapy background preferred to apply that therapy in supervision.

> I have a family therapy background, so I always come from that position of no blame. I really like that way of thinking for child protection, so I encourage my workers to think of, well, what's underneath the behaviors, how does this behavior serve the parents or the child? So, the usual family therapy theorists, I like Michael White, even going back to Steve de Shazer, what's Virginia, what's her last name? She wrote People Making, Satir, Virginia Satir. I encourage my workers – and this is actually really hard to do – but if they can just remember the motivational interviewing … So, mainly family therapy, but you also have to be risk aware, you have to be forensically aware, so you've got to look into the history, like, okay, you've got a 10-year-old with 18 reports, have a good look at that history, and does it make sense? What you're hearing, does it make sense with what the information is on the file?

Taking clues from family therapy, the supervisor appreciates the position of neutrality while working with supervisees. Suggesting supervisees to look behind symptoms and behaviors, be risk aware, and thoroughly examine the documents to ensure consistency between what is observed and reported indicates the complexity of working in the child protection system and with families. The supervisor appreciates the difficulties but also tries to encourage supervisees. When supervisors are committed to a particular model of work, in this case family therapy, supervisees must explore whether such expertise meets their needs before committing to the supervision.

Sensorimotor Psychotherapy

According to Ogden and Fisher (2015, p. 3), "sensorimotor psychotherapy, often referred to as a "body-oriented talking therapy," blends theory and technique from cognitive, affective, and psychodynamic therapy with straightforward somatic interventions, such as helping clients to become aware of their bodies, to track their bodily sensations, and to implement physical actions that promote empowerment and competency." Drawing initial insights from neuroscience research, it is designed to address the cognitive-emotional aspects and the bodily and autonomic symptoms of traumatic stress and attachment-related disorders (Fisher, 2011). A supervisor referred to the use sensorimotor psychotherapy to deal with the transference issue in practice.

> … so with the sensorimotor psychotherapy training, I use that in supervision. So if they reflect on something and there's transference issues that come up for them with their clients or participants, whatever term they use, I say "Well, do you feel comfortable talking about this?"

In clinical practice, some practitioners, while working with clients, often experience transference and counter-transference issues as certain events or situations related to clients trigger similar past experiences of the practitioner, which may interfere with their practice. Being aware of it and discussing it in the supervision may help the supervisee. However, we are not sure whether supervisors can use sensorimotor psychotherapy with supervisees, though they can discuss how this therapy can be used while working with relevant clients.

Psychodynamic Lens

Psychodynamic ideas have significantly influenced social work practice for many decades, particularly among individuals. The roots of these ideas may be traced to psychoanalysis and Freudian concepts of how identity, ego, and super ego develop, how these may be linked to relational and related issues, and how such an understanding may be used to work with clients and people (Danto, 2013; Payne, 2021). Over the years, however, psychodynamic ideas in social work have incorporated social environmental factors that contribute to the development of individuals and their psycho-social functions. Unlike clinical psychology and psychiatry, the psychodynamic lens in social work "looks not only at apparently problem behaviours, difficulties in childhood development and social dysfunctions, but also at clients' strengths and assets, their family, community and social environments and resources available to help clients" (Payne, 2021, p. 117). Psychodynamic ideas are complex, criticized, and have limitations, but they appear to be useful in interpreting, understanding, and working with human behavior, at least in some cases or situations (see Pierson & Thomas, 2010; Danto, 2013; Payne, 2021). A supervisor with a background in psychodynamic analysis narrated:

> … my background is probably psychodynamic more than anything else and I often talk to people about thinking about cases from that lens, even if we're operating in a different way, you know, even if … but in being able to choose the strategies that we might implement, being able to think about what, something from a more psychodynamic lens and also I think that, you know, again that really strong emphasis on the role that what I bring to this – what I bring to this experience for the client rather than just what the client is bringing or what they're experiencing.
>
> So, I would use a critical reflection framework and a psychodynamic framework to flesh that out.

This narration suggests that the supervisor has knowledge and skills of the psychodynamic lens and uses it in practice and supervision. It also appears to suggest that the supervisor is driving the agenda of supervision, which is contrary to a point made earlier that the supervision should be led by supervisees and their agenda. The supervisor asserts that even if the supervisee is "operating in different way," they will ask them to consider the psychodynamic lens. Similarly, "strong emphasis on the role that what I bring" may be interpreted as the dominant presence of the supervisor. On the other hand, some supervisors may argue that they are presenting an alternative lens—a kind of reframing from a different perspective. It is also important to note the use of a reflective framework, which may be useful in identifying these perspectives. However, with such expert supervisors, it is important and useful for supervisees to check in advance whether they are interested in learning and applying psychodynamic ideas and make a supervision decision accordingly.

Cognitive Behavior Therapy

Cognitive Behavior Therapy (CBT) is well known in clinical practice. Derived from theories of learning and cognition (Craske, 2010, as cited in Weaver et al., 2014), CBT collaboratively develops problem-focused cognitive and behavioral strategies to bring change in thought and behavior to enhance the well-being of people. According to Dobson and Dozois (2001, as cited in Weaver et al., 2014), three principles common to the CBT model are as follow: (1) One can access and become aware of the content and process of one's own thinking. (2) Cognitive mediation occurs between events and experiences and how a person responds to them. How one thinks, perceives, interprets, and gives meaning influences behavior and action. (3) The process of accessing and knowing how one thinks (no. 1 above) and mediating meaning from one's events and responses (no. 2 above) can be constructively and positively changed to achieve adaptive responses and social functioning (see Weaver et al., 2014). Some of the strategies include psychoeducation, appropriate behavioral reinforcements and activation, social skills, problem and relaxation training, exposure, and cognitive restructuring (see Weaver et al., 2014). Despite the merits of CBT, environmental and structural factors cannot be ignored; sometimes it may be necessary to know the background of the current situation. One supervisor was of the view that CBT is useful in supervision.

> I use a bit of CBT sometimes, because I think that's got application across the board. I think it's quite useful tool to draw upon even for ourselves.
> … so my main clinical discourse is CBT, cognitive behavioral therapy. But I do a lot of brain science …

This supervisor is of the view that CBT can be applied "across the board." The statement, "quite useful tool to draw upon even for ourselves," suggests that the supervisor and supervisee can use CBT during supervision. However, the supervisee learning to use CBT in the practice context is one thing, and using it for themselves is another. It appears that CBT is useful in normal situations without serious issues, and some practitioners use it to change problematic behavior.

Crisis Intervention

Most social workers encounter or are familiar with working with crisis situations. According to Roberts (2005, p. 779, as cited in Roberts, 2013), crisis is "An acute disruption of psychological homeostasis in which one's usual coping mechanisms fail and there exists evidence of distress and functional impairment. The subjective reaction to a stressful life experience that compromises the individual's stability and ability to cope or function." Although there are several intervention models (see Roberts, 2013), one model developed by Roberts (2013) has the following seven stages: Plan rapid crisis assessment; build rapid rapport with respect and reassurance; examine and define the dimension of the problem; explore feelings and emotions; find and assess past coping strategies; restore cognitive functioning through the implementation of an action plan; and follow-up as required. One supervisor had a crisis-driven approach to supervision.

> Often there is a need to have a very crisis driven focus. I'd like to think that doesn't happen often, but it does and that sometimes is related to that particular customer or particular incident in an office or an individual personal matter that's going on for someone or the work performance. So, it just depends, and often it's about dealing with the crisis and then moving on to the other so there is that element of crisis intervention that we do in our workplace just as much as we do in supervision.

To one supervisor, often supervision was dealing with the crisis. The statement, "I'd like to think that doesn't happen often, but it does," suggests that, for some supervisees, supervision is provided only when there is a crisis. It is important to research to what extent it is a prevailing practice and how it can be prevented, and planned supervision may be offered.

Supervisee-Led Model

As many supervisors have expressed, the supervisee-led model has some currency. Many supervisors think that supervision is the supervisee's space and time and should be planned and led by them. Based on the following response, a supervisee-led model may be conceptualized.

> No, if there are areas that I think, if there are elephants in the room, I think they can be important, but no, I don't have a strict format in terms of what we must attend to or a format in terms of session structure or whatever.
> I make that really clear at the start. This is your time. It needs to work for you. The agenda is your responsibility. I will meet you as best I can and I will tell you if I think there are gaps, but hopefully this is something that people enjoy and feel they are getting something out of yeah.
> I guess that's what I'm saying about, it has to work for the supervisee, because that's like you know, mum and dad fighting and, I certainly might have a different perspective, but I would see that as my role then, would be in talking through with the supervisee what fits for them and what do they want to do with the fact that there are perhaps two different ways of looking at this, what might be the next step. So, for me anyway, I think it's about putting that stuff on the table. Not shying away from it, because otherwise, it reduces the benefit I think, that can come from supervision.

In the supervisee-led model, the supervisor has a passive role, though they need to guide and facilitate when needed. The supervisee takes full responsibility for planning and preparing the agenda. The supervisee needs to honestly discuss the practice issues, and the supervisor will frankly and constructively discuss the gaps and guides to address them. Supervisees need to ensure that supervision is working for them and meeting their needs by offering regular feedback and changing the nature and content of supervision when necessary.

Family Approach

The concept of a family approach to supervision is an interesting one. The family approach may connote many things to many people depending upon their construction of the family. A supervisor said the following about using a family approach for supervision.

> I think another part of my approach from a theoretical perspective is very much around the family. What I see with my work colleagues is an extension of my family in that I have a group of my staff whom I see as my siblings, so they're the other supervisors, and then I see a whole lot of other children you know, who are the what we call the five and six staff members, social workers who are basically the supervisees at the end of the day, and I see that there's a real structure within the family of how supervision needs to be provided and how the supervisees need to present to the supervisors. You know I think there is that structural family structure that I see with my own family at home that I do bring into the supervision environment as well.

What the supervisor has implied in the above narrative is difficult to decipher. On the one hand, the supervisor states that colleagues are treated like family members, which may suggest offering care, protection, and support to supervisees. On the other hand, like the family structure, there is a structure between the supervisor and supervisee, and the supervision needs to occur within that structure. This suggests that line-managers can integrate the care, support, and educational functions of supervision with administrative accountability functions, though this may be challenging for some.

Best Practice

To Roberts and Yeager (2004), best practices in social work "often refers to recommendations/guidelines regarding the practices most appropriate for routine use in service systems with particular populations and problems" (as cited in Mullen et al., 2013).

However, best practice in social work and professional supervision is difficult to define and conceptualize as it is, more often than not, time and context specific and depends upon the conceptualizer, with whom others may or may not agree. From a critical perspective, Ferguson (2008, pp. 17–18) states that "best practice is about social action, process and the nuances of how practice is done. It includes critical attention to those processes which may not be amenable to or even seen as relevant to measurement, but which are essence of what social work is." Further, Ferguson elaborates the best practice that may range from "the use of gestures, types of questions, the management of emotion, the constructive use of statutory powers, to changing professional attitudes and dominant beliefs about situations, management and organisations, providing advocacy, practical and material support, and changing users' beliefs and behaviours" (p. 17). Best practice is more than outputs and outcomes; it does not constitute "idealised images of practice, but attainable ones within the possibilities of current working realities" (p. 18). To one supervisor, best practice was the focus of their supervision.

> But I think it's, looking at, looking at best practice, I think that's really the theme, or the model, that I try to (pause) making sure they get the best out of it, you know.

With the above understanding of best practice, what could be the best practice in professional supervision? Best practice in supervision should not be based on outputs and outcomes, though these are objectives. Best practice in supervision is about social action, processes, and how practice is done. It is about using gentle gestures, learning to ask questions and/or learning to listen to questions posed by people and communities, changing attitudes and beliefs of relevant stakeholders, advocacy, and providing practical support. Mullen et al. (2013) believe that the idea behind best practices is to improve quality and accountability.

Eclectic Approach

The eclectic approach "involves the use of any procedures, concepts, and theoretical principles that seem appropriate to a particular problem" or need (Scott, 1988, p. 123). A supervisor stated that they use an eclectic approach.

> I have a strengths-based perspective, so, I use a bit of an eclectic approach. So, I have, I use a solution-oriented perspective, I have training in acceptance and commitment therapy (ACT). One of my newer perspectives, or approaches, that I really love, is psychomotor, sensory psychomotor therapy. And I haven't actually gone to formal training with that, but my supervisor uses that, and I've got books that I've been reading up on that. Plus, I have been to numerous trauma model therapy training.
> It's nothing pure, it's probably a lot of different things … But I think it's, looking at, looking at best practice …

This supervisor's eclectic approach includes strengths-based and solution-oriented perspectives, ACT, sensorimotor psychotherapy, and the trauma model. The description of "a lot of different things" and "nothing pure" suggests that the supervisor does not follow a particular concept or theory by fully focusing on it. However, the main focus on the "best practice" and the use of whatever concepts and theories by the supervisor to achieve the best practice suggest the significance of practice in supervision. It is also important for supervisors to use any concept or theory because they are pertinent to the supervision issue being discussed, not simply because they like that particular concept or theory.

Conclusion and Summary

The analysis of conceptual and theoretical approaches used in supervision suggests that supervisors use a wide range of concepts and theories in supervision, which confirms the findings of previous studies (O'Donoghue et al., 2005; Harris, 2017, as cited in Harris & Slattery, 2021). Generally, the concepts and models provide some directions to both the supervisor and supervisee (Sloan &Watson, 2002). Some models such as Kadushin's and Margaret Morrell's model focus on the purpose of supervision and often cover many other approaches like strengths-based and reflective practice. Many supervisors also use a combination of several approaches, generally known as an eclectic approach. Of the 24 concepts and theories presented in the chapter, over a half relate to social work clinical practice theories, which were categorized under "casework, clinical practice, and therapy-oriented supervision models' in Chap. 4. In relation to therapeutic or clinical approaches, it appears that supervisors use them mainly because they specialize in them. This approach may be advantageous to some supervisees who plan to specialize in a particular area offered by supervisors. However, such specialized concepts and theoretical approaches are relevant if supervisors and supervisees find them useful in their practice. In the context of using clinical practice models, it is necessary to guard against the likely transference of the social worker-client relationship in the supervisor-supervisee relationship. Some concepts and models such as reflective practice, supervisee-led, family approach, and best practice are generic and can be used in any supervision context.

However, the analysis of narratives does not directly indicate any concept or framework that focuses on the development of qualities or virtues in supervisees, though some frameworks may include ethical issues. On the other hand, some supervisors' responses included phrases such as "strengths-based practice, reflective framework, helping supervisees to think, creating comfortable environment for supervisees, building relationship, unpacking issues in-depth, having a plan, keeping a balance between free flowing and structured approaches, responsibility to help, advocacy and support, loving or liking a particular framework, allowing supervisees have control over the supervision process, awareness of the purpose, humanness, connecting, nonhierarchical, solving problems together and respectful." Thus, it may be favorably inferred that some supervisors' work implicitly includes virtue or quality aspects, though their focus may not be purposefully developing these in supervisees.

As clarified in the introduction, the purpose of the chapter is to develop an understanding of what concepts and theories supervisors use to supervise supervisees but not to discuss those theories in detail. Qualitative research allows for deeper interpretations of narratives, so readers may interpret the same narratives differently and more meaningfully. However, we have kept our comments to a minimum so that narratives themselves speak louder. We hope both supervisors and supervisees find their views useful. The next chapter will discuss the use of practice wisdom in supervision.

References

Bruner, J. (1991). The narrative construction of reality. *Critical Inquiry, 18*, 1–21.

Clifford, D. J. (1995). Methods in oral history and social work. *Journal of the Oral History Society, 23*(2), 65–70.

Cojocaru, S. (2010). Appreciative supervision in social work. New opportunities for changing the social work practice. *Revista de cercetare [i interven]ie social, 29*(1), 72–91.

Craske, M. G. (2010). *Cognitive-behavioral therapy*. American Psychological Association.

Danto, E. A. (2013). Psychoanalysis. In T. Mizrahi & L. Davis (Eds.), *Encyclopedia of social work*. Oxford University Press.

Dobson, K. S., & Dozois, D. J. (2001). Historical and philosophical bases of cognitive-behavioral therapies. In K. S. Dobson (Ed.), *Handbook of cognitive-behavioral therapies* (2d ed., pp. 3–38). Guildford Press.

Ferguson, H. (2008). The theory and practice of critical best practice in social work. In K. Jones, B. Cooper, & H. Ferguson (Eds.), *Best practice in social work: Critical perspectives* (pp. 15–36). Palgrave Macmillan.

Fisher, J. (2011). Sensorimotor approaches to trauma treatment. *Advances in Psychiatric Treatment, 17*(3), 171–177. https://doi.org/10.1192/apt.bp.109.007054

Franklin, C., & Hopson, L. (2013). Family therapy. In T. Mizrahi & L. Davis (Eds.), *Encyclopedia of social work*. Oxford University Press.

Goldberg-Wood, G., & Tully, C. T. (2006). *The structural approach to direct practice in social work: A social constructionist perspective*. Columbia University Press.

Hall, J. C. (2016). Narrative therapy. In T. Mizrahi & L. Davis (Eds.), *Encyclopedia of social work*. Oxford University Press.

Harris, T. (2017). *Excellence in supervisory practice: Developing a supervisory capability framework for effective professional supervision in social work practice in Australia*. Unpublished thesis. Griffith University.

Harris, T. (2018). *Developing leadership excellence: A practical guide for the new professional supervisor*. Routledge.

Harris, T. (2020). *Successful supervision and leadership: Ensuing high-performance outcomes using the PASE model*. Routledge.

Harris, T., & Slattery, M. (2021). The PASE supervision model. In K. O'Donoghue & L. Engelbrecht (Eds.), *The Routledge international handbook of social work supervision*. Taylor & Francis Group.

Holloway, E. (2016). *Supervision essentials for a systems approach to supervision*. American Psychological Association.

Homberg, A., Mink, J., Karstens, S., & Mahler, C. (2019). Learning about professional theories, models and concepts within an interprofessional seminar for undergraduate healthcare students. *Journal of Interprofessional Education & Practice, 17*(December), 1–6. https://doi.org/10.1016/j.xjep.2019.100272

Kadushin, A. (1985). *Supervision in social work* (2nd ed.). Columbia University Press.

Kadushin, A., & Harkness, D. (2014). *Supervision in social work* (5th ed.). Columbia University Press.

Knowles, M. (1989). *The modern practice of adult education: From pedagogy to andragogy*. Prentice Hall.

Kolb, D. A. (2015). *Experiential learning: Experience as the source of learning and development* (2nd ed.). Pearson.

Merrill, D. M. (2006). A task-centered instructional strategy. *Journal of Research on Technology in Education, 40*(1), 5–22.

Merrill, D. M. (2012). *First principles of instruction*. Wiley.

Middleman, R. R., & Goldberg, G. (1974). *Social service delivery: A structural approach to social work practice*. Columbia University Press.

Morrell, M. (2003). Forethought and afterthought-two of the keys to professional development and good practice in supervision. *Social Work Review, Autumn/Winter, 15*(1/2), 29–32.

Morrell, M. (2005). Supervision-an effective partnership: The experience of running workshops for supervisees in 2004–5. *Social Work Review, Summer, 17*(4), 39–45.

Mullen, E. J., Bellamy, J. L., & Bledsoe, S. E. (2013). Best practices. In T. Mizrahi & L. Davis (Eds.), *Encyclopedia of social work*. Oxford University Press.

O'Donoghue, K., Munford, R., & Trlin, A. (2005). Mapping the territory: Supervision within the association. *Social Work Review, 17*(4), 46–64.

Odgen, P., & Fisher, J. (2015). *Sensorimotor psychotherapy: Interventions for trauma and attachment*. W. W. Norton and Company.

Okitikpi, T., & Aymer, C. (2010). *Key concepts in anti-discriminatory social work*. SAGE.

Payne, M. (2021). *Modern social work theory* (5th ed.). Red Globe Press.

Pierson, J., & Thomas, M. (2010). *Dictionary of social work*. Open University Press.

Roberts, A. R. (Ed.). (2005). Bridging the past and present to the future of crisis intervention and crisis management. In *Crisis intervention handbook: Assessment, treatment and research* (3rd ed., pp. 3–34). Oxford University Press.

Roberts, A. R. (2013). Crisis intervention. In T. Mizrahi & L. Davis (Eds.), *Encyclopedia of social work*. Oxford University Press.

Roberts, A. R., & Yeager, K. (2004). Designing, searching for, finding, and implementing practice-based research and evidence-based studies. In A. R. Roberts & K. R. Yeager (Eds.), *Evidence-based practice manual: Research and outcome measures in health and human services* (pp. 3–14). Oxford University Press.

Scott, W. P. (1988). *Dictionary of sociology*. Goyal Saab.

Sloan, G., & Watson, H. (2002). Clinical supervision models for nursing: Structure, research and limitations. *Nursing Standard, 17*(4), 41–46.

Szymanski, D. M. (2003). The feminist supervision scale: A relational/theoretical approach. *Psychology of Women Quarterly, 27*, 221–232. https://doi.org/10.1111/1471-6402.00102

Thomson, N. (2016). *Anti-discriminatory practice: Equity, diversity and social justice*. Palgrave.

Weaver, A., Himle, J., Steketee, G., & Muroff, J. (2014). Cognitive behaviour therapy. In T. Mizrahi & L. Davis (Eds.), *Encyclopedia of social work*. Oxford University Press.

White, M. (1991). Deconstruction and therapy. *Dulwich Centre Newsletter, 3*, 21–41.

White, M., & Epston, D. (1990). *Narrative means to therapeutic ends*. W. W. Norton.

Chapter 10
The Use of Practice Wisdom in Supervision

Introduction

This chapter discusses the use of supervisors' practice wisdom in their supervision sessions with supervisees. Unlike other concepts, practice wisdom is difficult to pinpoint, define, and quantify. Practice wisdom is a loaded concept; it is not one thing; it is not one quality or virtue; it is not one practice experience. It is a mix of complex factors such as the worker's being, practice and life experiences, learnings, and cultural upbringing. It is difficult to dissect and explain it, but one can see its use and result. Rooted in experience and thought, it appears to come spontaneously and proficiently.

By engaging in practice over a period, workers gain insights and develop skills to make decisions, exercise judgment, and offer advice. Through such practice experiences with variations in different contexts, they keep reflecting in and on action and refining their practice knowledge and skills, which may turn into their practice wisdom (Hugman et al., 2021; Payne, 2021). One way of understanding practice wisdom is by looking at Dodd and Savage's (2016) delineation of its three components: "tacit knowledge, critical reflection, and intersubjectivity." According to Austin (2008, p. 580), tacit knowledge exists in the minds of practitioners, "manifests itself through their actions, and is not easily articulated," but it is a meaningful and important source of information that influences the decisions and actions of "practitioners." Critical reflection is about "reflecting in action" mode where practitioners notice that they have been doing something right, and that sense or feeling allows them to do that something repeatedly (Schon, 1995, pp. 54–55; as cited in Dodd & Savage, 2016; Pawar & Anscombe, 2015). Insights gained from reflections help practitioners to build tacit knowledge. "Intersubjectivity is knowledge derived in the course of the practice interchange. It is the mutual knowing between two people of the other's experience, including meaning, intentions, and emotions (i.e., subjective experiences) based on a shared state (Bråten & Trevarthen, 2007;

M. Pawar, A. W. (Bill) Anscombe, *Enlightening Professional Supervision in Social Work*, https://doi.org/10.1007/978-3-031-18541-0_10

Trevarthen, 2009)" (as cited in Arnd-Caddigan, 2011, p. 373; as cited in Dodd & Savage, 2016). Intersubjectivity "can guide the worker in making decisions within the practice, helping to identify the shifting goals in treatment, aid in choosing strategies that contribute to the overall improvement of the client, and document the client's improvement" (Arnd-Caddigan, 2011, p. 372; as cited in Dodd & Savage, 2016).

With this understanding, we tried to explore whether and how supervisors use their practice wisdom in their supervision. The question was "What kind of practice wisdom do you use in supervision?" It was not surprising to see a couple of supervisors' initial responses as follows:

> I think it's something I need to reflect on and focus on myself.
> Okay, I like the term but I'm not quite sure what you mean in this context.

These responses confirm how problematic the phrase "practice wisdom" is. However, after further probing, many supervisors could think in their own ways and share their practice wisdom. Their responses were categorized under three broad themes. The first theme mostly relates to drawing on their experiences, including sharing relevant experiences, reflectively learning from those experiences, sharing what has not worked, and appropriate self-disclosure. In the second theme, the supervisors' practice wisdom was identified in some of their statements, such as "we cannot be good at everything"; "not just jump in, think"; and "if in doubt, throw them out." By further analyzing their narratives, a list of principles and techniques used in supervision practice was identified in the third theme. Accordingly, these three themes are presented in the chapter with the supervisors' voices, along with our brief comments. Finally, the chapter ends with a conclusion and summary.

Use of Practice Wisdom by Supervisors

Experience

The first theme of practice wisdom of supervisors related to their experiences. Under this, four sub-themes are presented: sharing relevant experience, reflecting on and learning from your own experience, sharing what has not worked with humility, and appropriate self-disclosure.

Sharing Relevant Experience of Supervisors

Life experiences include practice experiences, and together these contribute to experience-based knowledge, which is the major source of wisdom. However, not all experiences contribute to wisdom (Weststrate & Glück, 2017), as this depends upon how individuals or practitioners treat their experiences. Similarly, supervisees gaining from others' experiences depend upon how they receive, perceive, and make or construct meaning from and relate to those shared experiences. Many supervisors stated that their practice wisdom comes from their experiences, and they share their relevant experiences in supervision to help supervisees. To them, it not only demonstrated learning but also affirmed and validated their practice.

> Look, if it's relevant, if there's a similar case that I've experienced, for sure, I would be talking about what I found helpful, or what I've found useful. So, practice wisdom is relevant. I think that there's some learning and validation there when you share practice wisdom.

> … the thing about doing supervision I think is that it's very affirming of your own practice. You know, when you hear people struggling with the kinds of things you know you've struggled with and that you can help them think about that, that's really affirming. When you hear yourself talking about the work that you might have done in the past that's really affirming.

> Often, I will say, oh so say there was something that was happening in a group, or that they didn't feel that they were getting … able to get that point across, I would often go back to my own experience of being a learning group worker. You know, that reminds me of a time that I was in that situation. So, I think it's important to show your own vulnerabilities too.

> So, some of those things I'll often talk about, my early experience of being in … being a new worker to group work, or I've got a female facilitator who … we've talked about what it's like to be the only woman in the room.

> But I will certainly say sometimes, someone else I've seen for supervision who was in a similar situation found that and I don't know if that's helpful for you?

> I think I use, some of my learnings from practice I share with people. The other thing that I think workers really appreciate of my practice wisdom, so stories of what I've done and how I think in practice, but I think also that they really like the fact that I've worked hard over the years to translate some really, I call it some very academic ideas into very ordinary language that are usable and I think workers really like that. So, I think that's part of my practice wisdom also that I've, it's been 20 years of trying to teach these ideas in ways that are, I don't think ideas are very useful unless they mean that you can put them into action the next day or do something with them that's useful.

> Oh, a lot, I think. I think that practice wisdom is a good way of explaining something to someone …

From the above narratives, a few points may be noted. First, supervisors should share their relevant experience to supervisees. It makes sense to share similar case experiences and difficulties so that supervisees can find them useful. Most importantly, sharing practice wisdom leads to learning and validation. Second, while sharing experiences, the practice wisdom of affirming is insightful. When supervisees present their practice struggles, supervisors sharing their past struggles in similar contexts helps both affirm their practices, which may lead to mutual comfort, further questions, or new resolutions or actions. Third, while sharing experiences, supervisors presenting situations about their own vulnerabilities, whether it is facilitating a group for first time or being a lone woman in the room, would help supervisees. Fourth, sharing experiences should include practice stories showing how supervisors think in practice. Finally, sharing experience entails supervisors translating (complex) theories/ideas in a simple and usable text. Doing this in itself is a practice wisdom, which, we think, can only be acquired by practicing.

Reflecting on and Learning from Your Experience

As discussed in the introduction, critical reflection is one of the important components of practice wisdom. Any experience without reflection may diminish the potential of learning. Morrell (2003, p. 29) has observed that a lack of discipline to reflect regularly, a lack of time, a lack of commitment to "thinking time" by agencies, and a tendency to be swayed by case material can create hurdles for reflective practice. Weststrate and Glück (2017) contend that self-reflection to make sense of personal and practice experiences and one's own role in them is conducive to wisdom development. To some supervisors, sharing their experience was also a way to draw on practice wisdom of supervisees to enhance their knowledge and skills.

> I am very mindful of the need to draw on the practice wisdom of the person that you are supervising … because of the fact that I actually believe that you can learn from your own experiences, then I do that in supervision as well. I would look at have you had to deal with a similar sort of situation in the past?
>
> What are some of the things that you did well, and this is where aspects of appreciative inquiry come into that, where it is about enhancing people's knowledge and skills while at the same time identifying certain things that they may not be completely aware of.
>
> Yes, so it is about your own experiences and grounding some of the learning on lived experiences either of the worker or of myself that I can offer without saying, "I did it this way and therefore it's the only way to do things."

Here, the supervisor's practice wisdom is that "you can learn from your own experiences." To use this wisdom in supervision, supervisors have to facilitate supervisees' self-reflection on their experiences in similar situations, what supervisees did and did not do well, and identify in that reflection certain matters supervisees may not be aware of. Ultimately, supervisors have to facilitate learnings from self-practice experiences without imposing a particular way of doing things. The practice wisdom is self-reflecting on one's own practice to learn, and there is not "only one way" of doing things in practice.

Sharing What Has Not Worked—Humility

In social work education and practice, we often refer to "learning by doing" and "learning by doing mistakes." In addition to reflecting on what has worked well, reflecting on what has not worked well can contribute to effective learning and practice wisdom. Weststrate and Glück's (2017, p. 810) study found that "Wisdom-fostering forms of self-reflection require that individuals explore their own role in the occurrence of negative life events, confront and examine negative feelings, and do the effortful work of finding meaning in the difficult experience." Many supervisors stated that they not only shared what has worked for them but also what has not. To one supervisor, this kind of experiential sharing helped to demystify the myth that senior supervisors have all the answers and show their humility.

I tend to be fairly open to share some of the things that haven't worked for me in the past. And that sharing, I have found, has had two major aspects of impact. One, I think it has demystified the position to some staff who have come and sort of thought, you know, you're the team leader. You're the know-it-all. You've been there before. You've done it and therefore whatever you say is correct. So that has actually demystified that.

The other thing is that it has actually then demonstrated that a certain amount of … and somebody actually said to me at one stage that one of the things they like about my supervision sessions was my humility. And I said to this person, "What do you mean?" because we often use terminology and word, "What do you mean by my humility?" And then he said, "Look, it's your capacity to be humble about the things that you have done well but also to be open about the things you haven't done well." I don't think that I had actually realized until that time what I had been doing. Oftentimes it takes somebody else to tell you. I think, as I've said before, I think that I have always … what we strive to get a learning out of every supervisory session, for me.

So, I do bring to supervision a lot of my own experience; things that have gone well, things that have gone terribly, you know.

And, I guess the other part of the practice wisdom that I bring is my own experiences of supervision. What is it that has been useful and helpful for me and what is it that has been terrible because I've also got a file of terrible supervision experiences, you know.

So, yeah, the experience is as important, sometimes more important, than the knowledge, I think.

Or maybe the experience is the way of living out the knowledge or … yeah. I think the theoretical things become understandable or real when we're talking about experience.

In the supervision, both supervisors and supervisees should share their practice experiences of what has worked well and what has not and critically reflect on both contexts. When supervisors share what has not worked and why it has not, supervisees not only learn from that reflection but also observe and perhaps cultivate humility and humbleness of the supervisor and share and reflect on similar practice experiences in supervision. We can make better sense of theoretical knowledge by reflecting on practice experiences that have not worked well.

Appropriate Self-Disclosure

Social work is a relationship-based profession. Whether one works with clients, families, groups, or communities, social workers need to develop and maintain rapport and relationships to practice. Mutual trust is an important element in appropriately self-disclosing in practice. In the professional supervision relationship, trust and safety between the supervisor and supervisee are needed. When the line-manager is a supervisor, there is an asymmetrical power relationship between the supervisor and supervisee, and sometimes honest disclosure on the part of the supervisee is an issue. Supervisors appropriately self-disclosing may help supervisees to do the same. One supervisor found the wisdom in appropriately self-disclosing in supervision but with a caution about power relationships.

> … the danger I think is, when you've been around as long as I have, that you've got a war story for everything, and that's really not what it's about. So, I guess it's about, in a counseling construct we'd be talking about appropriate self-disclosure. I think the same thing applies, so there is a place for some of my experience, but I think it's something I would use with a bit of caution because there is a power issue in the relationship and I'm not in any way wanting to say this is what you should do.

The wisdom for line-managers, and non-line-managers, is appropriately self-disclosing with supervisees, whether it is about their practice or personal experiences. As line-managers have power and authority, self-disclosure needs to be done so that the supervisee does not take it as an authoritative directive. Line-managers have a delicate balancing role of being a guide, mentor, and supporter and being a work manager. We believe that the wisdom of appropriately self-disclosing would help the former and facilitate the latter.

Overall, the supervisors' wisdom for professional supervision suggests that practice experience is vital, though all experience is not helpful. The wisdom of critically sharing relevant experiences, helping supervisees learn from their own reflections, learning from difficult experiences and practice that have not worked well, and appropriate self-disclosure all enhance professional supervision.

Practice Wisdom Statements

By analyzing narratives of supervisors, eight practice wisdom-oriented statements were identified. These are like practice idioms or adages with a figurative, profound meaning different from the lexicon. While these statements represent the supervisors' wisdom, the meaning one derives from them depends upon readers' thoughts, perceptions, and interpretations. What follows are their wisdom statements with narratives along with our brief comments.

"We Cannot be Good at Everything"

Social work and its practice scope are very broad. This is evident in Chap. 3, which discusses wide-ranging government and non-government organizations and practice settings. The practice scope of social work suggests that it is nearly impossible for any practitioner to excel within all these organizations and settings. However, in any professional practice, it is critical to be good at and have expected competencies and proficiency in one or a few areas according to one's own interest, passion, and commitment. One supervisor's practice wisdom was that it is good to focus on what you are good at, as one cannot be good at everything.

> I think the wisdom is that we can't be good at everything. And clinic, whilst mental health sounds like it's a small sector, when you get into it there are so many variations. And different ways that you like working. And so, what actually came down to me is I'm actually strongly behavioral change. That just seems to work with me, that's part of, that's just part of my likes and dislikes. So that's the stuff that I, like you've asked about, that I've worked through.

For example:

> I, because I've done so much work with perpetrators of violence, and perpetrators of domestic violence, I am no good with victims of domestic violence, because all I want to say is no, leave now, leave now. You've got to leave; you've got to leave.

> And in the end, I actually realized that, and as soon as I had someone that was a victim of domestic violence, I would try and help them with their anxiety and their fear but worked very hard to refer them out. So, whilst I certainly don't reject those clients, I will only accept them as a transitory thing, because I know that my own fear for them gets in the way. Because I've seen and read so many court documents about what people have done.
> … I've noticed it the other way too. People that have worked with victims, they're no good working with perpetrators.

The above narrative suggests that it is important for practitioners and supervisees to identify their strengths and what they are good at and hone them in terms of developing knowledge, skills, competencies, and practices and pursue what they are good at. "We can't be good at everything" may also mean we should be good at something; mediocrity has no place in professional practice as we cannot risk the quality of service to and well-being of the people and communities we serve. While the statement offers comfort, it also raises the expectation that practitioners must be good at what they do.

"The Story That a Person Tells About Their Experience is not the Experience. It's a Story They Tell About It"

Social workers often deal with complex cases, live situations, and decisions, whether it is related to child protection, domestic violence, abuse, mental health, disability, or involuntary clients. In such practice contexts, people present their problems and needs to social workers by sharing their experiences of what they are going through in their lives. As a practitioner, it is critical to carefully listen to those clients' stories to appropriately support, help, and enable and empower them. A supervisor over a long period of practice experience has developed the following strong belief and wisdom, which appears profound.

> … a statement I said the other day to somebody, she was talking about a woman who had a story of trauma. Many traumas and many sexual abuses, and lots of domestic violence over many years. And this worker was feeling swamped by it all. And I said to her a line that I've, took me years to come up with and I said "You know, one of the things I believe is that the story that a person tells about their experience is not the experience. It's just a story they tell about it." So that little statement is one that it took me a long time to come up. And she said, "Can you say that again?" So, I said "Well I think it's, I really do believe that the story that this woman is telling, all those stories, they're not the experiences she's been through. They're just the stories she tells about it."

> And I said "We could look at what, there are lots of other possible stories that she could be telling this woman." Like how she got away from each abusive man. How she survived each period of crisis and trauma. What she knows about protecting her kids. What she would like to be able to do to protect her kids, even if she can't manage it, etc. And we looked at all the other stories that she could be telling and we wondered about ways that this worker could help this woman get in touch with some of those other stories. So, I think that was kicked off by me by saying, "Well this woman is telling stories, she is simply speaking about her trauma. That is, it not, it's only the stories that she's telling. That is not the actual …

We recommend reading and rereading the above narrative and question. What does that statement mean? What is the wisdom in it? Although the supervisor has explained it, a deeper insight may be gained by reflecting on it for practice purposes. When clients present their problematic life experiences, perhaps, that is only the tip of the iceberg. They may have so many experiences and so many versions of experiences. Rather than "getting swamped" by one story, concluding by listening to one story, a version of the whole experience, social workers need to tactfully question to gather relevant experiences to understand the full story as much as possible as the full experience may not be known at all. Such an exploration will help practitioners to critically reflect and develop different ways of working with vulnerable people and communities.

"Not Just Jump In, Think"

Phrases such as "solution-focused" and "problem-solving process" generally give the impression that social workers are "problem fixers." Out of enthusiasm, social workers sometimes may not resist the temptation to help and try to solve the problem quickly. However, this supervisor cautions that it is important to pause and think before jumping into action. As an employee, it is also necessary to follow the organization's guidelines to offer help.

> ... but the learning for me was to not just jump in and I think as a supervisor what I often say to people now is I ask them to think of a swan sitting on the water of a lake. On the lake they look serene. When you look at them from afar they just look like they're swimming gracefully across the lake but underneath they're often, their feet are flapping at a million miles an hour but on the top of the surface everything is calm and resolute and my supervisor said to me, "What you've got to do is, with that incident with the young girl, your brain is going at a million miles an hour but you need to be thinking calmly and serenely as to what is the appropriate way to deal with something and not just (directly)respond because you happen to see a picture in the paper." So that's probably, when I think about one of the things that I've talked with some of my supervisees about.
> ... I'm really mindful that that's something I often say to my staff you can't just, you know we have emergencies, we have bushfires, we have floods, you can't just run out to a recovery center and put your badge on and say, "I'm here on behalf of the department," when in actual fact you've got to be invited in to be a part of that environment.

In the above narrative, the swan-lake analogy is insightful. As pointed out earlier, social workers are often presented with complex and emotionally impacting individual and family circumstances, and there may be a natural urge to quickly make decisions and help. The wisdom, "not just jump in, think," suggests that while the brain is flapping, reflecting in action, it is critical to remain calm and composed; gather all the necessary information, different stories, and different experiences; and reflect and think about the information, rather than just jumping into decisions and actions. People's natural urge to help and to receive timely help and organizational constraints to doing so are real dilemmas that must be addressed sensibly.

"Listen to the Gut, But Look for Evidence to Support It"

There is a constant challenge in balancing the epistemological bases of making decisions in social work and similar fields. The significance and relevance of both subjective and objective data and the culture of the dominance of objective data, usually referred to as epistemic bias or injustice, are not unfamiliar in social work research and practice. In the child protection context, one supervisor's practice wisdom suggested that it is important to listen to gut feelings, but it should be supported by evidence.

> Look, I think what I like to do is encourage my workers to listen to their gut, and then, well, what's the evidence that supports that gut feeling? I like them to unpack the information that they get, especially from the first visit. The first visit is an extremely important part of the work we do, it's almost a work of art, if you're going to get any information it's usually in that first visit, yeah, so how you approach it, how you get in the door, how you elicit the information, you've got to give people the information about the report, what are the protective concerns, as we call them? Why were they reported? You've got to be able to negotiate around the people's curiosity as to who reported, because we can't give any information that would enable the parent to realize who has reported them, unless we've got the express permission of that person. But how the workers use their sense of self, how they bring in their theoretical orientation, and how they use that as a vehicle to develop their understanding of the risk within that family.

Although the above narrative is in the context of child protection and home visits, the message from this practice wisdom is very clear. It is important not to ignore your gut feelings, but you should not be swayed by them nor make decisions solely based on them. A good balance needs to be developed between both subjective and objective data, that is, gut feelings must be supported by evidence or data to validate them. Integrating the sense of self with theoretical knowledge suggests that social work practice is both a science and an art, heart and head, and it is important to guard against undermining or ignoring one against the other. In any setting, home visits are good examples to learn and show how gut feelings and observed and gathered information can be knit together and analyzed to point out inconsistencies. So, in practice, it is important to value gut feelings consistent with information and evidence.

"Open to Being Challenged"

For supervisors, both line-managers and non-line managers, here is an important message. A supervisor was open to being challenged and encouraged supervisees to do so.

> So, look I would say to the staff, "You know because I've got longevity in the job doesn't mean that I've got all the right answers," and I really encourage people to challenge my decisions. And a lot of the time they do and they're right. But I think even that, being open to being challenged and stuff like that, even that is really helpful as an approach.

"Open to being challenged" suggests supervisees critically discussing supervisors' ideas, decisions, and alternative approaches and asking supervisors to justify their explanations. That is what healthy professional supervision should be. However, as discussed earlier, there is often a power imbalance and fear of authority, particularly in the line-management context. To translate this wisdom, supervisors need to create trustful, reassuring, and safe supervision environments, so supervisees can embrace this approach. Open to being challenged is generally a good virtue or quality because it not only shows the modesty of the person but also a willingness to re-examine one's decisions and actions and correct, improve, or affirm practices, from which both supervisors and supervisees are likely to gain more knowledge and skills.

"Focus on the Person, not Tasks Alone"

From organizational behavior, management, and productivity perspectives, this practice wisdom statement poses an important challenge and ethical dilemma. Under the influence of liberal ideology, market, and rationalization, many organizations have cultivated the culture of "do more with less," which has taken a significant toll on workers and has often resulted in valuing the work rather than the worker, burnout, compromising processes, low quality, and sometimes resignations. One supervisor's practice wisdom suggested that focusing on the person, not the task alone, is important.

> I concentrate less on, tasks and more on the person who's being supervised. And I think that is because when I worked as a child protection worker, I had supervisors who no kidding one after another, year after year in both Victoria and South Australia … you could have died at your desk and they would have just swept up the file and put them on someone else's desk. And it was just, there was no interest really in quality, and there was no interest in the person delivering the service. It was about, deliver a service. It doesn't matter how or who, just deliver it. And I remember you know as a young social worker, I was really concerned about you know the – how my colleagues and I, how we cut corners because we were exhausted all the time. And no one ever said, "Are you okay?" Or "Can I help you?" Everyone was in the same focus, get it – it was quantity. And so that's really informed my approach to work which is, that I need to honor the person who's doing, the person first and then the quality of the work improves exponentially.

Supervisors need to focus on workers and their well-being equally. The suffering that is narrated above is terrible for any employee. Organizations, supervisors, and managers not caring for their employees and just expecting work from them, even at the cost of processes and quality, poses an ethical dilemma. The insight and wisdom shared by the supervisor is that it is important to value the person, provide care and support, one of the core functions of supervision, and then, naturally, productivity follows.

"If in Doubt, Throw Them Out"

This practice wisdom relates to decision-making and judgment in practice, which are not easy in complex cases and situations. It is also linked to gathering all necessary information and reflecting in action, "not just jump in, think." Doubtful decisions and poor choices in practice will have negative consequences. A supervisor said:

> … one of our little things there was, "If in doubt, throw them out," and I will often talk with supervisees who might be in selection type situations who will be agonizing over, are we giving this person a fair, you know, blah, blah, blah. And, I'll say, look when I was in that setting because it's much easier to say no to people than it is to deal with the consequences of a poor choice.

In practice, often workers encounter uncertainties and many life circumstances and events that do not have clear answers or explanations. In fact, uncertainty and doubtfulness are a norm in certain settings, rather than an exception. If in doubt, making decisions can be problematic. Perhaps, it is necessary to examine why the doubt arises and what information would be needed to resolve it. Without adequate information and proper assessment, doubtful decisions should be avoided.

"There is no Perfect Theory"

In social work, education and practice as the link between theory and practice and practice and theory is relatively overemphasized (Pawar & Anscombe, 2015). However, the field realities, practice contexts, or a particular case situation often defies theories, pushing us to correct existing theories or discover new ones. With well-informed theoretical knowledge, it may be a good idea to approach practice with this wisdom as it helps to see situations with openness. A supervisor's practice wisdom is that, as there is no perfect theory, one must be aware of what theory is being used in what context. There is often a danger in doing without knowing.

> My practice wisdom is that there's no perfect theory. And that we can utilize all different forms of data as long as we know what we're doing, as long as we're explicit about that …
>
> I often find that practitioners that are new to me will have been practicing and they'll be mixing up theories and not explicitly stating what they're doing. And I'll also find that often they're using some empirical theories in an inappropriate way.
>
> So, if we're using an empirical theory, then there is a rationale and a, I call it treatment dose, because that's what in CBT, so a number of hours that you need to do to get clinical effect. You actually need to know that stuff and not just mix it up. And so, I'm pretty clear on, if you're only seeing a client for short therapies, then you can't do attachment theory, because that would be harmful to that client.

> And often social workers are really confused by that, because they learn pots of theory, which is good, as I did, but I think that in clinical mental health work, all of those clinical theories come with a bit of a rider. So, there are, we're using an evidence-based theory, we need to use it in the group and in the way the evidence base says. So, funding comes into that too. So, I would often, even when I was a clinician, and I would tell my supervisees, yep, you don't like this theory, it's not your preferred theory, this is what you're funded for, let's work out how you can use it in a way that you like.

In practice, we need to know what we are doing and be explicit about it. The example in the narrative shows that practitioners need to use theories appropriately in clinical practice and generally as well and follow the necessary implementation guidelines. Although there is no perfect theory and practitioners' preferences or liking to theories may differ, if a funder prescribes a particular theory to be followed, it is important to follow the theory, if one is part of such a team. "Let's work out how you can use it in a way that you like" suggests a crucial role of supervisors to help supervisees apply a theory their way in the imperfect theory world. As no perfect theory exists, one should not rigidly commit to any particular theory.

For example, these eight practice wisdom statements convey profound messages to supervisors and supervisees. Each one has a clear guide for practitioners. It has taken years of hard work and practice experience of supervisors to offer this wise advice. They also demonstrate the supervisors' qualities and virtues. These narratives may motivate readers to undertake further research to discover practitioners' wisdom.

Supervision Practice Principles or Techniques

As stated in the introduction, this is the third theme of practice wisdom analyzed from the supervisors' narratives. Our reading and rereading of their narratives appeared to us as principles or techniques. They also appear as dos and don'ts. Or they may be considered wise advice to supervisors and supervisees. A few of them may seem familiar, but they certainly reinforce and facilitate the practice of supervision. The following is a brief description of them.

Start with Their (Supervisees') Experience

This principle or a piece of advice is closely connected to the first theme, experience. Sharing experience, reflecting on it, and looking at what has and has not worked are necessary first steps in supervision. A supervisor suggested beginning with supervisees' experiences.

> I'm cautious around that and really probably my first line of approach would be, "Well, what have you tried so far?" Or "What do you know hasn't worked?" Or really start with them and their experience and then you know make some judicious decisions, I guess, about whether it is wise to drop in my tuppence worth, but I think it is an interesting line because it's not about withholding but it is about what's actually likely to be most useful here.

To begin with, supervisors exploring supervisees' experiences help supervisors understand the context better and make judicious decisions to offer help relating to administration, education, and support or any other area useful to supervisees.

Active Listening

Social workers are familiar with the knowledge, skill, or technique of active listening and are well trained to do so in their practice. Active listening is both a principle and basic skill, and, as a competency, active listening ability needs to be purposely developed by training and practice. A supervisor stated that they bring "active listening" to supervision.

> And I guess what I really bring to it is the active listening. You know, like, listening empathically and asking questions to expand and explore the issue a bit more fully. So that's the base line, I guess.

Active listening requires being free from a mind preoccupied with professional and personal engagements and events. It also requires a presence of mind with full concentration on the supervisee. Although it is not a "client-social worker" situation, active listening involves observing both verbal and nonverbal communication. Genuine empathy and compassion give life to active listening.

Never Say "I Know How You Feel"

Empathy is taught as an important principle in social work education and practice. Accurate empathy is difficult to achieve, and the skill of empathizing can only be developed by practice, by trial and error. Operationalizing empathy is necessary while working with clients or people, but is it needed in the same way while working with supervisees? We are of the view that, generally, empathy is a good humanistic trait when interacting with and relating to people. As a general guide or principle, a supervisor suggested the following:

> Never say "I know how you feel." Never. Not with clients and not with [laughing] your colleagues.
>   Because, yeah, you can say "Well I empathize" but you will never know how somebody else feels.

Empathizing by expressing "I know how you feel" or "I empathize" may appear mechanical and to some extent unreal. Some people or clients (for example, the homeless, chemically dependent, incarcerated people, and sex workers) can challenge practitioners that they cannot know how they are feeling. While juxtaposing this issue with the supervisor-supervisee context is problematic, the scrutiny of effective skills for the use of empathy is called for. In whatever way it is expressed, genuineness, warmth, and compassion may bridge this gap, but this is a matter for another discussion. However, the supervisor's advice is clear: "Never say I know how you feel."

Acknowledging and Validating

Although offering service is the foundation of social work (see social work codes of ethics) and there is an element of selflessness, the need for recognition, appreciation, and affirmation is human. A supervisor suggests it is important to acknowledge and validate supervisees and their practice regularly.

> And acknowledging, normalizing maybe some of those feelings, acknowledging what they're going through, and validating the work that they're doing as beneficial and useful and affirming that they're on the right track. You know, that's the approach I'd take as my base line.

Supervisors can and do play an important role in building the confidence of supervisees. Along with providing educational support, validating, and affirming knowledge and practice skills of supervisees, reassuring them that what they are doing is beneficial will help supervisees learn more and do better. At the same time, appropriately acknowledging supervisees' difficulties, feelings, and uncertainties may offer them some support and comfort.

Do Not Get Bogged Down to One Thing; in Crisis, Look for Opportunities

Whenever difficulties, challenges, or complex cases are encountered, there may be feelings of getting stuck, not able to see alternatives or options. Under such circumstances, a supervisor suggested looking for opportunities rather than being engulfed by just one thing.

> Don't get bogged down in one thing. That might be the practice wisdom, I suppose. And then, if there's a crisis on, what opportunities are there here? Not just to see it as a big problem. (pause) I suppose that's just come from a bit of recent reading and that sort of thing.

This is sound advice and a good principle to follow in practice. Otherwise, one serious incident in practice may stop the whole process. It is useful in terms of making further progress for supervisees to develop this perspective. Looking for opportunities in crises provides hope, which helps people get through such difficulties.

Don't Bring Too Much of Yourself in; It Is Not About You

This theme is repeatedly observed in supervisors' narratives. Thus, it may be considered a principle of professional supervision. Supervision is never about supervisors; it is all about supervisees and the outcomes for people and clients. Supervisors should not dominate supervision. It is important that supervisors remain other-focused rather than self-focused.

> … don't bring too much of yourself in. Bring some sometimes, but it's not about you. It's about the supervisee who's come to you. They don't want to listen to your story. That time is short, and it needs to be about them. So, being really clear about that, so, that's been something I've learnt across time.

With a wealth of accumulated experience and expertise, it may be difficult for some supervisors to hold back, and they may inadvertently dominate through their power and authority, particularly in the context of line-management. This principle is an important reminder to all supervisors that supervision is about supervisees and people and client outcomes, and it should be driven by them. Supervisors have a facilitative role only of making contributions as required.

Ask Hard Questions

This principle, technique, or skill is linked to the wisdom of "reflecting on and learning from your own experience" discussed earlier in this chapter. Asking hard and bold questions is necessary to find answers and new answers or insights. Hard questions facilitate reflection and make one think critically. On the other hand, the response of "do not know" may make one defensive, passive, and wait for others' help. A supervisor suggested the following:

> So, stop saying "We don't know" because we're perpetuating this myth that we don't know. So, that just really makes me cranky. So, I will challenge, I do challenge people in supervision. And I ask hard questions and I go places. My supervisor said to me once "(Participant name), you go places that nobody else would go" because I'm not frightened to ask the hard questions or go to those hard places, that people get uncomfortable with and don't want to talk about. Yeah. And yet I think that's the most interesting bit because then you're really getting to the core of the problem. So, the practice wisdom around that is that you can't push people, don't push them too fast or too far. Because I might have an idea in my head about "Oh Lord, I think this is about this" but it's up to them to name it first. So, you got to be very careful about that. Don't come on too, don't be too all knowing.

Supervisees should stop saying "I do not know" and begin thinking and reflecting. Supervisors should raise challenging questions to "get to the core of the problem." Instead of supervisors providing answers, by raising questions, supervisees can be helped to look at the presenting problem differently, practice options, and find solutions or further questions on their own.

Upside-Down Brainstorm—Discussing the Opposites

Sometimes, to emphasize a point, to reinforce a particular practice or think creatively, a technique of using the opposite logic or opposite way of thinking may be useful in supervision. What a supervisor has narrated below appears to be a creative and effective way of helping supervisees realize certain dos and don'ts in practice.

> … it was like an upside-down brainstorm. So instead of saying – instead of brainstorming things that would work, we brainstormed things that would definitely not work. So, I think this person came with a problem of feeling like she wasn't – the team, multidisciplinary team, didn't value her contribution. And she felt like she was having to really fight for her methodology to be accepted by the team. And so, what we did was – yeah, so we all – we did it like a role model. So, we – there were actually a couple of things we tried. So, she sat in the chair as the – well, I'll talk about the first way first of all, where we all threw out ideas

of what – instead of saying, "Well, have you tried talking to the team about your approach and some of the theoretical values?" we would say the opposite to that. Yeah. "Have you tried just not listening at all and talking over your colleagues and telling them they're idiots?" We tried all the opposites – we suggested all the opposite. So, what came out of the discussion was all the things you should not be doing, which made her think about – okay, well she's doing some things right, she's not doing any of those things so what she's doing is probably good, it was, like, finding the exceptions. Yeah.

Reverse brainstorming is a technique that helps to see causes of the problem, which in turn helps to find solutions. An example in the above narrative shows how the supervisor used the reverse brainstorm technique to help the supervisee affirm practices they should and should not be doing. It is a creative way of helping supervisees to think outside the box or laterally (de Bono, 2009) and may be carefully employed when suitable.

This section has discussed eight principles and techniques shared by supervisors. These are insightful and helpful to both supervisors and supervisees to facilitate better professional supervision. There may be many similar techniques supervisors may be using in their supervision, which need further exploration.

Conclusion and Summary

In this chapter, experienced supervisors have shared their supervision practice wisdom. Although wisdom is an important quality or virtue (Hugman et al., 2021), it is a complex concept and difficult to delineate and explain (Dodd & Savage, 2016). However, as clarified in the introduction, supervisors' narratives of wisdom tend to capture the knowledge and actions embedded in their experiences (tacit knowledge), critical reflections linked to past and prospective actions, and certain strategies in terms of wisdom statements and principles or techniques (intersubjectivity). Each supervisor has shared different practice wisdom because their supervision practice settings and practice experiences differ. The practice wisdom of working in large public sector organizations such as the child protection and mental health fields of practice is quite different from working in small non-government organization settings. That range and difference are well reflected in the above-presented narratives. However, through those narratives, the invaluable wisdom they have shared generally appears to be useful for both supervisors and supervisees. Valuing relevant experience as the fundamental basis of wisdom, critical reflection in and on actions, learning from what has and has not worked, eight practice wisdom idioms or adages that have profound implications for supervision practice, and eight practical supervision principles or techniques will help further think and improve professional supervision in social work.

As the chapter is about the practice wisdom of supervisors, their qualities and virtues are well portrayed in their narratives. Talking of or reflecting on practice wisdom in itself is a virtue. Many supervisors used terms such as "strive for learning, affirming/validating practice, careful self-disclosure, putting into action, enhancing knowledge and skills, humility and humbleness, exploring opportunities, listening to the gut, challenging decisions, encouraging hard questions, open to being challenged, active listening, making judicious decisions, and keeping on the right track," which suggests the presence of implicit qualities or virtues in supervision practice. It appears that there is scope for purposefully developing these and similar qualities or virtue in supervisees through professional supervision practice. We have significantly gained from interviewing supervisors and rereading their narratives and supervision wisdom. We hope readers may be able to better reflect on these narratives, find new meanings and insights beyond our interpretations, and further contribute to supervision practice. The next chapter will discuss the use of virtues or qualities in supervision.

References

Arnd-Caddigan, M. (2011). Toward a broader definition of evidence-informed practice: Intersubjective evidence. *Families in Society: The Journal of Contemporary Social Services, 92*, 372–376.

Austin, M. J. (2008). Strategies for transforming human service organizations into learning organizations: Knowledge management and the transfer of learning. *Journal of Evidence-Based Social Work, 5*, 569–596.

De Bono, E. (2009). *Lateral thinking: A textbook of creativity*. Penguin.

Dodd, S. J., & Savage, A. (2016). Evidence-informed social work practice. Psychoanalysis. In T. Mizrahi & L. Davis (Eds.), *Encyclopedia of social work*. Oxford University Press.

Hugman, R., Pawar, M., Anscombe, A. W., & Wheeler, A. (2021). *Virtue ethics in social work practice*. Routledge.

Morrell, M. (2003). *Forethought and afterthought- two of the keys to professional development and good practice in supervision*. Social Work Review, Autumn/Winter 2003, p. 29–32.

Pawar, M., & Anscombe, A. W. (2015). *Reflective social work practice: Thinking, doing and being*. Cambridge University Press.

Payne, M. (2021). *Modern social work theory* (5th ed.). Red Globe Press.

Weststrate, N. M., & Glück, J. (2017). Hard-earned wisdom. *Developmental Psychology, 53*(4), 800–814. https://doi.org/10.1037/dev0000286

Chapter 11
The Use of Virtues or Qualities in Supervision

Introduction

As stated in the first chapter and referred to in the conclusion and summary of relevant chapters, one of the objectives of this book is to explore whether supervisors focus on developing character or qualities in the process of supervision. Earlier, we have observed that in the supervisors' narratives presented so far, we found the implicit presence of some virtues or qualities, though there was no evidence of systematically and purposely developing them in supervisees. This chapter discusses whether and how supervisors try to develop virtues or qualities in supervisees as part of professional supervision.

Our focus on the virtues or qualities aspect of professional supervision is in recognition of its general neglect relative to principle and rule-based ethics in the social work profession (see Pawar, 2014; Pawar & Anscombe, 2015; Hugman et al., 2021) and its relevance to supervision, which is all about developing the supervisee as a good practitioner for the ultimate benefit of the people and communities they serve. Virtues are human qualities or characteristics that are regarded as good or right in a cultural context (see Hugman et al., 2021) and enhance individuals' moral nature and capacity to do their best in adherence to and beyond principles and rules, which are not sufficient in some contexts. Complex and challenging field situations need virtuous practitioners who can analyze and make decisions to work with and address those challenges. We believe professional supervision is one of the best opportunities to reinforce and strengthen some of the virtues and qualities of supervisees. Thus, this chapter examines the supervisors' views and attempts to develop supervisees' virtues and qualities.

The first part of the chapter presents some social workers' qualities perceived by supervisors. These include finding one's own answers or self-determination, strengths-based thinking, a non-judgmental approach, human rights, empowerment, honesty and accountability, patience, tolerance, understanding, care, compassion,

© The Author(s), under exclusive license to Springer Nature Switzerland AG 2022
M. Pawar, A. W. (Bill) Anscombe, *Enlightening Professional Supervision in Social Work*, https://doi.org/10.1007/978-3-031-18541-0_11

good relationships, links to the wider world, and shared learning. The second part discusses how supervisors develop some qualities of supervisees. The analysis of the narratives suggested their efforts in developing the qualities of strengths, honesty, reflection, good listening, decision-making, warmth, confidence, and humor. The last part concludes the chapter with a summary.

Social Workers' Qualities Perceived by Supervisors

We tried to directly explore whether supervisors draw on social workers' qualities in relation to their practice. Most supervisors stated that they do, and a couple of them were unsure. The supervisors' ambiguity in relation to the use of social workers' qualities in supervision is reflected in the following response. *"Yeah, I think I probably do. Again, it's probably not something that I intentionally do ... "* It is important to note that some elements of qualities and character are inherent in social work due to the helping nature of social work and codes of ethics; however, intentionally focusing on developing qualities is different from their subdued presence. From the other supervisors' narratives, the following qualities were identified.

Finding Their Own Answers/Self-Determination

A couple of supervisors emphasized the quality of helping people find their own answers rather than directly offering help. Valuing people's knowledge and skills and helping them determine answers are important values or principles in social work.

> I want to expand, make them conscious, the principles of the clients being the expert in their own situation. Not having the answers for people, that people have to generate their own answers ...
>
> I draw on things like, you know, the values of the profession, that capacity to identify but very aware of people's self-determination. For me, self-determination is a critical issue.

Valuing people's knowledge and skills means treating them with dignity and respect and helping them self-determine. These remarks suggest supervisors can link the values and principles to social workers' qualities. The connection between social work values and principles and social workers' qualities needs further exploration (Banks, 2012).

Strengths-Based Thinking

Although a strength-based approach to supervision was discussed earlier, a supervisor identified strengths-based thinking as a quality.

> I like to use strengths, strengths-based thinking and … the use of self and what you bring to your client. So, I use their strengths and say, 'righteo, what is it about you that you're able to do well? What things do you find easy? What things do you find rewarding?'

Looking at one's own strengths as a social worker, that is, using self from the strengths-thinking perspective and working with clients, people, and communities from the perspective of their strengths, can be developed as a quality of strengths-based thinking.

Being Non-judgmental, Human Rights, Empowerment

Another supervisor perceived being non-judgmental and following human rights and empowerment approaches as qualities that need to be developed.

> … always watching to ensure that those qualities of being non-judgmental and you know, a human rights approach and empowering individuals to be the experts in their own lives, that those things are present and happening.

These approaches are often discussed in social work, but it would be interesting to explore how these can be developed as qualities.

Honesty, Accountability, and Trust

A line-manager referred to the qualities of honesty, accountability, and trust so that there is no need to check whether a worker is working or not.

> …I'm constantly trying to get them to practice in a way, you know, perform in a way that is just professional and adult and human decency, you know, being honest and being account-able and …
> … turning up on time and you know, if you tell me you're going to do this, actually me being able to trust that it will be done rather than feeling like I have to check up on you.

This is the essence of developing qualities. Once honesty, accountability, and trust are developed or ensured, good work and relationships flow on their own. The supervisor describes these qualities as human decency.

Patience, Tolerance, Understanding, and Care

A supervisor referred to patience, tolerance, understanding and care as human qualities.

> … I keep coming back to that word, those human qualities and the "Let's have patience, tolerance, understanding, and care for each other, irrespective of hierarchies." Because I just think that transcends everything, really. [Laughing] I just think it does. [Pause] But not everybody sees it like that.

It is important to underscore the supervisor's remark that these qualities are relevant irrespective of hierarchies and transcend everything.

Compassion

A supervisor referred to compassion as a quality of social worker. *"I have a particular quality; everybody tells me I'm really compassionate."* Compassion is a composite attribute that includes careful listening, kindness, caring, support, giving, love, and empathy.

Good Relationships/Links to the Wider World

In a mental health setting, a supervisor highlighted the importance of focusing on the qualities of good relationships and connecting to the wider world.

> … we as social workers in mental health do wider service, so we will make links to Centrelink, we will make links to CASA, we will have them in our speed dial, so that we've got colleagues that we can get our clients help with. I had a particularly good relationship when I was in general practice, with Centrelink …

> And there's always this link to the wider social world. So, you know, and normalizing my supervisees' clients' behaviors and responses in context of their wider social context.

Here, the supervisor perceives cultivating contact with practice and the client's wider context and maintaining good relationship with them as qualities.

Shared Learning

A supervisor perceives sharing learning among staff members as a quality.

> … I'm always encouraging people to not only go and do that sort of training, but to also then develop their colleagues around them and to actually share their experience and their learning so that it then becomes a part of everyone's practice.

In the organizational context, helping and encouraging colleagues to share their learnings with others is a good quality and practice.

Inherent Personal Traits and Characteristics

In addition to the above-listed social workers' qualities perceived by supervisors, we asked them to name some of the qualities of social workers. A couple of supervisors narrated as follows:

I think that there are some inherent personal traits and characteristics.

You know, well, humility, compassion, a sense of righteousness, a sense of social justice. A sense of doing what is right, a sense of openness, vulnerability, transparency, the capacity to feel … the capacity to feel for the other person without taking ownership of their feelings and that's a tricky one and that's one that I often pick up with some stuff.

Patience, tolerance, care, understanding, [pause] good communication which isn't just about talking, the listening [pause] very much. [Pause] Just always being human. Don't forget we're all people. We're all trying our hardest. [Laughing] We all make mistakes. We all get it wrong sometimes. That's what being human is about. And so, let's keep that front and center for social work because I think that's what makes social workers really. And at the back of my mind, just as I said that I thought oh and let's be radical sometimes.

These qualities not only confirm some of the above perceived qualities but also show that supervisors are aware of the qualities that social workers need in social work practice. Generally, most of the qualities identified relate to professional practice. The emphasis on "capacity to feel without owning," "being human," and the recognition of "making mistakes" or "getting it wrong sometimes" show the complexities, challenges, and uncertainties of social work practice. From the projection perspective, the above listed qualities may be interpreted as qualities of the supervisors. Having identified these qualities and assumed that these are supervisors' qualities, we further explored how supervisors develop some of these qualities in supervisees.

Developing Supervisees' Virtues/Qualities in Supervision

The following section discusses how supervisors develop supervisees' qualities. We asked supervisors to share some supervision examples of how they draw on and develop supervisees' qualities. After some contemplation, they presented the following examples from their supervision sessions. By analyzing those examples, we have identified and discussed several qualities. However, it may be noted that these examples and qualities are not in any particular order, as each is important in a given context. A few qualities are repeated in different examples as they cannot be separated according to the categorization due to the nature of the narratives.

Using Strengths of Supervisees

In the following example, a social worker/supervisee could not find a place or role in a multidisciplinary team and was on the verge of withdrawing from the team. The supervisor drew on the supervisee's strengths, helped the supervisee communicate openly, plan not to give up, and be proactive and assertive, which all emanated from the supervisee's strengths. It also shows the significance of not focusing on certain vices, such as being negative or reactive.

I had a recent client that I saw. Who was working in a medical model, working alongside nurses, and she was the only social worker on the team. She was coming to the decision of whether, "I stay in my role, or whether I leave?" She just didn't feel she could be part of the team because she didn't feel that she had a role. So, using strengths, I sort of said to her, "Well, you either try to make it work by being proactive."

Because she said, "I like to try and think through things, and I like to try and problem solve, and work out solutions." So, I said, "Well, how about you just try and figure out if there's a possibility by speaking to your manager?" She said, "Oh yes, I've actually spoken to the manager about it and she's going to have me join in on assessments when there's any new referral to come through." But I felt I encouraged her more by, believing in herself to do that, that she could actually accomplish change by using her strengths in making her work more appealing to herself.

Because it was a palliative care and the nurses have been trained to do everything. It's been historic that if a social worker was on that team, that you didn't even have a, didn't ever have her own desk. She was just a, was floating, across all kinds of rooms where she could find her, a table and a chair. I don't think that's, you've got to be able to feel belonged when you're in an organization.

… previously before she became employed there, she had done her social work placement there. So, I said, "Well how are things different when you were a student, now you're an employee? What do you find, what's changed? What's the same?" Looking at comparisons all the time and seeing, "Well, what do you think you now could do, to create an environment where you feel that you can contribute and be a part of that team?"

So, at the end of the day we ended up talking through that she will give it another go until the end of the year. But by communicating more openly to her line-manager more openly about options that she could see herself do. Rather than being reactive to the negative vibes and not feeling wanted, or not having a role where she can openly contribute. Because she said, "I know all this stuff, I know that I can, I know about medication, and I've worked in pharmacies before and did all that." So, I said, "Well this is really important that you use your knowledge, this is really great."

Because nurses and social workers don't always get along. (laugh) Then I brought back my experience of working in medical model and in a multidisciplinary team … So, I made similarities, comparisons to this, how things can change, how things can improve by your strengths.

That gave her a lot of encouragement to carry on with her plan of not giving up, but by putting forth some suggestions, with, strengthened with the ideas we've discussed, to give it another go. But she can actually prove her worth as a social worker. Break down that barrier of what is perceived as a social worker. That they are useful, that they're not just there to tick boxes and find you, you know, financial support, or (laugh) housing. A lot of that can still impact on people as they don't quite understand, from other professions, what we do.

But I've said, "It's about being proactive and being assertive enough to say, that these are the things I can see myself doing as a social worker." And allowing that to, and of course that's up to the manager to allow that to happen. But it's to also create a better culture for social workers in moving forward.

The above example shows that the supervisor helped the supervisee be proactive to make it work, encouraged them to believe in themselves to make changes, compared the previous experience, and contributed to creating a new environment and using previous pharmacy knowledge. Most importantly, the supervisor shared the previous experience, discussed similarities, and showed how things could change and improve by using one's own strengths. By performing the social worker's role, asserting oneself was also a good strategy of strength.

Another supervisor also said that if supervisees are doubting their capabilities, it is good to draw on their strengths:

> I think if someone was showing that they were doubting their own capabilities I think I'd – I'd like to draw out the strengths that I could see so that they were feeling like they have got something positive to offer and that they are doing a good job. So, I'd bring out – I'd draw out from them – you know, social workers can feel that they're not being very successful, they're not making change quickly enough, or they're not helping a family. So, I think it's important to bring out the qualities that are legitimately theirs that they're bringing to the situation, that might be qualities such as, "But you're such a good listener," or "You've done a good job of assessing that family. You know, you've really got a really good concept of what's happening in that whole system." And so, I think noticing the things they do well, even if it might be something small.

The above example shows that removing self-doubt is a good step in building strengths. Supervisors can build supervisees' strengths by positive reinforcement, encouraging, appreciating, and recognizing when they do well, even small things.

Be Open and Honest and Non-judgmental

In the following supervision situation, a supervisee worked in two organizations simultaneously with the same client. When one organization realized this, it made the supervisee angry and upset. The supervisee raised the issue during supervision, where the supervisor pointed out a conflict of interest and how it was important for the supervisee to focus on openness and honesty and yet remain non-judgmental.

> A worker is seeing a client there, and also seeing a client somewhere else. In a different job. And I said, "What are your policies around this? Maybe that's something that's really important for you to have a look at. To make it very clear. And to be open and honest. So, have a conversation with this person." So, this person was very, came to me and I could see was very upset and angry about this. And so, exploring this issue and having a look at what was happening around this conflict of interest. Every situation is different, and you need to really tease out what's happening here. How did this person find out that this worker is working over here? They may have independently searched this person out. Do we have a right to stop someone searching out a worker somewhere else?

> You can't really control this worker in what he's doing, or he or she's doing, at this other organization. You can however have a conversation, an open non-judgmental conversation with the worker about your concern, about maybe the impact on your organization, maybe future insurance claims? 'Cause that can happen. I put that out there. So, I said "All these things are out there."

In a practice situation such as this, the supervisor is asking the supervisee to follow the organizations' policies and be open, honest, and non-judgmental, which may help the supervisee develop these important qualities.

Experiential Learning, Reflection, Non-judgmental, Good Listening, and Observing

In the following example, a supervisor shows how a supervisee was helped to learn from past experiences and reflect on them. The supervisor also focused on the skills of good listening and observing and remaining non-judgmental.

> There's a young woman who I supervise at the moment who's got a little bit of experience of mental illness and she's also supporting other people, and she's employed. I get her to think about, what her learnings are from her own experience. And how if she's talking to someone who's worried about going to hospital. She's got direct experience of that. If she's talking to someone who's having hallucinations and wondering what that's doing to their social life, because it interferes with that sort of thing.

> To use her own experience to think about where the person's coming from and what might be. Their qualities, that she has for self-reflection and to be non-judgmental, to be a good listener. She's all those sorts of things. When I'm talking to her about that, I said, 'Talk about the person and what they're telling you. How did you observe that?' Get her to be specific about non-verbals and relate that to her own experience. She said, 'I know that you would be feeling that, because that's what I felt.' So, what did you see that reinforces that for you?

Learning from one's own experience, reflecting on it and using it in practice to relate to people's experiences, and developing communication skills in terms of listening, observing, and focusing on the person are excellent clinical social work practice skills. Further deliberation is needed to determine whether these skills, by practice and habit, can be developed and considered as qualities, or whether they remain as practice skills.

Developing Clarity About Issues and Decision-Making

In a family court setting, social workers often work with complex and challenging cases. In addition, their work situation may be demanding, and it may be difficult to juggle all these issues. In such circumstances, the following examples show how supervisors have enabled a supervisee to develop clarity about issues and decide not to offer their service.

> I'm thinking of the family court reporter who was a social worker who now works privately and has had two situations recently where judges have asked, where children are going to be handed from one parent to another, and have asked that this report writer oversee that handover at his office. He did one of them and it was just shocking for him, so he's now looked at, if understandably so, and so what we've looked at is I guess around advocacy in part for himself but also for this family, what could he do other than be in the situation where the judge makes that demand of him, because he doesn't see that as a purposeful thing to be doing. You know, we talked to, "Is it actually better for the kids that you're there blah, blah, blah?" In his particular circumstances he doesn't see so, so and we're looking at how can he actually stand up in that system appropriately and say, "This is a piece of work I'm not available to do," and what might be the strategies for that and some of it is about you know, having a full diary.

I guess that's one of the pieces where that original conversation about "where do we draw the line?" on this continuum comes into sharper focus, so, I would certainly be working with someone to identify if there was some challenge in their practice that seemed to be related to some personal situation. To get that conscious and concrete and then look at, "Well what do we do about it? Is that something that we'll talk about some more here?" Is there somewhere else that you would take that but to make that a conscious decision. I'm really fine about that occurring here, in theory. Sometimes, in practice it wouldn't be wise, but I would certainly always make that a decision-making process, but I'd probably go as far as with the person, getting clear about what the issue was so they could then decide what to do with it.

In another setting, mental health, the following example shows how a supervisor empowered supervisees to be assertive and take it as a challenge.

I just think of one case, one supervisee, who mainly saw women. And she had a man referred. And she started seeing him and so we had a whole session on "what is it about seeing men?" Because this man actually had the same mental health condition as the women that she was seeing. But she felt that she actually wasn't helping and she felt that she didn't like it. She didn't know how much she was helping.

So, actually a lot of that was in the end, we decided that she could either just look at this as a challenge and look at this as a way to extend her skills, or she could just refer it back. And so, a lot of it is empowering social workers to say actually, "You know what? I'm really, really good at this client group." And yes, you might be similar, but you're not.

In both examples above, the supervisor has helped the supervisees think, develop clarity about the issue, and, by asserting themselves, make a decision to continue working with a presenting issue or not to continue. It appears that by developing clarity and helping the supervisee to be assertive, the supervisor has tried to empower the supervisees to make tough decisions. Decision-making and right or appropriate decision-making are critical attributes of a social worker, but they can only be developed by practice and with the necessary and appropriate support.

Affirming Braveness

In organizations, there may be situations where workers must deal with complex and sensitive collegial issues through no fault of their own. Talking about such issues with a supervisor or manager calls for courage. Under such circumstances, a supervisor affirmed the bravery of a supervisee, as illustrated below.

It's just a recent one where – she's a new graduate social worker, but she's a very, very confident and competent young woman, and in her team is someone who feels a bit threatened by her. And I think she was – yeah, she was not sure about – she was feeling as if this person was trying to sabotage her work, because that person had been there for a bit longer and was more senior than her. But this new girl – she was working much harder and getting more done and having very complex cases and having good successes and people were coming to her to talk about – instead of to the senior person. And the senior person was feeling very threatened. And she felt very guilty talking to me about this because she felt that she was a little bit out of her – or she felt, you know, she should be looking up at this person, respecting this person more, and she felt a little bit bad talking about – negatively about her colleague to me. And so, I affirmed her for sharing it. Affirmed her braveness for sharing it, because I could see that she felt uncomfortable sharing it …

Yeah, yeah. She felt uncomfortable. And she felt that she shouldn't be sharing it because she was, I suppose, she was criticizing her senior person. And she felt uncomfortable. So, I commended her braveness and I commended her for her obvious hard work and her strength. And then we talked about some ways that she might tackle that in a respectful and ethical way.

When issues occur or are noticed or experienced in a practice, community, or organization, naming and raising them is not easy. Many people tend to overlook such issues, even if it is directly hurting them. However, social workers are trained to locate, discuss, and mobilize people and call out issues of injustice. The proportion of workers that engage in such practice is not clear. The above example shows how the supervisor appreciated and affirmed the bravery of the supervisee in discussing a sensitive staffing issue within the organizational context. This is one way of showing how the quality of courage can be encouraged and developed by taking small steps.

Warmth and Power

Warmth and power, in some respects, are important interconnected qualities; often the former can generate the latter. The absence of the former and misuse of the latter can lead to disasters in any professional practice and more so in social work. In the following example, a supervisor shows how an attempt was made to develop the quality of warmth in a worker. It also shows how the supervisor developed awareness of the worker's being relating to the use of power and helped the worker to carefully use the power of warmth in practice.

So, I do all that all the time, I think, in terms of, whether its people's, we're talking about personal qualities of warmth, or some people have a beautiful openness they bring to social work. And it's powerful. They bring a powerful presence without meaning to into a relationship with a client or a community. And, but I think there's lots of other sets of qualities, again like I was saying, people's ability to, someone might be not such a warm person but can do some really straight talking. I'm thinking of one social worker I supervised a few years ago who really was not a warm soul. And I am. I work through warmth and I like to think of myself as a strong and very gentle social worker. But with strength, whereas this woman was just not gentle and warm, she just didn't operate like that. Really blunt, really open, said it as it was, but deeply caring.

And so, we tried to name how she operates. Importantly, I think, because lots of people, she, that was her, one of her ways of being. She also had a really amazing knowledge of the networks available for people. And a good set of relationships with referring workers. And other organizations. So, again, just naming those up, exploring them, but with this young woman as well, questioning some of the impact of some of her ways of being, because lots of people would be really drawn to her, and a couple of people would be a bit frightened of her. So, we looked at, whether or not, how she uses her power, how she exercises her power might just be a bit off-putting for some people, and how she could be perhaps be aware of that more without losing her really lovely way of being.

Genuine warmth, love, and "a beautiful openness" are great qualities. Having them as part of one's being is one thing, but genuinely expressing them is another. Both are critical. All these have undeniable power in developing and maintaining relationships. Here, the supervisor is helping the supervisee think about their communication, the use of power, and its unintended impacts. By raising this awareness, the supervisor is helping the supervisee demonstrate and develop warmth and "a beautiful openness" as a quality; the flow of power from that would be quite different.

Reassuring/Building Confidence

Social workers often work with wicked problems, and it is difficult to see immediate and tangible results, and, sometimes, that may not be the objective. Under such circumstances, some social workers may question their ability to do good work or doubt what they are doing. One supervisor said it was important to reassure them and build their confidence.

> Well, you know, sometimes social workers that I supervise will come and they'll think that they haven't done a really good job. And actually, when you pull it apart, they have. And start talking about the qualities that they've brought to that relationship. So, they will have developed trust. They will have used their really good interpersonal skills to build rapport. They will have allowed the client to maybe get a wider picture of the issue that's confronting them. They'll have, and social workers in mental health, because we're mandated using empirical stuff, will have given them some psychoeducation usually.

> And so, while the social worker may not have solved the person's problem, they may have actually helped them on their way a bit or enabled them to go on for another day … So, in mental health a lot of it is accepting that you ease the way. You give people some skills, you ease the way.

By helping social workers to recognize what they have done, their confidence can be enhanced. When supervisees undervalue their own work, supervisors can identify and show supervisees' successful efforts and achievements such as building relationships, trust, and rapport and making a difference for a day. Small successful steps in the process and developing a sense of confidence are important, and supervisors, as demonstrated above, can help achieve that.

Humor

Developing a sense of humor as a quality and its use in professional supervision is under-researched (Gilgun & Sharma, 2012; Jordan, 2017, 2019a, 2019b) compared to the use of humor by leaders in organizations (Robert et al., 2015; Tan et al., 2020). The use of positive humor between the supervisor and the supervisee, social worker, and the client or people may lighten any workplace unhappiness or stressful situations, at least for some workers and people. One supervisor said that, by observing supervisees, they might be encouraged to use their sense of humor.

> I suppose through observations, you might get some people who've got that sense of humor, and you can ask them, or you can encourage them to use that sense of humor appropriately in the relationship they have with clients. I suppose I just always encourage people to use their own personality and their strengths, so if you've got a very gentle worker, well, they don't have to change, they don't have to become strident, they can use that gentle approach, but that persistent approach.

Whether humor is a quality or a skill is unclear, but both are important in some situations. Jordan (2019a, p. 90) believes that "Humour can be used to think differently and innovatively, and, in the end, positive and shared humour enables a practice that can be both more social and more humane." Positive humor can be used constructively between the supervisor and supervisee, social worker, and people by recognizing and developing it as a quality and skill. Although there are merits of using humor in suitable contexts, it is important to take note of cultural appropriateness, the level of existing relationship, communicating intended meanings, and the no harm principle (Gilgun & Sharma, 2012; Jordan, 2017).

Gentleness

The quality of gentleness is linked to many other qualities such as kindness, compassion, and empathy. Some social workers can sometimes be quite strident for many reasons (one's own nature, an abusive or aggressive client or people, a stressful setting or case, etc.). In the following example, the supervisor highlights how it is sometimes necessary to change from strident to quiet and become a good listener.

> If you've got a more strident worker, I suppose, I would just match the cases with the worker, as well, in terms of allocation, and what I might do with my workers is, at times I might ask them if they needed to flex their style, and strident people can become more quiet and they can become active listeners, they don't always have to rush in, but you also have to challenge your workers too. I do find the more strident workers more difficult to supervise, I must say.
>
> I think child protection has got a reputation for being very strident, almost aggressive, but when you work here you see that isn't actually the case.

Do we need a strident quality in a social worker and what kind of social work needs a strident quality? The supervisor has found strident workers difficult to supervise. It is important to develop the quality of gentleness and quiet listening (see Marques, 2013); changing a strident style may produce better outcomes for clients and people.

Capacity to Face Challenges and Make Difficult Decisions

Some social work practices are more challenging than others. A supervisor gave an example of how supervisees are helped to face challenges and make difficult decisions under value conflict situations, particularly in the child protection setting. These are important qualities but are not easy to learn.

> I think, yeah, in a lot of the work that one does in child protection, I think that it gives you an opportunity to be challenged in terms of your professional values and your professional framework, as well as when there is a potential conflict between what you're actually required to do. So, making decisions about removing children from their parents is a fairly big issue and there's a whole lot of issues related. There is the best interest of the child. There's social justice. There's a clear need to be able to determine who the client is because oftentimes we work with parents and children and we have at some stage or another had to determine who is the client, who is the primary client.
>
> Sometimes there are dilemmas as to whose needs you are actually serving. So, there have been a number of cases where we have to be very clear about managing that conflict and using social work values in terms of how you do these things. There are certain things that you have to do because of the organization and because of the legislation. How do you do them? What are the values? What is the empathy? What are some of the things that you do that actually enable you to do that and to hold your professional identity alongside?

The purpose of focusing on and strengthening virtues and qualities is to develop the capacity to face challenges and make appropriate decisions under the given circumstances. In the child protection context, several factors relating to social, cultural, legal, organizational, family, child, parents and guardians, and practice values need to be considered. Often due to conflicting interests, these factors can interact in complex ways and pose ethical and decision dilemmas. Supervisors can significantly contribute to developing the capacity of supervisees to face and think through these challenges and make decisions.

Overall, under this section, supervisors have narrated what virtues and qualities are crucial for social workers and how they develop them in supervisees. Most emanate from their practice experiences; some can be linked to social work codes of ethics, theories, and clinical practice. The qualities of being honest and non-judgmental can be linked to the code of ethics; strengths-based perspectives and reflective practice are taught as social work theories; and the knowledge and skills of listening, observing, warmth and gentleness, and decision-making are very much needed in clinical practice. In addition, the other qualities discussed are bravery or courage and the use of humor. As told by supervisors, these are not exhaustive and not listed in any particular order, and most of them are important in any practice. However, what the analysis suggests is that supervisors try to develop virtues or qualities in supervisees, in their own ways.

Conclusion and Summary

The main purpose of this chapter was to explore whether and how supervisors try to develop virtues and qualities in supervisees as part of professional supervision. We have focused on social workers' virtues and qualities because this area of work is neglected, social work is mostly dominated by principles and rule-based ethics (Pawar, 2014; Pawar & Anscombe, 2015; Hugman et al., 2021), and the conscious cultivation of virtues and qualities is likely to help social workers make decisions in complex situations and contribute to better practice.

In the first section of this chapter, supervisors' perceptions of the qualities of social workers were presented. As stated earlier, most of the qualities perceived by the supervisors relate to professional practice. These included being honest, accountable, non-judgmental, patient, tolerant, and compassionate. Further, they emphasized supervisees sharing, caring, developing good relationships, using a self-determination approach, and finding answers on their own. As these are perceived by supervisors, we tend to think these are their own qualities. The second section explored how supervisors try to develop such qualities in supervisees. The supervisors narrated supervision examples to show their attempts to develop virtues or qualities in supervisees. These included the use of strengths and challenges; reflective practice; warmth; gentleness; humor; bravery; being honest, non-judgmental, a good listener, and observant; developing clarity and confidence; and decision-making capacity. The comparison of the supervisors' perceived qualities of social workers and their efforts at developing certain qualities in supervisees showed similarities or consistency between the two regarding the use of strengths and being honest, non-judgmental, patient, and compassionate. In terms of contrasts in their supervision, the supervisors tried to develop the qualities of reflective practice, decision-making, bravery or courage, confidence, and humor, which were not reflected in perceived qualities. Irrespective of the similarities and differences, most of these qualities are rooted in social work (clinical) practice and codes of ethics and can be linked to core qualities such as courage, compassion, integrity, and wisdom (see Banks, 2012; Hugman et al., 2021).

However, we think the questions posed were difficult as supervisors paused, contemplated, and then responded. Each supervisor shared whatever they remembered at that time. Different examples presented by supervisors show different practice contexts of supervisees, and accordingly they have shown how they have tried to draw on some of the qualities of supervisees. These qualities only came to light when direct questions were asked about how they develop virtues or qualities. In the responses to earlier questions, as stated elsewhere, the use of virtues or qualities was not explicit or apparent. From this, it may be inferred that the development of virtues or qualities of supervisees does not occur through planned and purposeful professional practice. Nonetheless, it does occur in a spontaneous and ad hoc manner, perhaps, buttressed by the professional code of ethics and related principles and values, which are relevant to forming virtues and qualities of social workers to the extent that they become their second nature. They do not think about them, as they are what social workers are. Toward that end, we think that there is scope for purposefully focusing on developing virtues and qualities of social workers both through education and training and professional supervision. In that process, the following questions are worth considering: Should these and similar virtues or qualities be formed as an integral part of being of a social worker as a person and as well as a professional social worker? Or, are they two different beings, the being of a person and the being of a social worker? This issue is further explored in the next chapter.

References

Banks, S. (2012). *Ethics and values in social work* (4th ed.). Palgrave Macmillan.

Gilgun, J. F., & Sharma, A. (2012). The uses of humour in case management with high-risk children and their families. *British Journal of Social Work, 42*(3), 560–577. https://doi.org/10.1093/bjsw/bcr070

Hugman, R., Pawar, M., Anscombe, A. W., & Wheeler, A. (2021). *Virtue ethics in social work practice*. Routledge.

Jordan, S. (2017). Relationship based social work practice: The case for considering the centrality of humour in creating and maintaining relationship. *Journal of Social Work Practice, 31*(1), 95–110. https://doi.org/10.1080/02650533.2016.1189405

Jordan, S. (2019a). *The uses and abuses of humour in social work*. Routledge.

Jordan, S. D. (2019b). How many social workers does it take to change a light bulb? One to hold the bulb in place and the rest to incite revolution: Subversion, social work and humour. *Critical and Radical Social Work, 7*(1), 73–86. https://doi.org/10.1332/204986019X15491042559673

Marques, J. (2013). Understanding the strength of gentleness: Soft-skilled leadership on the rise. *Journal of Business Ethics, 116*(1), 163–171.

Pawar, M. (2014). *Social and community development practice*. SAGE.

Pawar, M., & Anscombe, A. W. (2015). *Reflective social work practice: Thinking, doing and being*. Cambridge University Press.

Robert, C., Dunne, T. C., & Lun, J. (2015). The impact of leader humor on subordinate job satisfaction: The crucial role of leader-subordinate relationship quality. *Group & Organization Management, 41*(3), 375–406. https://doi.org/10.1177/1059601115598719

Tan, L., Wang, Y., & Lu, H. (2020). Leader humor and employee upward voice: The role of employee relationship quality and traditionality. *Journal of Leadership & Organizational Studies, 28*(2), 221–236.

Chapter 12
Developing Supervisees' Being

Introduction

This chapter discusses supervisors' views about the supervisee as a person and professional social worker and how supervisees' "being" can be developed. The dynamic concept of being includes interconnected dimensions of physical/organic, mental/emotional, social/relational, and spiritual/existential (see Pawar & Anscombe, 2015, p. 29). Sometimes, "being" is also referred to as "self of a social worker," which Dewane (2006, p. 544) delineates in terms of the use of the social worker's personality, belief systems, relational dynamics, anxiety, and self-disclosure. Virtues and qualities or character are one aspect of being and are connected in a complex way to all these aspects of being or self. Regarding strengthening the virtues or qualities of supervisees, this chapter explores whether supervisors should contribute to building being of the supervisee as a person or as a professional social worker. Are they separate? Can they be separated? Or are they interconnected?

The supervisors' views on these questions are discussed in the first section of the chapter. Most supervisors emphasize the significance of integrating the two as they cannot be separated, though other voices were suggesting that it is a gray area and they may need to be separated. The second section of the chapter includes the supervisors' views on how the supervisee's being can be developed. An analysis of the supervisors' narratives suggests that the supervisee's being can be developed by role modeling, discussing supervisees' qualities, creating a safe environment, caring, family value conflicts and influences, comparisons of previous situations, the code of ethics, goals, legal and human aspects, and both personal and professional issues. The other suggestions included assigning matching cases or work, a graduated return to work, preventing value conflict situations, and seeking additional external support. Finally, the chapter conclusion and summary are presented.

Supervisee Being as a Person and Professional Social Worker

In the previous chapter, we raised with the supervisors whether it was possible to develop the supervisee's sense of being both as a person and a social worker. Most supervisors thought the two were interconnected, whereas one supervisor believed that only focusing on the "professional social work being" appeared mechanical. Another thought distinguishing between the two was a gray area. Their narratives with our brief comments are presented below.

Person and Professional Being Are Intertwined

Generally, in social work, as we try to look at everything comprehensively, one supervisor stated that looking at the person as a whole is what social work is about.

> I think it's really important to not just focus on the work. I think that's why you look at the person as a whole. Which is what social work is about. I think that's the benefit about being a social worker. We look at the whole system, we don't look at clinical or just the person themselves, we look at everything.

The supervisor suggests looking at the supervisee as a whole person, not focusing just on work aspects, as social workers are trained to view others holistically.

In the next narrative below, a supervisor stated that personal and professional being are interrelated, and one cannot be two different persons in two situations, whether personal or professional.

> (pause) … Well I think they're very closely related, you know. The sense of being as a person, one's self and a social worker, because for me anyway, the same qualities of being a good social worker are internalized, pretty much. Personally, don't leave those behind when you're dealing with people outside of work. (laughter) … If you've got a non-judgmental attitude, or a, which one would hope most social workers will have, is that you don't judge people when you meet them in other circumstances. So, it's about reinforcing that attitude when you're supervising people. I see that as certainly developing as a social worker, but I think you develop as a person at the same time. Holistically.

> And that's the thing about social work, we don't be a social worker at work only; we're a social worker everywhere. That's the tiring bit about it. So, I think that whenever we're doing work with … a social worker, then we're also developing them personally.

Once virtues or qualities are internalized, they become an integral part of the person. They become part of their second nature. The narrative clearly states that developing as a social worker and developing as a person occur simultaneously, so they are interrelated. Thus, the being of a professional social worker is the being of a person as well.

Further, the following narrative suggests that to start with the being of a person is basic, perhaps because, even when one becomes a professional social worker, the being of a person already exists and the being of a professional social worker builds on it.

I'm always interested in the sense of being as a person to start with and that's as basic as how are you and where does that go, because I think you can't divorce that from, you can't, that's a strong word. It is unlikely that if someone's sense of being is not in too good a spot that that won't have some impact on their work, so I'm interested in that. Their sense of being as a social worker usually people will be talking about, at least implicitly, in the conversation. So, the example I gave of the court report writer and the legal system, one element of that conversation was about his being as a person, but another element was about his being as a professional and what he was being asked to do, and it was both bits that needed attending to and this is a father of young children, you know it was enormously impactful for him. So, I think both bits needed attending to and the sense of being as a social worker, like it was quite clear to see in that conversation, but sometimes it's not so clear. In some of the situations where people are having difficulties with policies or organizational regulations or whatever, then sometimes it's about making it explicit, that their distress is around their sense of being as a social worker because they came into this job, they trained for four years with a vision …

The above example suggests how the being of a person and the being of a professional social worker are intertwined. Due to countertransference, professional work can impact a social worker's being as a person. A social worker engaged in removing a child from parents may get stuck with the thought of their own children, and, for some, that may be a terrible moment. Therefore, the supervisor suggests attending to both the social worker as a person and a professional social worker.

Focusing Only on the Professional Being Is Mechanical

If supervisors are only concerned with the work of the supervisee and only keep checking and supporting work or attending to the professional being, such an approach may appear mechanical, suggesting that there is no life or humanness in it. A supervisor stated:

I'm always interested in how they're going as individuals first because I know that's important. So, I think stating that every time – instead of just bouncing into business, I think I always take time to say, "How are you going?" and you know, "How's your workload?" and "You feeling on top of things?" and "You're feeling like things are okay?" I always start off like that so, they feel – they feel that I'm seeing them as a person, not just as a machine.

Supervisors must first look at the supervisee as a person, ensure their personal well-being, and then balance it with their professional work. This is basic humanness. Supervisees should not feel that their supervisor is looking at them as machines, not human beings. It is necessary to integrate a worker's personal and professional being.

Essential to Integrate the Personal and Professional

In the following narratives, supervisors refer to the self of a social worker and the significance of self or individual development. It shows how the whole self is involved in work and how work impacts the whole self.

… my answer to that is absolutely. I'm not sure that it's possible to develop someone's sense of being as a social worker without their sense of being as a person being developed as well. I think that we bring our whole selves into our work. And our work impacts upon our whole selves.

Yeah, absolutely. I think that's an important element within supervision in terms of developing that sense of self; that sense of their individuality, that sense of being a practitioner and sometimes you know whether it's from a feminist approach or whether it's from another theoretical perspective that they're strongly coming from. You know, I think it's so important to develop that person as an individual, and I think it's important that the supervisor is helping to guide that.

Due to their interconnectedness, these narratives show supervisors attending to the whole self of supervisees and facilitating their individual development, so they do well in their professional work.

In the following narrative, the supervisor highlights how the social worker's personal and professional being are intertwined, and one cannot do without the other.

… I mean they're not two – they're not – I know exactly, I know what you're saying but in lots of ways they're not two different things are they, because once you're social work trained you can't, be a social worker without being a person. And I think one of the great things about social work as a profession is it actually asks you to bring something of yourself, not just intellectually but personally to the table. And – which is one of the things that always really appealed to me about social work. And so yeah, I don't think you can do one really without the other. And I reckon most social workers know that.

The session is for them but the learning is for both and the session is about a professional decision but there are elements of the profession and then the personal that make you the social worker that you are.

I think they integrate because I think they do influence our practice so long as they don't override each other.

I think again, our personal sense of self that comes into the professional has to remain separate to a certain degree, but I think the values and what we've been brought up on, that's what makes us a good practitioner … so, I don't see them as two very separate entities that never entwine. I think they definitely do entwine yeah.

Here, the supervisors say that everyone brings their "self" to the profession, and, without that, they cannot become social workers. Indeed, both are intertwined and important, but the supervisor cautions that we should not allow the two to override each other. Personal and professional values contribute to becoming a good practitioner, but there is also the suggestion that there needs to be a certain degree of separation between the two.

Gray Area

For another supervisor, separating the personal and professional being and mixing the two is a gray area. It is the responsibility of the supervisee and supervisor to discuss what, how much, and under what circumstances the separation may occur.

So, there is that sort of gray space and I never want people to feel that they can't talk about … I think it's really important for practitioners to reflect on where they're at personally, whether it's something that's pushing their buttons or whether there's stuff going on. You know, like "My partner's left me and I just can't focus on my clients." Again, I think that's important to be able to think about that and hear that and provide some support around that within the supervision relationship but in terms of working to resolve whatever that might be creating that should be happening somewhere else.

Yeah, and I do think that that's probably, you know, in my head I think there are things that lie clearly with the supervisee so I think I think it lies with them to bring something along to talk about but that's something that I think probably lies more with the supervisor; not exclusively but I think that it is a supervisor's responsibility to kind of monitor that grayness and be supportive of hearing the information but also being clear about when it might need to be dealt with elsewhere.

This narrative suggests that it is important for the supervisor to know what is happening to the supervisee in terms of their personal being and personal situations impacting that being and their consequences on the professional being and work and to provide some support or comfort. However, if the issues are serious, that may not be the remit of the professional supervision. The supervisors may advise supervisees to seek appropriate support as self-care is critical from a personal and professional point of view.

The above narratives of the supervisors unequivocally make the point that the supervisee's being as a person and a professional social worker are intertwined, and we cannot think of one without the other. While they are social workers, they bring their "personal being" into their work. Also, they bring professional social work into their personal being. Their personal and professional values and virtues must converge. They cannot and should not display one quality in a professional social work setting and another or contrary quality in a personal setting. This may be a deeply debatable topic to some. There are other supervisors' voices that have rightly cautioned that some separation between the two may be needed and suggested guarding against the dominance of one over the other. This is where supervisors can play a critical role in developing the consonance, care, control, and balance between the two by focusing on virtues and qualities of supervisees as part of their being.

Developing Being of Supervisees

Further, we explored supervisors' views about developing the being of supervisees, both personal and professional, through professional supervision. The analysis of their narratives suggested several ways of developing supervisees' being. These are presented below with our brief comments.

Role Modeling Oneself

Role models have a great influence on people. One suggestion to develop virtues and qualities is to observe and learn from those with such qualities. One supervisor believed that supervisors should demonstrate certain qualities so supervisees can learn and internalize them.

> Yes, look, I think that you do that by, I guess, walking the talk, by the way in which you actually … as a supervisor, you are a role model. I think as a supervisor you need to be aware of the impact and be very responsible of the impact that you have on other people. I think that you need to, therefore, be able to share, not just your professional but also your personal. By that I don't mean that you're going to then use the supervising session as a counseling session for yourself because you have had a bad day or because you've got problems with your personal life or whatever.

Role modeling is an effective way of influencing others. Learning from what one does differs from learning from what one says. The suggestion from the supervisor above is to keep the congruence between their talk and walk. Supervisees observing certain virtues and qualities in supervisors will greatly impact them. Sometimes, careful personal disclosure may be needed to achieve that. Although role modeling is an effective way of developing the supervisee's being, it may not be easy and may be too demanding.

Talk About Supervisees' Qualities

A couple of supervisors try to focus on the qualities of supervisees and refer to them during supervision as sometimes supervisees themselves may not be aware of them. Directly talking about certain qualities of supervisees may help develop their being.

> I'll often talk about how his personality, his gentleness and his disarming way absolutely doubles up. And he's very congruent. What you see of (supervisee) is what you would see when you were down the street, or wherever. He's completely authentic.

> … his honesty and his authenticity. And I think that shows to the people we work with too, to our people, to the people we work with.

> … because sometimes obviously as their supervisor you get to see their skills in a way that they don't. But you can say, "You do this in a really good way." Like I had a guy who used to work with and he was terrific with families and everything, but any time he spoke about a problem that related to the family he could not just see the individuality of that family's problem, or those young people. He had this fantastic big picture and overview and he could see all the systemic issues. He was very vitally interested in politics and he could see, all the historical and contemporary barriers and so we could discuss them in supervision and eventually I remember saying to him, "Have you ever thought of going into policy and advocacy, because you would be fantastic?" And that's what he did. And he's now a, you know a fantastic advocate and – so it's sort of developing that. That was about him personally. He had the interest and capacity to see the big picture.

The above narrative is insightful about one role of the supervisor, who needs to skillfully identify the qualities of supervisees and discuss and reinforce them during supervision. The supervisor also suggests doing it in a good way – perhaps in a positive and constructive way – as in the above example of how the supervisee was encouraged to consider advocacy.

Creating a Safe Environment

Creating a safe environment helps supervisees be more transparent and share with supervisors freely and comfortably. The following narratives highlight the importance of supervisors creating a safe environment for supervisees.

> Well again I think that if you feel safe in an environment then you are going to flow, then you are going to flourish more, you are going to feel safer, you are going to feel more transparent, and so you're going to talk about issues that you've got, and you're going to share how you're feeling. And so that gives you an opportunity to develop as a practitioner, and perhaps as a person. I really do think that they're both …

> … but I mean that you provide an environment by which the person feels safe and free to bring up some of the dilemmas that they have in their own professional development.

Supervisors need to create a safe environment, emotionally and psychologically, so supervisees can express themselves without fear or doubts. It will also help in discussing professional or personal dilemmas and ways of resolving them.

Encouragement to Discuss Discordant Views

For a couple of supervisors, one way of developing supervisees' being is by encouraging the discussion of discordant views or different approaches to addressing the presenting issues. They said:

> … and I really encourage people to bring these things to supervision because I think it's really helpful to talk about, and really interesting to talk about, and pull it apart, and wonder about, "Well, if you did," "If you didn't," you know, what would happen then. And what are the outcomes for each and weigh it all up. I think those dilemmas, or those discordant views make really interesting conversation. Yeah. So, I really enjoy those type of conversations.

> So, we've talked a lot about her learning from Aboriginal people. And learning from their culture and taking the learnings from social work and trying to blend the two and seeing where they don't blend. And deciding what to let go of. So, lots of conversations over two years. But also again, lots of conversations with her about managing her organization, which is poorly managed from her point of view, she gets limited support.

These supervisors think that discussing discordant views or differences with supervisees helps supervisees analyze consequences of each view or approach and take appropriate steps or decisions. It also helps to decide what to pursue and "what to let go of." Rather than progressing unidirectionally, looking at issues from different perspectives and carefully weighing them helps develop critical thinking abilities. Such discussion is likely to contribute to building the intellectual being of supervisees.

Discussing Family Value Conflicts and Influences

A supervisor stated that the supervisee's family background was an important part of their being, and sometimes it may impact the work with clients and people if there are value conflicts. Discussing these conflicts helps to develop supervisees' being.

> … the prejudice of growing up at home with a family where perhaps the father and mother always had an environment of a family that was a dynamic group of people who always had a very strong work ethic, who never relied on a government hand out as they were growing up and then they're working with someone who has been a long-term unemployed person for 10 or 15 years who totally conflicts with what your own values and personal identity that your family has raised you on, and how do you marry the two? So, I think that's really important, so it's about being able to have the conversation in supervision that you can still talk about your value add in terms of what you've grown up with, but then how do you influence that longer-term unemployed customer to see that it's not about what they can't do, but what they can do and maybe what they can do is volunteer work or maybe what they can do is training to get themselves eventually into employment, but it's not about just recognizing the fact that they've been long-term unemployed. So, it's about flipping it and making it a more positive conversation, but with the influence of what we've learnt in a family for instance.

An example in the above narrative clearly shows how certain families' values and qualities – a strong work ethic – internalized in supervisees may interfere with work or change their perceptions of unemployed clients and their practice approaches. Compared to the family in this example, there are also families with opposite values. Having a positive and open conversation about such values or qualities during supervision and providing the clients with enabling perspectives helps supervisees think about how values and qualities, and the social worker's being, influence practice.

Demonstrating Care

The following narrative shows that supervisors can develop supervisees' being by demonstrating care for them, even when it may involve referring their clients to other agencies.

> So, we put our heads together and we, I helped her get through that time, one of the things that I think I do well, is care. So, caring in a way that she knew I cared about what was happening for her. But also, insisting that we talk about what she's learning and also insisting

that we look at what she does do and what she had been able to achieve in each of the interventions.

And when the interventions, she had a couple of situations around suicide that were simply, as far as I was concerned, and she, ethically wrong that she was there on her own managing those. I helped her refer them back to the larger organization and gave the responsibility back to the managers.

As discussed, offering support to supervisees is an important function of professional supervision. By experiencing and observing how supervisors care for supervisees, in words and deeds, supervisees can develop the quality of caring for others. The supervisor seems to interpret allocating inappropriate cases or overloading as unethical, and preventing such practice demonstrates caring for the worker, clients, and people. Such experiences would help supervisees develop a caring being.

Comparing Previous Situations

A supervisor tried to develop the being of supervisees by encouraging them to compare how they were when they first came for supervision and how they were now.

... And I just said to her, "Listen to you, can you hear how different you sound now managing this than you sounded two years ago." And she said "Yeah." And she talked a lot about how she's grown in herself as a person, in her social work knowledge, in her ability to be with her clients, in her skills acquisition but also in her depth of being as a person in those relationships. And then she said, "And a lot of that's you (supervisor name)." And I thought oh, and then straightaway we need to well, 'cause, I want to give that back to people too.

Comparing oneself between the past and present helps one to be introspective and see the dynamic being, in professional and personal terms. Such an exercise helped the supervisee to see as a person and grow in their knowledge, skills, and capacity to build relationships. Supervisors can play an important facilitative role in making such methodical and periodic comparisons. It certainly helps the supervisee to think about the growth of their being as a person and social worker.

Linking to the Code of Ethics and Career Goal Planning

To develop the supervisee's being, one supervisor thought of drawing from certain values from the social work code of ethics and focusing on their career goal planning.

I will link in particular back to the three values, which are professional integrity, social justice and respect for persons.

And so, I will often reframe what supervisees have told me in terms of those values, to make an explicit link back to the code of ethics.

The other one is much more existential. I'm not an existentialist. So, for me, I replace existentialism with more plans and goals ... So, in terms of building this sense of self, it will be much around goal planning and where do they want to go? But also interrogating those goals and making sure those goals are aligned with their values and my values, which are the social work values if I'm doing social work supervision.

Strengthening virtues and qualities is not an alternative or substitute to social work values and principles. We have argued that virtues, social work values, and principles are interwoven (Hugman et al., 2021, p. 13). Likewise, to develop a supervisee's being, the supervisor suggests using the code of ethics and drawing from values of integrity, social justice, and respect. In addition, career planning and goal orientation in conjunction with values, and periodically interrogating them, is an innovative way of developing the being of the supervisee.

Weighing Up Between Legal Being and Human Being

To a supervisor in the child protection context, a supervisee's being may be developed by engaging in difficult decision-making situations and processes where legal directions require making certain decisions that may not coalesce with the supervisee's being. Discussing these situations and the risks involved contributes to developing the supervisee's being.

> I think the two are quite intertwined, and it's actually quite a tough call in many situations where the work that you do, and the decisions that you make, especially if you're looking at legal intervention and removal, are the last thing that you want to achieve, so what you could see from a risk perspective, as being in the child's best interests is never just a straightforward victory, okay, it always comes with a cost, so, as a social worker in child protection, you can see the risk, and as your being, you have almost a sense of dread that you know what you have to do, you have to go out to the home with the police, often, not always, but often, and you have to give those parents the paperwork and then, as a social worker, you have to negotiate how you safely remove those children from the parent, okay, and if you can use your relationship, and your words and your negotiation skills, that's all very well and good. The worst cases, and sometimes they have to happen, is when you almost have to do a snatch and grab, and you have to get a warrant to go in with the police and serve the paperwork, and then remove the child from the parents, and you have to weigh up, like, as a human being, that's a very difficult thing to do, but you have to weigh up what's the greater good.

> I suppose my job as a supervisor is teasing out the tipping point of risk, because we all sit with some risk, but when does it tip over into unacceptable risk, and then it's a job to be done, and society expects us to assess risk and take the appropriate steps, and no one wants child protection to come knocking at the door, but everyone wants to know that there's child protection in the society, so my job is to tease out what's the risk. Is it at that tipping point of the unacceptable, in terms of what that child's life is like, and then talking through with the worker, despite all your hard work, and all the, I suppose, the nice conversations that you may have had, the rewarding conversations where you felt you were moving this parent along, despite all that, is your sense that the line is in the sand and we have to go to the Children's Court to get a decision, and just going to the Children's Court doesn't mean to say you're removing a child, it might mean that you're going to the court to get conditions, but you're going to the court to get a statutory conditions, rather than working voluntarily.

In legal and contested legal contexts, how does the supervisee's being shape and contribute to child protection and welfare decisions? How do qualities of empathy and compassion balance with risks and the child's best interests? Supervisors and supervisees discussing the legal domain, evidence and factual domain, social and emotional domain, and cultural domain and how these contribute to decision-making and whether any of these domains dominate or override (e.g., legal domain) the other domains may help the supervisee's being to sensitively consider conflicting interests and contribute to decisions under given circumstances.

Assigning the Case that Goes Well with the Worker

Sometimes, supervisees' being may be reinforced by supporting what they are comfortable with and where they can work best. This may involve assigning particular kinds of clients or cases. A supervisor said:

> My supervisor said look that's okay, because there's a whole lot of other people, other prisoners out there that I know that you can work with. And so, this person then was referred to someone else.

Transference and countertransference and other personal and professional issues can adversely affect supervisees' quality of work, which in turn can impact the being of the supervisees and service to clients. Openly discussing this with supervisors and supervisors changing or assigning appropriate cases may strengthen the being of the supervisee in terms of knowledge, skills, and relationships and benefit all stakeholders (clients, organizations, management, colleagues). It is relatively straightforward when the line-manager is the professional supervisor. In the case of a non-line-supervisor, liaison with the line-manager is desired to make such changes. At any rate, supervisors have a critical role in creating a safe environment where supervisees can flourish.

Preventing Core Value Conflict Situations and Settings

Value conflicts are the fundamental causes of many other problems and can lead to internal struggles for supervisees. Being aware of these value conflicts and preventing situations and settings where such conflicts may be triggered are ways of nurturing the being of the supervisee.

> … I can remember saying to this worker, "There will be situations in your professional life where you may have to withdraw from the decision-making process because your professional identity and your personal beliefs clashes with what's happening".

> And I offered an example of myself. I became very aware very early in my learning as a social worker that there were certain decision issues that I would not be able to work with and that I would professionally withdraw from certain cases. So, for example, I wouldn't

see myself working in a pro-abortion service because it's just something that I wouldn't be able to manage honestly in terms of my personal beliefs and that I didn't believe that professionally it would be appropriate for me to place myself in a situation where I would be in a struggle, in a dilemma, ethically for myself, where I would be forced to do what the agency … because that was my employment.

Approaching and making decisions about such situations can present an ethical dilemma because one believes in the core values. Whether it is abortion or euthanasia and another issue, some supervisees have strong values, beliefs, and attitudes, and both sides have sound arguments and justifications based on their moral positions. In the above example, the supervisor advises the supervisee to withdraw and prevent core value conflicts, so the supervisee's being is not shaken, and their value base or being is strengthened.

Attending to Personal and Professional Issues

As discussed in Chap. 6, balancing the personal and professional needs and issues of supervisees is an important part of professional supervision. Here, the supervisors' view is that this element of supervision is necessary to develop the being of supervisees. They said:

… I don't want to be nosey as to what's happening in their life, but if there's anything that's going to spill into their work life, I'd like to know, just the bare bones, so I can offer some support, maybe someone needs to go a bit early, maybe they need to come in a bit late, are they having any health issues, any of their own relationship issues, are they a parent and they have to go early for whatever reason? So, I like to know a little bit about how are they going, as individuals, and then would start working through the cases, where they think they're at, what's their vision for the cases?

Sometimes people say, "Is it alright to talk about something that happened to me personally, because that's really impacting on me this week." And I say, "Well that's up to you. I'm fairly fluid like that. I think that we bring our whole selves into our work. And if something that's happened to you once is impacting on your ability to work with somebody now, then we will deal with that." So, we look at the factors that are getting in the way of their work.

You know, we spent a fair amount of time because I was aware that these would have been impacted by that information at a number of different levels, personally and professionally, and I needed to acknowledge the personal, but I needed to focus on the professional, which was the role.

For example, the following narrative shows that such support may also include graduated return to work depending upon the issue.

The supervisee works in a child protection organization. Her husband of 30 something years, over the Christmas break, basically said, "I'm not into you. I'm going." Total, total shock to her. She has line-supervision and fortunately she has a really good line-supervisor, but what she did was come here to talk about how she was going to manage that and then went and put that plan to her line-supervisor who, bless his cotton socks, took it on board. So, what it looked like in practical terms was a graduated return to work, but in reality, what she was saying is, "This is not a safe place for me to fall apart. I cannot do that in this environment, so I've got to know that I've got a return to work that I can manage intact." You know. There are no guarantees but something that will allow me to be able to do the job professionally while I'm there and then go and fall apart and not have the falling apart happen at work. So, I would add to those two things that you added some of those unexpected personal things. Sometimes it can be health things that just come out of the blue, death of children. There's a range of things that are just, where people can't hold it together and deal with what's occurring personally and what's required professionally, I think.

Crises like these are not uncommon in some supervisees' lives. Supervisors' support can make a significant difference to supervisees' being. Several supervisors stated how it is important to attend to personal issues of supervisees in the interest of their professional work, though it must be done carefully and be balanced. Supervisors must be flexible and sensitive to accommodate supervisees' personal-professional connected needs or issues. Implicit in the process of demonstrating it is conveying the supervisor's care, kindness, concern, compassion, and interest in the supervisee's well-being and work. Experiencing this kind of support will help the supervisee develop their being. The supervisors' choice of terms such as attending to the "individual first and work next," "the need to acknowledge the personal and then focus on the professional," and "bring our whole selves into our work" suggest a commitment to offering support to supervisees and thereby developing their being.

Seeking Additional External Support

Supervisors providing balanced support to supervisees also call for decisions to direct supervisees to seek additional support from other relevant sources when required. A few supervisors believed that some personal issues of supervisees cannot be addressed during supervision and that needs to be respectfully communicated.

> I think people do kind of their professional growth and development and exploration of practice issues I think also impacts on where people are at personally. And I think that's the thing that if supervision doesn't have a space for reflection on what I bring to it, then that stuff does get missed, you know. And I mean I said that the first supervisor I had was excellent and taught me how great supervision can be and I remember very clearly a conversation that he had with me that said "I've noticed when we talk about these particular cases, you have this response and, you know, I'm wondering whether that's something that you need to kind of think about and explore with a counselor that won't be me; you know, this is supervision."
>
> And I remember at the time kind of going, "Oh my goodness. I never thought anyone would say that to me" but then, some months later going, "Yeah, he's right about that and I need to do that" and I did it.
>
> And if he hadn't have had the conversation with me what would the impact have been? Would I have become dysfunctional in how I had coped or, you know, would I have burnt out or would I have become … would it have had a negative impact on my professional life and work if I hadn't have dealt with what was happening for me personally?

We don't discuss much about their personal life really, it's all pretty much clinical. But if it does come up, we then find commonalities, or links to ways that may impact on their decision-making or the way they process things.

And, you know, we talk about how there can be a grayness around that so if somebody's seeing a particular client and it's really pushing their buttons because of their own experiences, that's a helpful thing to talk about, to identify and talk about in supervision. If, as part of that identifying, I think or the supervisee thinks that's something that they need to resolve in some way for themselves then I might sort of name that that's my sense with them or if they name it, you know, I would encourage them to seek that out. But that would be with someone else; that that's not something that happens within the supervision relationship.

Usually not. [Pause] And I don't encourage that either. So, in the contract I say, "Look if you've got personal issues that are impacting on work, then it might be useful for us to talk about that just for me to know but I don't need the detail and that you need to get help outside of professional supervision for that. That's not the purpose of supervision".

Advising supervisees to seek additional support is a complex and contextual decision. It depends upon each supervisee and supervisor and the nature of the issue. Some supervisors may address the issue during supervision; others may recommend seeking support elsewhere. In the interest of supervisees, these supervisors are clear that, after informing and initial discussion, some personal issues of supervisees are not the remit of professional supervision, and supervisees must approach other professionals for help, which may resolve the issue and strengthen their being.

To sum up this section, it is insightful and useful to see the supervisors' suggestions to developing supervisees' being. There are several ideas for supervisees and supervisors, from role modeling to seeking additional external support. They do not necessarily directly refer to any virtues or qualities, but implicit in them are several virtues and qualities that are integral to the personal and professional being of supervisees.

Conclusion and Summary

This chapter has discussed supervisors' views of the supervisee as a person and professional social worker and how supervisees' "being" can be developed. Although there is a gray area between the personal and professional self of the supervisee/social worker, most supervisors think the two are intertwined and we cannot think of one without the other. There must be congruence between the two. That view is consistent with the supervision literature that emphasizes the integration of personal and professional selves (see Aponte & Winter, 2000; Ingram, 2013). Supervisors have a critical role in helping separate the personal and professional being when necessary. It is also necessary to ensure that one being does not dominate the other. Supervisors shared several ideas relating to developing the being of the supervisee. These included supervisors themselves role modeling, discussing supervisees' qualities, creating a safe environment to encourage transparent conversation and discussion, looking at early influences and value conflicts, demonstrating care, comparing and contrasting with previous situations, career goal planning, reflecting on difficult decision-making contexts, drawing on social work values and principles, respecting personal circumstances, choice in assigning cases, preventing value conflict situations, and advising to seek additional external support when necessary. Examples shared in the narratives bring to life many of the points made by supervisors.

Most supervisors' responses did not include any direct focus on developing certain qualities or virtues of supervisees. A few supervisors did refer to qualities or personality, caring, and decision-making, which are important. However, several qualities are implicit in their narratives. Their ideas relating to several ways of developing the supervisee's being may be useful to many supervisors and supervisees. Focusing on developing personal being in supervision is quite different from focusing on supervisees' personal issues. We intended to look at whether and how supervisors focus on developing personal being in normal circumstances. However, some responses suggested there was a misunderstanding of the question, as some supervisors specifically referred to personal issues faced by supervisees; some supervisors try to address such issues, while others do not. This revelation suggests that it may be a significant issue in supervision, and, in some ways, it does connect to the personal being of supervisees. Further delineation and exploration of this issue may be needed in future research. Overall, in line with Clark's (2005) analysis, developing and strengthening being, virtues, and qualities of supervisees/social workers will contribute to improved social work practice and better outcomes for people and communities.

References

Aponte, H. J., & Winter, J. E. (2000). The person and practice of the therapists: Treatment and training. In M. Baldwin (Ed.), *The use of self in therapy* (2nd ed.). Haworth Press.

Clark, C. (2005). The deprofessionalisation thesis, accountability and professional character. *Social Work and Society, 3*(2), 182–190.

Dewane, C. J. (2006). The use of self: A primer revisited. *Clinical Social Work Journal, 34*(4), 543–557.

Hugman, R., Pawar, M., Anscombe, A. W., & Wheeler, A. (2021). *Virtue ethics in social work practice*. Routledge.

Ingram, R. (2013). Emotions, social work practice, and supervision: An uneasy alliance? *Journal of Social Work Practice, 27*(1), 5–19.

Pawar, M., & Anscombe, A. W. (2015). *Reflective social work practice: Thinking, doing and being*. Cambridge University Press.

Chapter 13
Action for Professional Supervision

Introduction

The need and demand for social work and professional social work are growing globally. Have society and the social work profession kept up to meet such needs and demands? Based on our own life and professional social work experiences and observations, we do not think so. Similarly, the need and demand for professional supervision in social work are growing. However, our limited survey in this book and reflections on our interviews with social work practitioners and supervisors suggest that professional supervision in social work is practiced with great variation, from a mix of quality supervision to little or no supervision. However, it has great potential and is emerging as its own independent field of practice in terms of knowledge and skills toward meeting the growing demand for professional supervision. In this concluding chapter, we highlight what can be done to realize that potential and establish professional supervision as much needed practice across the sectors beyond social work. Our concluding thoughts are presented under five sections and themes. The first section includes the recapitulation of chapter conclusions, tacit development of virtues and qualities in supervision, a few limitations of the study, and suggestions for future research. In the second section, we summarize our understanding of the main trends in the dynamics of professional supervision. These trends relate to supervision in accredited training and clinical practice, inconsistency in organizations and line-management approaches, the influence of neoliberalism and new managerialism, the growth of private practice and external supervision, the standard set by the professional bodies, and organizations without professional supervision. In the third section, we justify professional supervision as an emerging area of practice. The fourth section refers to the apparent need for professional supervision beyond social work. Finally, we contemplate coordinated action to enhance access to professional supervision for all who need it.

© The Author(s), under exclusive license to Springer Nature Switzerland AG 2022
M. Pawar, A. W. (Bill) Anscombe, *Enlightening Professional Supervision in Social Work*, https://doi.org/10.1007/978-3-031-18541-0_13

Professional Supervision and Voices and Virtues of Social Workers

This book's e main purpose was to share experiences and views of social work practitioners as supervisors and explore whether they focus on the virtues and qualities of social workers during supervision. Toward that end, it clarifies the concept of professional supervision used in this book. It suggests that professional supervision in social work revolves in an interconnected manner around seven professional attributes (purpose, knowledge, skills and techniques, codes of ethics, professional autonomy in decision-making, self-governance, and public recognition, Henrickson, 2022, p. 187), agency of the practitioner and supervisor, people and communities, and organizational and institutional contexts. Practice experiences, challenges, and opportunities in each of these make a critical platform for practitioners to discuss, reflect, and develop their human and professional being. Thus, professional supervision in social work has emerged out of necessity as it develops practitioners to deliver quality services to people and communities, which is the main focus and purpose of organizations and professional bodies. However, professional supervision in social work is not singular or linear. The nine types and related contexts of supervision (students, license/registration/accreditation, line-management, group, peer, academic, independent, mentoring, and coaching) show the scope of supervision with respective motivations, features, and limitations. Of all these, line versus non-line-management supervision has generated much debate and discussion due to the neoliberal, managerial, and organizational dynamics impacting the supervisor and the supervisee and the quality of supervision.

Generally, the way professional social work has spread around the world has also impacted professional supervision as it is dominated by the casework model or clinical practice. Thus, it is important to consider professional supervision in the context of colonized social work and in light of neocolonization and decolonization, deprofessionalization, populism, nationalism and welfare chauvinism, digitalization and online trends, and the sustainable development goals, climate change, and disasters. The colonized history of social work and challenging changes and trends have profound implications for how professional supervision is and should be practiced in a range of government and non-government organizations and practice settings. In most of these organizations and practice settings, professional supervision seems mostly limited to clinical practice, case management, and therapeutic work. Thus, we argue that such supervision should be extended to nonclinical practice organizational contexts and practice settings such as the community, social enterprises, and policy practice. Despite the contribution of professional social work and the progress and development of many countries relating to human development indicators, major global problems such as poverty and hunger, ill health, a lack of access to basic services, climate change and disasters, and wars continue to persist. So, extending professional supervision in nonclinical practice contexts makes sense.

Although line-management supervision is ideal, if it is done the way it should be done by addressing all the purposes and functions of supervision, many line-managers are unable to meet that ideal and cannot address all the purposes of supervision. In such situations, non-line-management supervision has emerged as a default arrangement where it is feasible. As both approaches have strengths and limitations, it is important to reduce the limitations to enhance the quality of supervision.

To provide professional supervision to social workers (irrespective of their work designations), several supervision models have been developed and used over the years. We have analyzed the models and divided them into three categories. The purpose and goal-based models include any combination, sometimes overlapping, of the seven purposes of supervision. These are to ensure administrative/managerial accountability, offer education, help manage the job, make a professional impact, provide support, realize better outcomes for clients and communities, and meet license or practice accreditation requirements. To achieve these purposes and goals of supervision, several paths have been followed in combination – path-based models. These include line and non-line-management supervision and a mix of the two, contract-based supervision, supervision in private practice, digital/online supervision, casework, clinical practice and therapy-oriented supervision, supervision through reflective learning, peer group and group supervision, systemic supervision, portfolio supervision, appreciative supervision, cultural competency supervision, supervision through critical conversations, and feminist supervision. They are practical models because they have emerged out of necessity, and supervisors and supervisees employ them. It may be noted that some of these models, such as contract and digital, are methods of organizing the supervision, but not the actual supervision. The final category is the integration of purpose and path-based models, which includes a comprehensive model of supervision and an evidence-informed model of social work supervision. However, these are literature review-based models yet to be tried in the way they are conceptualized. Overall, our three categories of supervision models provide a new perspective on understanding supervision models. As already commented, most of these models have a clinical practice orientation, but our review is not comprehensive and might not have included all existing models. However, we believe that professional supervision should be systematically extended to other areas such as community organizations and development, policy practice, welfare administration, research training, and education. Notwithstanding a range of supervision models, timely and appropriate supervision is still unavailable for many practitioners who need it. Also, the purposes and goals of supervision are not fully addressed and not achieved as line-management supervision is dominated by administrative or management matters. In the case of other types of supervision, the nature of supervision is often determined by the prevailing contexts and motivations, mostly on an ad hoc and needs basis.

These and similar issues are well reflected in the dilemmas identified by supervisors. Some supervisees have no choice as only line-management supervision is available. Many line-managers or supervisors who are qualified to offer supervision and are aware of the need cannot find time to offer professional supervision due to excessive administrative demands. Therefore, the educational and support functions of supervision are largely neglected. Many supervisees have disclosure issues with line-managers due to hierarchy, power, and surveillance issues. Balancing surveillance and support is a critical issue for supervisors. Although private practice with its strengths and weaknesses seems to fill an important gap in professional supervision, it also poses ethical, adequacy, and affordability issues. When a human-centered profession such as social work is forced to use only digital technology without meeting people in-person and when organizations are forced to follow digital technology, it may pose practice, moral, ethical, and human issues, notwithstanding some advantages. As all supervisees may not be professional social workers and all supervisors may not have supervision experience, there is the possibility of mismatches and, therefore, the need for individualized supervision. Professional bodies need to play a further role in enhancing professional supervision. Developing qualities and the character of supervisees and social work practitioners is an unaddressed issue in professional supervision that needs to be systematically explored.

The analysis of the general process, essentials, themes, and content of professional supervision followed by supervisors provides valuable insights. The supervisors followed varied and flexible, informal, and formal processes, mainly determined and led by the supervisee. The supervision process must be a two-way commitment focusing on clear goals and tasks and issues. Several essentials of supervision narrated by the supervisors were linked to administrative, educational, and support functions of supervision. They suggest that supervisors and supervisees be clear at the beginning and facilitate reflection, positives or strengths, presence of mind, listening, sharing experiences, empathy, building relationships and trust, identifying themes and issues, and posing curious questions. The range of themes and content covered in supervision suggests a shift from client or practice-focused issues to organizational issues, at least in some contexts. Those issues must be addressed in the interests of people and communities, workers, organizations, and the profession. Reflective supervision stood out as it was referred to under the process, essentials, and theme or content of professional supervision. The ending process of supervision appears to be neglected and needs to be explored in future research.

The supervisors' perception of supervisees' expectations showed that supervisees expect support, space for ventilation, direction and advice, problem-solving, learning more, and counseling from the supervision. Similarly, supervisors expect supervisees to prepare well, be punctual and serious, raise ethical dilemmas, be aware of issues and defend practice, and have a vision, sense of responsibility, passion, risk orientation, and a clear focus. Comparing the supervisees' and supervisors' expectations revealed congruence relating to being reflective, looking at issues and cases from different perspectives, keeping continuity or follow-up, and being honest. The remaining expectations that did not match were complementing rather than contradicting. The analysis of expectations may help supervisors and supervisees to prepare well for supervision.

The range of issues discussed during supervision was varied. Organizational policies and procedures, conflicting values, the shortage of staff members, and interpersonal issues were posed during supervision. Practice issues included personal caring for people or clients, complex cases, critical decisions, and work-related stress. Issues relating to developing competency, both in terms of skills and knowledge, and maintaining boundaries were discussed. When supervisees bring personal issues to supervision, it is important to attend to them in a balanced way. The use of a reflective practice framework is common. Supervisees discussing different theoretical frameworks relevant to their practice issues help them have different insights and perspectives. It is emphasized that supervision is not just issue or problem oriented; good things, good aspects of the work, and achievements also are discussed. The organizational issues were more challenging to practitioners than the issues they experienced in their practice with people/clients.

The supervisors used a wide range of concepts and theories, including the purpose and goals and path-based models discussed above. For example, they employed ideas from reflective practice, adult learning, the task-focused approach, systems theory, postmodernism, strength-based practice, anti-oppressive practice, social constructionism, feminism, narrative therapy, family therapy, sensorimotor psychotherapy, psychodynamic, cognitive behavior therapy, and an eclectic approach. Of the concepts and theories used by supervisors, over half relate to social work clinical practice theories – many supervisors use these theories because they specialize in this area. This approach may be advantageous to some supervisees who plan to specialize in a particular area offered by supervisors, whereas, for others, it may not be relevant. In using clinical practice models, it is necessary to guard against the likely transference of the social worker-client relationship in the supervisor-supervisee relationship. Some concepts and models such as reflective practice, supervisee-led, the family approach, and best practice are generic and can be used in any supervision context. Most supervisors use these models in combination or by mixing them with other ideas.

In the narratives, the supervisors shared their supervision practice wisdom, emanating from their practice experiences, critical reflections, and learnings from what has not worked. So, in the supervision, sharing relevant practice experiences and reflecting on them is critical. Several practice wisdom statements such as "we cannot be good at everything"; "not just jump in, think"; "open to being challenged"; "there is no perfect theory"; and "if in doubt, throw them out" are insightful and useful in practice. A few principles or techniques identified in their practice wisdom were as follow: start with supervisees' experiences, listen actively, never say "I know how you feel," acknowledge and validate, do not get bogged down on one thing, look for opportunities in crisis, don't bring too much of yourself in, it is not about you, ask hard questions, use upside-down brainstorming, and discuss opposites. The invaluable wisdom shared by the supervisors is generally useful for both supervisors and supervisees. There appears to be scope for purposefully developing these and similar qualities and virtues in supervisees through professional supervision practice.

Our quest to explore whether and how supervisors try to develop virtues and qualities in supervisees revealed that the supervisors did identify qualities of social workers such as being honest, accountable, non-judgmental, patient, tolerant, and compassionate. Further, they stated that supervisees should be able to share, care, develop good relationships, use a self-determination approach, and find answers independently. They shared several supervision examples to show how they develop in supervisees certain virtues and qualities such as strengths and challenges, reflective practice, warmth, gentleness, humor, bravery, honesty, remaining non-judgmental, good listening, observing, clarity and confidence, and decision-making capacity. Although most of these qualities are rooted in social work (clinical) practice codes of ethics, they can be linked to core qualities such as courage, compassion, integrity, and wisdom (see Banks, 2012; Hugman et al., 2021).

In the final analysis, the supervisors' views about the supervisee as a person and professional social worker suggest that, though there is a gray area between the two, the personal and professional self of the supervisee/social worker are intertwined, and we cannot think of one without the other. The fundamental belief that the two must go together is consistent with the supervision literature that emphasizes the integration of personal and professional selves (see Aponte & Winter, 2000; Ingram, 2013). According to the supervisors, the supervisee's being can be developed by supervisors themselves role modeling, discussing supervisees' qualities, creating a safe environment to encourage transparent conversation and discussion, looking at early influences and value conflicts, demonstrating care, comparing and contrasting with previous situations, career goal planning, reflecting on difficult decision-making contexts, drawing on social work values and principles, respecting personal circumstances, assigning relevant cases, preventing value conflict situations, and advising to seek additional external support. Overall, the ideas relating to several ways of developing the supervisee's being may be useful to many supervisors and supervisees.

Tacit Development of Virtues/Qualities in Supervision

As stated earlier, one of the main objectives of our research was to explore whether supervisors focus on developing virtues and qualities of social workers in supervision. We tried to trace it by raising different questions to supervisors and analyzing their narratives to those questions. The analysis of supervisor and supervisee expectations did not indicate any direct focus on developing supervisees' virtues and qualities. However, we deciphered virtues and qualities in the narratives as supervisors referred to reflective practice, having vision and responsibility, taking risks and having passion, valuing time and supervision, committing to supervision, learning, and being truthful and honest. The examination of issues posed in the supervision did not make explicit reference to the development of the qualities and character of supervisees. However, the use of phrases, such as "working with client issues is a breeze" and "best practice, making relationships, keeping the customer at the center of work, focus on understanding, harnessing energy, transparent practices, holding on to values and change agent for the people, empowering customers and recognizing good work," suggests the presence of supervisors' virtues and qualities in their work. Although wide-ranging supervision concepts and models were employed by supervisors, we did not find any concept or framework that focused on the development of qualities and virtues in supervisees, though some frameworks may include ethical issues or aspects. However, their reference to "strengths-based practice, reflective framework, helping supervisees to think, building relationships, unpacking issues in-depth, having a plan, flexibility, responsibility to help, advocacy and support, loving or liking a particular framework, awareness of the purpose, humanness, connecting, solving problems together and respectful" may be linked to some virtues and qualities, but their focus may not be purposefully developing them in supervisees. In the narratives of the supervisors' practice wisdom, the use of the terms such as "strive for learning, affirming/validating practice, careful self-disclosure, putting into action, enhancing knowledge and skills, humility and humbleness, exploring opportunities, listening to the gut, challenging decisions, open to being challenged, making judicious decisions and keeping on the right track" suggests the implicit presence of qualities and virtues in supervision practice, but there was no evidence of purposefully developing them. To a specific question, supervisors shared supervision practice examples to show how they develop virtues and qualities in supervisees. The analysis of those examples did not suggest the planned and purposeful development of virtues and qualities. As earlier observed, it may occur in an ad hoc and implicit manner, perhaps, bolstered by the professional code of ethics and related principles and values, which are relevant to forming virtues and qualities of social workers. Similarly, in their narratives of developing the being of supervisees, certain virtues and qualities were implicit in the narratives, though a few supervisors did refer to qualities and personality, caring, and decision-making.

Based on these findings, we believe that, overall, our research and analysis are insufficient to conclusively state whether or not supervisors develop the virtues and qualities of supervisees. This is because the complex nature of virtues and qualities and many other early socialization factors contribute to their development. They are also assumed to have certain qualities oriented toward professional social work. Professional social work codes of ethics, values, and principles have certain elements of virtues and qualities, and they can contribute to the development of virtues and qualities of social workers, but it is unclear when and how professional social work contributes to developing virtues and qualities. However, drawing from our analysis, we can confidently state that planned and purposeful development of virtues and qualities in supervisees does not occur during professional supervision. We argue that there is scope for purposefully focusing on developing social workers' virtues and qualities through education, training, and professional supervision.

Limitations of the Study and Future Research

A few limitations of this analysis are that it is based on a small number of supervisors' narratives, though they were purposely selected to ensure representation from all states and territories in Australia. General limitations of qualitative studies apply to this research. Although we interviewed social work practitioners as part of a broader research project (see Pawar et al., 2017, 2020; Hugman et al., 2021) and significantly gained from their comments and insights, the analysis presented in this book is based predominantly on the supervisors' interviews. As already clarified, the supervisees' expectations are supervisors' perceptions of what supervisees expect. In the future, similar systematic research may be undertaken to ascertain supervisees' views and perspectives. It may also be useful to comparatively examine expectations of line and non-line-management supervisors and employed and self-employed supervisees, including in private practice. As the ending process of supervision appears to be neglected, it needs to be explored in future research. A few supervisors' narratives suggest that personal issues of supervisees do come up in the supervision, and some supervisors have different views about considering those issues in supervision. This revelation suggests that it may be a significant issue in supervision, and, in some ways, it connects to the personal being of supervisees. Further delineation and exploration of this issue may be needed in future research. Researching the process of developing virtues and qualities in supervisees is a complex problem, and what we attempted is preliminary. It would be interesting and valuable to explore further whether and how supervisors develop virtues and qualities in supervisees. What kind of virtues and qualities do social workers bring to the social work profession? What new virtues and qualities do social workers develop in the social work profession? What kind of existing virtues and qualities are strengthened and weakened in them? Are there any virtues and qualities unique to the social work profession? How can virtues and qualities be taught or developed innovatively? How do social workers develop as better people with professional training, practice, and supervision? Longitudinal studies may be needed to address these and similar research questions. Despite these limitations, we hope this study contributes to the literature relating to professional supervision and our suggestions and research questions stimulate further research in the future.

The Main Trends in the Dynamics of Professional Supervision

The following analysis, our reflections, and observations, in a way, are beyond the remit of this book, and, at the outset, we must admit that we are deviating from the limited and main purpose of the book. We are doing so in the interests of the profession and further strengthening and expanding professional supervision. In writing this book and reflecting on the supervision literature and our relevant experiences, we have identified and analyzed six main trends in the dynamics of professional supervision. They are not new; they are well reflected in the literature and prevalent in the field but, perhaps, not in the way we see and articulate them. Along with the supervisors' voices presented in this book, as social work educators and researchers, we are adding our voices to the professional supervision cause.

Mainly Focused on Accredited Training and Clinical Practice

Professional supervision in social work has evolved since the 1930s with its own checkered history (see O'Donoghue & Engelbrecht, 2021a). Over more than 90 years, one trend can be clearly observed. Professional supervision is relatively well established and followed in most accredited social work training programs and clinical practice settings. In almost all accredited social work programs, both in bachelor and master's courses, students complete field education under professional supervision. The only exception is that some new social work programs in some developing countries appear to have compromised this mandatory requirement due to resource constraints (a lack of resources, practice settings, and trained staff). According to the requirements of professional accreditation bodies and tertiary social work programs, every social work student must complete a minimum number of hours of field education under professional supervision.

Likewise, as discussed earlier in this book, after social work graduation, those who wish to register, obtain a practice license, or meet practice accreditation requirements must undertake the stipulated minimum hours of supervised practice under a qualified professional supervisor, who may be in private practice or employed in an organization or engaged in both. Most accredited social workers continue in clinical practice. This text notes that professional supervision is dominated by clinical practice for good reasons. However, the trend is clear that in both accredited training and clinical practice, professional supervision is consistently practiced and well established with specified hours and competencies.

Inconsistency in Organizations and Line-Management Approaches

The second trend is that the way professional supervision is valued and used in organizations, both government and non-government and practice settings discussed in Chap. 3, and by line-managers or supervisors is inconsistent and varies greatly. Some organizations and line-managers or supervisors regularly use it and try to achieve all the supervision functions (mainly administration, education, and support), and all parties involved (the organization, supervisor, and supervisee) are satisfied with supervision practices. This offers a compelling case for continuing the ideal of line-management supervision. In contrast, some organizations and line-managers or supervisors use it inconsistently, irregularly, and formally and informally (e.g., during tea and lunch breaks and travel). Some attend to only one or two functions of supervision, usually the administrative functions. As already pointed out, under line-management supervision approaches, some supervisees have experienced power, hierarchy, trust, and disclosure issues. Sometimes, it is left to supervisors and supervisees to work it out, depending upon their needs, interests, and motivations. So, the experience and use of supervision are mixed. Under this trend, important professional issues can be brushed aside, and workers and supervisors are left to themselves to cope or adjust to practice situations, which may need thorough professional attention. This broad trend has continued for some time.

Influence of Neoliberalism and New Managerialism

The third trend relates to the significant influence of neoliberalism, new managerialism, privatization, and the free market on organizations and professional supervision. Two critical consequences of this impact are employees being asked to do more with less due to resource squeezing and non-professionals being recruited to manage and supervise. One outcome has been the increased demands on line-managers or supervisors, particularly with administrative work. This has made it challenging for them to allocate time for professional supervision, even if they wanted to, so professional supervision has been significantly compromised. Another outcome has been that nonsocial work professionals or nonqualified supervisors have assumed line-manager and supervisor roles. This has resulted in social workers having limited options for professional supervision. Some approached social work colleagues or peers, some made non-line-supervision arrangements within or outside the organization, and some sought external supervision by spending their own money. Some organizations facilitated these and similar arrangements. Many social work practitioners were under significant pressure as the amount of work to be done in a limited time increased with little or no support from line-managers or supervisors. This trend has also significantly impacted the quality of services delivered to people and communities. Overall, this trend appears to have pushed the stakeholders (supervisees, supervisors and organizations) to find innovative and alternative ways of organizing professional supervision.

Private Practice and External Supervision

One of the innovative and alternative ways of organizing professional supervision was through private practice and external supervision, which we conceptualize as a fourth trend. It appears that private practice is gradually growing. It is unclear to us whether the growth in private practice is occurring serendipitously, due to the influence of privatization and the free market or to meet the increasing demand, which governments and relevant organizations are unable to address adequately, or due to policies such as mental health support under Medicare. It may be a combination of these factors. Social work practitioners in private practice are undoubtedly filling an important gap by providing valuable professional supervision services to individuals, groups, and organizations on a contractual basis. This trend has also helped to address some of the weaknesses of line-management supervision. As many organizations appear to be failing to keep up the ideal of line-management supervision, external supervision through private practice seems practical under the given neo-liberal and managerial milieu. While there is some comfort in seeking external professional supervision through private practice, it cannot fully substitute for line-management supervision and may be complementary. However, it does mean that supervisees must inevitably negotiate with both supervision systems. On the other hand, private practice has also created a demand for professional supervision as anyone entering private practice must complete the required hours of supervised practice. It also appears to have increased the use of online or digital supervision. It is unclear to us whether private practice has an element of negative discretion, cooption, or pecuniary motivation, which has the potential to compromise professional supervision. Professional supervision in private practice is not only a means for knowledge and skills transfer and support but also a tradable commodity in the market, where individuals and organizations must purchase it.

Professional Bodies and Supervision Standards

The fifth trend in professional supervision constitutes how professional bodies have responded to the above discussed trends. To ensure and maintain the minimum standards in social work practice and the profession, professional social work bodies have organized relatively well to develop supervision standards, worked with licensing and registration agencies, facilitated the registration of practitioners, and provided and created platforms for continuing professional development training programs. These important tasks and achievements notwithstanding, it appears that professional supervision is unavailable to many practitioners who need it. What else can professional bodies do? Do they want to become partners in transferring knowledge and skills and providing support to practitioners? Or do they want to become partners in trading professional supervision? Or do they want to do both? Despite these professional bodies' important contributions, their actions relating to professional supervision appear inadequate as many organizations and practitioners do not have access to professional supervision. Professional social work bodies in some countries have not developed to a level to facilitate professional supervision activities, and, in some countries, they are not organized or not established.

Organizations and Practitioners Without Professional Supervision

The sixth and final trend is that there are several organizations and many practitioners who continue to practice without any effective professional supervision. This may be due to a lack of awareness, the cost, or geographic location. It is also unclear whether they feel the need for professional supervision. They may only experience performance management supervision. However, this does not mean that some do not experience practice issues and do not need support and professional supervision. We assume that most face similar issues and aspire to both personal and professional growth and find their own ways to deal with issues – perhaps negatively adapt and when things become unbearable or leave the industry when burnout occurs. This may also impact the quality of services provided to people and communities. The challenge is how to reach out to such organizations and practitioners and enhance access to much needed professional supervision.

Professional Supervision as an Emerging Area of Practice

Amid these and similar ongoing trends in the dynamics of professional supervision, a significant body of knowledge and skills of professional supervision have been developed over the years. This is evident through the publication of several books, research articles in peer-reviewed journals, and an international handbook on professional supervision (O'Donoghue & Engelbrecht, 2021b). Some practitioners also have developed modules on professional supervision and regularly offer professional supervision training to supervisors and supervisees. It may be assumed that professional social work bodies, as already pointed out, are generally supportive of these developments since they also play a role by developing norms of and for professional supervision. A brief review and the use of concepts and models of professional supervision presented in Chaps. 4 and 9, respectively, further attest to the knowledge available in this growing field. This knowledge can be organized in terms of historical, organizational, and practice settings, conceptual and theoretical, interpersonal skills and support, engagement of people and clients and communities, and evaluation processes. Given this evidence from research, publications, and literature, professional supervision in social work is emerging as an area of practice in its own right, and it is critical to continue developing it.

The Need for Professional Supervision

As noted in the introduction, there is a great need for professional supervision in social work, but not all practitioners have access to it. In our survey, over one-quarter of social workers did not have professional supervision, and about 14% only had line-management supervision. This suggests that about 40% of social workers did not have professional supervision in terms of education and support. Many of those who had professional supervision found it inadequate due to line-management supervision issues, as all aspects of supervision were not addressed. The education, support, and career advancement functions of supervision are not only relevant to professional social work practitioners but also to employees and self-employed persons in most sectors, whether it is health, education, justice, or welfare. In our view, a lack of professional supervision raises health, safety, and self-care issues for most employees and self-employed persons generally, including social work practitioners. In some services sectors, workers can come under tremendous stress for various reasons: a mismatch between demand and supply, organizational pressures to do more, organizational restructures, ongoing technological changes, staff shortages, and demands from consumers, customers, or service users. The recent COVID-19 pandemic has exposed some of these issues. Some aspects of professional supervision involve mentoring, and there is a considerable demand for mentoring in most organizations. Several online mentoring platforms have been created to meet this demand. These developments appear to suggest that many people need education and support, and many organizations are failing to meet that need. Therefore, as some social workers have sought external supervision on their own, many people are looking for other sources to meet this important need. Thus, the need for professional supervision is greater than ever before, and it is critical to expand the scope of supervision beyond the professional limit to offer it to all people who need it in the general interest of their welfare and well-being. Toward that end, we propose the following coordinated action.

Coordinated Action for Professional Supervision

To meet the growing demand for professional supervision within social work and beyond, we propose the following coordinated strategies. Awareness raising and articulation of the issue is the first step. The need for professional supervision beyond social work is evident. There are good examples within social work that, through establishing senior practitioner divisions (e.g., in the child protection field) and providing professional supervision, job satisfaction, job performance, and job retention, have increased. Such successful cases should be used to make a wider case for professional supervision and mentoring for all those who need it across all organizations. It can be developed as an independent program or service like employee assistance programs.

Second, a range of training sectors, including universities, need to play an important role by developing and introducing appropriate short and full course training programs to prepare well-trained professional supervisors or mentors. Already some universities and private practitioners offer such training programs. These need to be refined, virtues and character-building content needs to be added, and they need to be scaled up to cross the boundary of professions.

Third, we raise the question of what more professional bodies can do. While their work relating to professional supervision has been important, it has not been adequate. Professional bodies also have a keen interest in ensuring the safety and security of the profession's clients, and professional supervision has implications for clients and client outcomes. They need to think about scaling up supervision and support activities creatively, not only within social work but more generally in society as a worker well-being issue. They can develop the minimum supervision standards for all organizations, including employers of social workers, and suggest monitoring mechanisms. They can also advocate for this cause.

Fourth, all organizational governance systems are mandated to implement governments' health- and safety-related laws and guidelines. It is critical to initiate the process of including the relevant functions of supervision in these laws and guidelines so that organizations gain legitimacy to allocate resources for the professional development and mentoring of staff members. Human resources or people and culture divisions within organizations appear to have similar programs, but they seem to be general, specific issue focused, and are far from adequate. From the viewpoint of most employees, these divisions are not trusted agencies to offer professional supervision as they are usually perceived to align with the organization rather than employees. As line managers cannot perform all professional supervision functions, this specific service needs to be independently developed, like employee assistance programs. While these assistance programs are generally problem oriented, professional supervision is proactive, regular, and developmental.

Fifth, employees' unions, where they exist, have a critical role to play. While negotiating enterprise agreements with organizations, the unions can include the provision of professional supervision and mentoring to staff members. Some related provisions may be there, but they are almost defunct for most employees as they are selectively used for targeted staff members. All those employees who need professional supervision should have access to it. Organizations need to allocate resources to it as already some organizations employ external staff to provide professional supervision to staff members.

Sixth, along with the efforts of the unions, employees can also play a role by collectively demanding access to professional supervision in the interest of the organization and the quality of services it delivers. As some employees do not receive any support, experience discrimination, get stuck in their career progression, and look helplessly for mentoring and support, it calls for organizing employees to make a collective demand for access to professional supervision.

Seventh, if existing policies and legislative provisions are inadequate to provide professional supervision, this issue needs to be placed on governments' agendas to introduce necessary legislation, amendments, policies, and programs. All stakeholders together need to play a coordinated role to work with respective governments to achieve this.

Finally, the eighth strategy relates to further research and knowledge building in professional supervision. As stated above, over the years, supervision knowledge has been developed, but this should continue as relative to other social work and social science topics; it is an under-researched area. Earlier, some research suggestions were made in the context of social work. Here, similar questions need to be raised beyond social work, cutting across all organizations and sectors. Through research, it is important to document the nature and magnitude of the problem and the need for professional supervision. Equally important is creating evidence of success stories where professional supervision is fully implemented.

We strongly believe that in the interests of the welfare and well-being of people and organizations, professional supervision and mentoring should be available, not as an ad hoc honorary activity but as a legitimate work provision to all those who need it.

References

Aponte, H. J., & Winter, J. E. (2000). The person and practice of the therapists: Treatment and training. In M. Baldwin (Ed.), *The use of self in therapy* (2nd ed.). Haworth Press.

Banks, S. (2012). *Ethics and values in social work* (4th ed.). Palgrave Macmillan.

Henrickson, M. (2022). *The origins of social care and social work: Creating a global future.* Policy Press.

Hugman, R., Pawar, M., Anscombe, A. W., & Wheeler, A. (2021). *Virtue ethics in social work practice.* Routledge.

Ingram, R. (2013). Emotions, social work practice, and supervision: An uneasy alliance? *Journal of Social Work Practice, 27*(1), 5–19.

O'Donoghue, K., & Engelbrecht, L. (2021a). Introduction: Supervision in social work. In K. O'Donoghue & L. Engelbrecht (Eds.), *The Routledge international handbook of social work supervision* (pp. XX–XXVI). Taylor and Francis.

O'Donoghue, K., & Engelbrecht, L. (2021b). *The Routledge international handbook of social work supervision* (pp. XX–XXVI). Taylor and Francis.

Pawar, M., Hugman, R., Alexandra, A., & Anscombe, A. W. (2017). *Empowering social workers: Virtuous practitioners.* Springer.

Pawar, M., Hugman, R., Anscombe, A. W. (Bill), & Alexandra, A. (2020). Searching for virtue ethics: A survey of social work ethics curriculum and educators. *The British Journal of Social Work, 50*(6), 1816–1833. https://doi.org/10.1093/bjsw/bcz106

Index

CPSIA information can be obtained
at www.ICGtesting.com
Printed in the USA
LVHW080046200223
739874LV00004B/178